CAGING THE BEAR:
CONTAINMENT AND THE COLD WAR

CAGING THE BEAR:
CONTAINMENT AND THE COLD WAR

edited by
CHARLES GATI

THE BOBBS-MERRILL COMPANY, INC.
Indianapolis and New York

Copyright © 1974 by the Bobbs-Merrill Company, Inc.:
"Introduction: But Was the Cold War Really Necessary"
and "Traditionalists, Revisionists, and the Cold War:
A Bibliographical Sketch."
Printed in the United States of America
First Printing

Library of Congress Cataloging in Publication Data

Gati, Charles.
  Caging the bear.

  Bibliography: p.
  1. United States—Foreign relations—1945–
—Addresses, essays, lectures.   I.   Title.
E744.G345   327.73   73–19522
ISBN 0–672–61351–4 (pbk.)

To Tommy, Stevie, and Susie,
for whom the Cold War is—
and should remain—history

CONTENTS

PART TWO: CONTAINMENT AND ITS ALTERNATIVES

THE CONTRIBUTORS

ZBIGNIEW BRZEZINSKI is Herbert H. Lehman Professor of Political Science and Director, Research Institute on Communist Affairs at Columbia University. Member of the Policy Planning Council of the Department of State, 1966–68, Mr. Brzezinski has written *The Soviet Bloc, Alternative to Partition, Between Two Ages, The Fragile Blossom,* and other books.

J. WILLIAM FULBRIGHT has been the United States Senator from Arkansas since 1945 and Chairman of the Committee on Foreign Relations since 1959. His books on American foreign policy include *Old Myths and New Realities, The Arrogance of Power,* and *The Crippled Giant.*

CHARLES GATI is Associate Professor of Political Science and Director, Program in Comparative Communist Studies at Union College and Visiting Associate Professor of Political Science at Columbia University. He has contributed to *The Conduct of Soviet Foreign Policy* and *The Behavioral Revolution and Communist Studies,* and to such journals as *World Politics* and *Foreign Policy.*

GEORGE F. KENNAN was head of the Policy Planning Staff in the Department of State at the time he wrote the "X" article in 1947. Since then, he served as U.S. Ambassador to the Soviet Union and to Yugoslavia. His studies include *American Diplomacy 1900–1950, Realities of American Foreign Policy, Russia and the West under Lenin and Stalin,* and *On Dealing with the Communist World.* Mr. Kennan's autobiographical works are *Memoirs, 1925–1950* and *Memoirs, 1950–1963.*

MARSHALL D. SHULMAN is Professor of Political Science and Director, Russian Institute at Columbia University. During the last years of the Truman Administration, he was a special assistant to Secretary of State Dean Acheson. Mr. Shulman's books include *Stalin's Foreign Policy Reappraised* and *Beyond the Cold War,* and he has contributed to *Foreign Affairs* and *World Politics.*

JOHN SPANIER is Professor of Political Science at the University of Florida. The sixth, revised edition of his *American Foreign Policy Since World War II* was published in 1973. Mr. Spanier has also written *The Truman-McArthur Controversy and the Korean War, World Politics in an Age of Revolution,* and *Games Nations Play.*

TOBY TRISTER is Project Director of the Parallel Studies Program with the Soviet Union at the United Nations Association.

HARRY S TRUMAN was thirty-third President of the United States, 1945–53.

DONALD S. ZAGORIA is Professor of Political Science at the City University of New York/Hunter College. He is the author of *The Sino-Soviet Conflict 1956–1961* and *Vietnam Triangle,* and he has contributed to *The American Political Science Review* and *Problems of Communism.*

WILLIAM ZIMMERMAN is Associate Professor of Political Science and Director, Center for Russian and East European Studies at the University of Michigan. He is the author of *Soviet Perspectives on International Relations* and co-editor of *The Shaping of Foreign Policy,* and he has contributed to the *Journal of Conflict Resolution* and *The American Political Science Review.*

INTRODUCTION:
But Was the Cold War Really Necessary?

1. BEYOND THE FALLOUT SHELTER

Two stories—one extraordinary, the other quite common—are worth telling.

At the time of the Cuban Missile Crisis of 1962, this otherwise highly intelligent but obviously rather tense high-school teacher was so convinced of the imminence of nuclear war that he resigned from his job, sold his house, packed up his family, and left for Australia. He thought he could survive the forthcoming nuclear holocaust in that distant, faraway land. (By the time he changed his mind and returned, his job had been taken.) Then there was the far more common experience of thousands and thousands of Americans who as late as the early 1960s sought to save their lives by building fallout shelters, encouraged as they were by the government to do so. Indeed, new businesses sprang up specializing in shelter supplies, selling rifles and handguns to keep out the enemy and perhaps one's own neighbors as well.

For two decades after World War II, the Cold War was widely believed to have been a prelude to a "Hot War." In this sense, the Cold War is over, for the expectation of a direct military confrontation between the United States and the Soviet Union or between the United States and China has dramatically declined. Much of what used to be called the Cold War mentality, typified by the fallout shelter syndrome, is now passé. In the improved political climate, the leaders of the United States, the Soviet Union, and China have begun to explore common interests. The kind of anti-communist rhetoric which used to distinguish American discourse on foreign policy has virtually disappeared. Despite or perhaps because of the unrelenting Sino-Soviet rift, China and the Soviet Union have also toned down their abusive anti-American rhetoric. American-Soviet and American-Chinese talks about trade, cultural exchanges, the limitation of strategic arms (only with the Soviet Union), and a few other matters of substance and protocol have turned out to be promising. In short, international relations among the Great Powers have lately assumed a less volatile, more businesslike character.

To be sure, only the naive would conclude that conflict has been eliminated from the fabric of the international system or that it has been replaced by trust and harmony. Far from it: if conflict means discord, tension, or the pursuit of mutually exclusive goals and interests—and not necessarily war or the expectation of it—then it remains a seemingly permanent feature of international life and indeed of the relations among the Great Powers. Their search for power, influence, prestige, and economic advantage, as well as their desire to meet needs of national pride, has long characterized their behavior and continues to do so today. The resulting conflict of national interests thus persists as the norm rather than the exception of international politics and of Great Power relations in particular. What has changed, more than anything else, is that international conflict is no longer identified with the possible occurrence of global and nuclear war.

With the belligerence of the past at least suspended and the artificial conviviality of the present reflecting more anxiety than confidence, an uneasy truce has been declared. The underlying conflict of interests and ideas has been put into abeyance.

2. THE COLD WAR IN THREE PHASES

Another way of discerning the dimensions of change is to identify its dynamics and trace its historical development. Let us therefore tentatively sketch what might be called the three phases of the Cold War.

The *First Phase* witnessed the establishment of Soviet-imposed Communist regimes in East-Central Europe (1945–48), extending from Albania to Czechoslovakia, as well as the formation of what was initially a pro-Soviet but subsequently became an independent communist system in Yugoslavia. Contrary to original wartime expectations, the unification of Germany was not merely postponed, but two Germanys with divergent political orientations came into permanent existence. In the Greek civil war (1945–49), the Soviet Union provided aid to Communist guerrillas, while the United States supported the royal government's forces. In Berlin, the Soviet attempt to compel the West to abandon that city in 1948 and thus eliminate the embarrassing as well as unsettling Western presence from the heart of East Germany, led to the dramatic American airlift—the first of several Berlin crises which brought the world to the threshold of major war.

Lasting from 1945 to 1949, the First Phase of the Cold War can therefore be described as a *confrontation,* primarily between the United States and the Soviet Union; its main geographic locus was *Europe*; and the most important instrument of foreign policy used or expected to be used was the *military*. Both sides perceived the world in sharp black-and-white terms. Stalin emphasized the two-bloc doctrine, classifying nations as either allies or enemies, declaring that countries which were not for the Soviet Union were considered to be against it. As for the United States, President Truman enunciated the policy of containment, which represented not only an expression of American determination to stop or contain the expansion of Soviet power abroad—although that was its primary purpose—but our official conclusion that the Communist way of life itself was alien as well as dangerous to us. In short, with profound distaste toward each other's values and a commitment to oppose each other's foreign policies, the First Phase concluded with the ominous prospect of a military confrontation in Europe.

During the *Second Phase*—from the Korean War (1950–51) to the Cuban Missile Crisis of 1962—the theater of the Cold War significantly broadened. It may well be that the implicit lesson of the Berlin airlift was the mutual recognition of stalemate in Europe, and as a result both the Soviet Union and the U.S. earnestly began to look beyond the old world for new gains. The emerging tendency found expression in the Korean War, the Suez conflict of 1956, and particularly the Soviet and, to a lesser extent, American reappraisals of the non-aligned or neutralist Third World in the early 1950s.

Unable to break the European impasse and unwilling to risk a show-down with the U.S. in Europe, the Soviet Union set aside the sharp Stalinist dichotomy contained in the two-camp doctrine and began to represent itself as a friend of the Third World. Gone were the days when the leader of India, Jawaharlal Nehru, for example, would be called an "imperialist hireling" in the Soviet press; he and others like him were now wined and dined, visited by such high-ranking Soviet leaders as Khrushchev and Bulganin, given economic assistance, and co-opted, with or without their concurrence, in the "anti-imperialist" struggle. For its part, while the United States continued to express disapproval of neutrals and fence-sitters in the Third World, we nonetheless commenced an extensive and generous foreign-aid program and, during the Suez crisis at least, we took what amounted to a firm anti-colonialist, pro-Third World stance.

True, the steady upgrading of the two military alliances in Europe and the Korean War in particular served as vivid reminders of the continuing danger of military confrontation in Europe and Asia. Yet, during the Second Phase, the two sides increasingly began to view the Cold War as a *competition* (as well as a confrontation); reflecting this, the geographic locus of the Cold War was enlarged so as to include not only Europe but the non-aligned Third World and especially *Asia* as well; and reliance on the *economic* instruments of foreign policy rapidly increased.

THREE PHASES OF THE COLD WAR

	I. (1945–49)	II. (1950–62)	III. (1963–72)
MAIN FEATURES	Confrontation	Confrontation and competition	Confrontation, competition, and cooperation
MAIN LOCATIONS	Europe	Europe and Asia	Global
MAIN INSTRUMENTS OF POLICY	Military	Military and economic	Military, economic, and diplomatic

As the *Third Phase* unfolded, it was once again a peak in Cold War hostilities that served as a line of demarcation. Just as the Berlin crisis of 1948–49 had led to a transition from the First to the Second Phase, the Cuban Missile Crisis of 1962 marked an end as well as a beginning. The Third Phase still featured military confrontation and economic competition in Europe and Asia, as did the previous ones, but at the same time Soviet-American *cooperation* began to evolve on a *global* basis, with both sides increasingly relying on the *diplomatic* instrument of foreign policy.

The extraordinary complexity of the Third Phase—which lasted from the aftermath of the Cuban Missile Crisis to the winding down of the Vietnam War in 1972—stemmed from the concurrent pursuit of seemingly contradictory policies by both powers. Even as they continued to prepare for war (the U.S. actually waged one), they began to anticipate peace. For the unmistakable lesson of the Cuban Missile Crisis was the unthinkability of nuclear confrontation. True, suspicion did not give way to trust, harmony did not replace conflict, and swords were not turned into plowshares. Military strength continued to provide the foundation of diplomatic moves. Despite spectacular and often-successful summit meetings and repeated public assurances by both American and Soviet leaders, this was not *the* era of negotiations. Indeed, this was not the era of cooperation *or* competition *or* confrontation; it was the era of all three at the same time. Neither the U.S. nor the Soviet Union relied on diplomacy *or* economic aid and trade *or* war and the threat of war to solve their outstanding problems; they relied on all three instruments of foreign policy and did so at the same time.

Nor would it be accurate to imply that the Third Phase reflected an emotional love-and-hate relationship evolving between the two major powers. On the contrary, the intensity of hostile feelings generated by the Cold War began to subside, giving way not to a sudden burst of affection but to an attitude of calculated cordiality at best and calculated coolness at worst. The Cold War thus officially yielded to the "Cool War," with the tempers of yesteryear apparently in the deep freeze. But unofficially, on the popular level, the relative clarity of the Cold War was replaced by the perplexity of the emerging era. In the United States and in the Soviet Union as well, some individuals and groups remained committed to feelings, and policies, of belligerence; they were the "mournful pessimists" who would not shed their Cold War mentality and would equate cooperation and diplomatic efforts with appeasement or capitulation. At the other end of the political spectrum were the "jubilant optimists," particularly in the United States, who vastly overestimated the dimensions and dynamics of change in the international system.

No doubt the Third Phase—because of its remarkable complexity—lent itself to public misjudgment and confusion.

One year, during the Cuban Missile Crisis, Soviet and American warships faced each other "eyeball-to-eyeball," as President Kennedy's Secretary of State, Dean Rusk, noted. The following year, the President called for the re-examination of *our* view of the Cold War and *our* attitude toward the Soviet Union. Then, while the United States would pour men and *matériel* into Vietnam to fight "communism," in Moscow —still the citadel if not the center of communism—the United States and the Soviet Union would agree to the partial Nuclear Test Ban Treaty. Similarly, President Kennedy, who led the way to such cooperative steps as the opening of the hot line between Washington and Moscow, would also remark (during the same year and, incidentally, only four days before his death) that,

> If it was not for the assistance which we have rendered to millions of people, if it were not for the alliances which we have made in SEATO, our association with CENTO, our alliances in NATO, our alliances in the inter-American system, long ago this globe of ours would have seen the communist advance sweep over much of what is now free.

Such contradictory perceptions of, and policies toward, the Soviet Union—and by the Soviet Union toward the West—continued throughout the 1960s. The war in Vietnam and, to a lesser extent, the Soviet invasion of Czechoslovakia in 1968 slowed down, though failed to curtail, the cooperative aspects of Soviet-American relations. Soviet assistance in helping the United States out of Vietnam without the appearance of immediate defeat was largely due to the growing Soviet desire for improved relations with the West in general and the United States in particular. Pressed by economic needs and technological backwardness at home and gripped by fear of being outmaneuvered by China abroad, the Soviet leaders favorably, if cautiously, responded to the discreet overtures of their major European adversary, West Germany, and their major global adversary in the West, the United States. By the time the first Soviet-West German and Soviet-American summit meetings concluded, in 1970 and 1972 respectively, the Soviet leaders succeeded in convincing the West that the evolving "mixed" relations of the present—more cooperation, some competition, less or no confrontation—reflected long-term mutual needs and interests rather than the short-term tactical requirements of the moment.

More specifically, the Third Phase also witnessed the realization of some of the historic goals of Soviet foreign policy since the end of World War II. Because of the American desire to extricate the U.S. from Vietnam and obtain a larger share in the profitable East-West trade; and because of the West German desire to end the European political deadlock, assert the maturity and independence of West Germany, and participate in promising East-West trade relations, the Soviet leadership could negotiate the following accomplishments:

First, by sanctioning the German Democratic Republic (East Germany) and consenting to separate representation for the two German states in the United Nations, the West has tacitly confirmed the most remarkable Soviet gain resulting from World War II—the division of Germany.

Second, by acknowledging the Oder-Neisse line as Poland's western frontier (as much of Western Europe has done) and the European *status quo* (as both President Nixon and Chancellor Brandt of West Germany have done), the West has tacitly confirmed the other main consequence of World War II—Soviet hegemony over East-Central Europe.

It may be argued, of course, that the political realities of postwar Europe had been shaped by World War II itself and that therefore implicit Western acknowledgment of these realities did no more than formalize the war's outcome. To argue this way, however, is both to state the obvious and to miss the significance of "formalities" in international politics in general and in East-West relations in particular. For what should be emphasized is that the West, having been drawn into the Cold War largely because of the twin issues of Germany and East-Central Europe, has now agreed to shelve these issues, thus indicating that—despite occasional statements or rhetoric to the contrary—it would press neither for German reunification nor for political independence in East-Central Europe.

To be sure, the understandings and agreements also contained Soviet concessions. First, by reassuming its responsibility for Berlin and assuring free access to and from that beleaguered city, the Soviet Union has tacitly acknowledged the permanence of Western rights and presence there. Second, by holding highly publicized summit meetings with the President of the U.S. and the Chancellor of West Germany, the Soviet Union has at least publicly removed these countries from its "enemy list," which may well be a risky precedent for a country that has historically blamed "imperialist encirclement" and German belligerence for its problems and difficulties. In any case, having been maneuvered by the West into the least-desirable corner of the emerging three-power U.S.-Soviet-Chinese triangle, the Soviet Union appeared to embark on the path of tempering its anti-Western stance, implying that it had more to fear of China than of the West. It was to be three for the seesaw, perhaps—undoubtedly an intriguing configuration in the international politics of the postwar world!

While the U.S.-China connection has rightly captured world-wide attention, its importance lies more in what it bodes for the future than in specific achievements to date. For the time being, what needs to be stressed is the importance of the modified Western position on Central Europe: that the West has acknowledged the Soviet concept of a divided Germany and Soviet hegemony in East-Central Europe. *Thus, to suggest, as was done earlier in this Introduction, that the Cold War is over because the expectation of a Hot War has faded may be accurate but incomplete; what needs to be added is that the Cold War is over mainly because these two troublesome issues—which, more than any other, provided the original justification for the U.S. entry into the Cold War—have been removed from contention.*

This conclusion in turn leads to two sets of controversial questions.

One has to do with the wisdom and propriety of the new Western position. Were the Western concessions significant? Were they necessary? Were the Soviet concessions "mostly bubbles," as *The Economist* of London claimed? Did the West realize the futility of rigidly holding on to policies whose implementation would have required military action? If so, if the West's new stance on Central Europe was based on such pragmatic considerations, should the West generally discard Cold War objectives, however noble, whose realization seems neither imminent nor likely?

The answer to these difficult questions depends on one's basic assumptions about the role of power and perhaps the role of morality in international politics. If one subscribes to the validity of the anti-communism of the Cold War era, or finds the Munich analogy about the dangers of appeasement pertinent, then the answer is likely to be critical of the United States and particularly of West Germany. For on balance the Western concessions were more substantial than those extracted from the Soviet Union, and, furthermore, essentially correct policies, in this view, should not be sacrificed on the altar of pragmatism.

If, on the other hand, one subscribes to what might be called the "anti-anticommunism" of the post-Vietnam era, or finds the Vietnam analogy about the dangers of overcommitment pertinent, then the answer is likely to be supportive of the United States and particularly of West Germany. For if the relaxation of international tension and the improvement of the cooperative dimensions of Soviet-U.S. relations can be attained by casting aside objectives of possibly less than fundamental interest to the U.S.—whose implementation, at any rate, is impossible without war—then "measuring" concessions is neither relevant nor necessary: what matters is the removal of issues of contention and the reduction of the danger of war.*

3. BACK TO THE ORIGINS: NEW QUESTIONS

Another set of questions will take us back to the origins of the Cold War. If the United States or the West in general could so significantly alter its policy objectives concerning the future of Germany and the fate of East-Central Europe in the early 1970s, could it not have altogether avoided assuming responsibility for such concerns in the 1940s? What was so vital about Central Europe in the 1940s that, judging by the ominous lack of a national debate now, could be so easily disavowed in the 1970s? Couldn't the United States have been as "understanding" of Soviet goals and aspirations in the 1940s as it was apparently becoming in the 1970s? Indeed, was containment really necessary? Was the Cold War then really necessary?

Such a new look at old events is an immensely difficult task. In the wake of the Vietnam fiasco, it is tempting to indict American foreign policy of earlier years as well, possibly discounting in the process the political climate under which it was shaped. Conversely, it is always

---

* On balance, this writer approves the new Western position—adding, however, a word of caution. If the danger of the Munich analogy—Never Trust an Enemy to Abide by an Agreement!—lies in its inflexible opposition to negotiated settlement, the danger of the Vietnam analogy—No More Vietnams!—lies in its inflexible opposition to U.S. military involvement under all circumstances (save a direct attack on the United States). Foreign policy by either analogy leaves no room for fresh initiatives, necessary maneuverings, and indeed the proper representation of this country's legitimate interests abroad.

tempting to argue that what was done had to be done, as if the U.S. could do nothing else but what in fact it did. As a matter of fact, these polar positions—discussed at greater length in the bibliographical sketch—framed the heated debate of the 1960s between the so-called "revisionist" and "traditionalist" historians about the origins of the Cold War.

Going beyond the revisionist-traditionalist debate probably requires that we further explore *the extent of Soviet objectives in the postwar era* and then assess *American sensitivity toward subtle differences within the Soviet, and later on within the Chinese, leadership over foreign policy.* Unfortunately, neither issue lends itself to easy answers or definitive judgment—only additional questions.

The difficulty with any analysis of the extent or scope of Soviet objectives lies not only in the usually mentioned "lack of information," but also in the analyst's disposition toward the validity of the Soviet leadership's *statements* on foreign policy. Nobody can seriously question that Stalin believed in the inevitability of a communist world based on the Soviet model or experience. Nor can anyone seriously question the Soviet leadership's identification with the Leninist view that even inevitable historical change requires hard work and united action. What is at issue, then, is not whether the Soviet leaders believed in the universal applicability of their cause, but whether in 1945 or 1947 or 1948 they were prepared to compel the West to accept their objective. Alas, political leaders everywhere are prone to present maximum goals which they themselves know cannot be readily realized.

Given the unreliability of Soviet statements about foreign policy goals, what about the *facts* of Soviet expansionism?

As of 1945, the picture was probably still unclear. The Red Army having reached the heart of Europe, the division of Germany was just taking place and pro-Soviet regimes were only surfacing in East-Central Europe. By February, 1948, however, when a *coup* imposed a communist government on Czechoslovakia, all of East-Central Europe, including East Germany, had been brought into the Soviet orbit by force. Should these acts have been interpreted as the beginnings of Soviet expansion aimed in the end at Western Europe, as the West was apt to believe, or were they merely grounded in the Soviet Union's own security, as some critics maintain?

An indirect but pointed answer might be to relate the well-known but only partly applicable story of the hotel burglar, a story Senator Henry M. Jackson is fond of telling. This burglar approached his job with the attitude of a cautious professional. So that he would not be caught, he tested every doorknob in the hotel, assuming that there were three possibilities. If the door was unlocked, he would walk in; if the door was firmly locked, he would walk away; if the doorknob was loose, he would jiggle it, play with it, try it—if the door opened then, he would walk in, if not, he would walk away. The basically cautious but ambitious approach underlying Soviet foreign policy—and the foreign policies of other major powers—may not be fundamentally different from that of this burglar, even though the burglar seeks access to gain money rather than influence.

At any rate, the more direct answer is that had it not been for containment, for the Marshall Plan, and for NATO, the Soviet Union was likely to have extended its influence into Western Europe. As Senator Fulbright suggests (Chapter 5), "by 1947, with the United States virtually disarmed and Western Europe in a condition of economic paralysis, the Soviet Union might plausibly have tried to take over Western Europe through the manipulation of Communist parties, through military intimidation, through economic strangulation, and possibly even through direct military action." The facts of Soviet expansionism in Central Europe between 1945 and 1948, combined with Soviet statements about the inevitability of a communist world, made a disturbingly strong case for this possibility. While there was no evidence, then or now, to identify Soviet foreign policy with unlimited or globalist expansionism, there was ample reason to conclude that the thrust of Soviet foreign policy in the second half of the 1940s was aimed at Western Europe.

But what about American reactions? Could it be that American foreign policy was so inciting in 1945–47 as to provoke subsequent Soviet truculence? Or, since both the Soviet and the Chinese political elites appear to have been debating the proper approach to the U.S. in the early postwar years, could we not have been more sensitive to their internal debates and skillfully supported factions more favorably inclined toward the U.S.?

These questions—dealing as they do with the issue of American overreactions, ineptness, or insensitivity—are explored at some length in Part Two of this book, and the authors' conclusions are not uniform. There is agreement, however, about the existence of some very subtle differences both within the Soviet and Chinese leaderships about the extent to which they should consider the United States their enemy in the postwar world. For example, in 1946 some high-ranking scholars in Moscow's official Institute of World Economy and World Politics—led by Eugene Varga and possibly supported by Stalin's deputy, Georgi Malenkov—did not see immediate prospects for, and by implication cautioned against, untimely "revolutionary advances" abroad. True, Varga was subsequently dismissed from his job and purged, and his heretical position was denounced, but that happened only after the Truman Doctrine had been declared. In other words, what was probably seen in Moscow as our hardening anti-communist stance might have contributed unwittingly to the anti-Varga case and made a more moderate communist position toward the U.S. unpalatable. Then, in addition, there is the far more direct, recently published diplomatic evidence that several Chinese leaders including Mao Tse-tung, hoping to avoid undue dependence on the Soviet Union, would have welcomed American recognition in 1949 and economic ties as early as 1945.

The United States did not explore these possibilities. In the Soviet case, the Varga controversy was probably considered an academic debate—and, for all we know for sure, in part it was. Moreover, our assumption of monolithic unity behind Stalin within the Soviet elite and within the international communist movement blinded us to the nuances of both intra-party and inter-party Communist politics. It was not until the Soviet-Yugoslav break of 1948—fully understood and successfully exploited by the U.S.—that some began to suspect that the notion of monolithic unity among communists had been a hoax perpetrated on an unsuspecting West ready to assign superhuman qualities to its adversaries. As to the Chinese, our lack of response to the 1949 initiative for recognition is particularly perplexing, for Mao was by then in power and it would have been to our advantage, of course, to maintain American presence in China. Unfortunately, the Western assumption of communist unity must have made American diplomats and analysts screen out information and disregard alternative policies which controverted their preconceived notions.

All in all, the conclusion may well be that the United States was not at all skillful, let alone ingenious or imaginative, in exploring opportunities for moderation within the Soviet Union and China. But in retrospect, at least, these opportunities appear to have been rather modest in the Soviet case, and even a country with far more experience in the subtleties of international politics than the U.S. then possessed could have missed the clues. On the other hand, our inept handling of the 1949 Chinese initiative demonstrates the extent to which the United States had by that time decided on an anti-communist posture both in Europe and Asia.

In sum, the United States neither sought to probe nor succeeded in exploiting whatever differences appear to have existed within the Soviet leadership and also failed to respond to Mao's exploratory signals. Thus, during the first few years of the Cold War, American sensitivity toward the subtle nuances of communist politics was conspicuously, if understandably, lacking, leaving open the ever-present possibility of missed opportunities. Yet it does not necessarily follow that the U.S. could have substantially moderated the course of Soviet foreign policy or that—in fact—it was American intransigence which had prompted Soviet leaders to do what they did. Nor can there be much doubt, finally, that, having consolidated its control over Central Europe without actual resistance from the West, the Soviet Union was indeed aiming in the direction of exploiting the prevailing weaknesses of Western Europe.

Under these circumstances, the containment of Soviet power in Europe seemed clearly warranted. Containment was required, however, not so much because of what was happening in Germany and East-Central Europe but because of what Soviet policies there portended for the future of Europe as a whole. Shedding crocodile tears over the fate of East-Central Europe and the division of Germany was the American politician's way of exploiting anti-communist sentiments; it was his way of lining up domestic support for the defense of *Western* Europe—as well as for his re-election.

However, once such domestic support was at hand and both the economic reconstruction and the necessary defense of Western Europe were therefore assured—by the early or mid-1950s—there was no longer any serious justification to prolong, let alone intensify, the Cold War in Europe. Especially between 1953 and 1955—in the aftermath of Stalin's death, the time of the Soviet-Yugoslav rapprochement, the Austrian Peace Treaty, and the Geneva summit of 1955—there were indications of an opening, of a serious reconsideration of Soviet foreign policy toward the West. That might well have been the first opportunity to acknowledge, however tacitly, the postwar political realities of Europe, and thus assure the Soviet Union of our disinclination to change the *status quo* by force. If the Soviet leaders had responded in kind, the Cold War, with its gruesome expectation of nuclear exchange, would have given way some twenty years sooner to the mixed pattern of the Third Phase—to the more promising combination of cooperation, competition, and cooperation in the international system.

4. TOWARD LIMITED DÉTENTE

If a date is to be assigned to the end of the Third Phase and the beginning of an era of limited détente or "relative normalcy," the years 1972–73 shall do. Despite over two decades of intense hostility, that was the time when the President of the United States went to China and China arrived at the United Nations. Despite the U.S. mining of Haiphong and the bombing of Hanoi, that was the time when the Soviet Union did not let the devastation of its Vietnamese ally interfere with the Soviet-American summit meeting in Moscow. And despite years and years of exhausting effort in Vietnam, that was the time when

the United States at last found it possible to withdraw from that beleaguered country.

Indeed, despite almost three decades of accumulated suspicion and
belligerence, Leonid Brezhnev could declare on American television
in the summer of 1973 that, "Mankind has outgrown the rigid Cold
War armor it was once forced to wear." The Cold War was officially
over. Agreement was signed on the limitation of strategic arms. The
West German parliament ratified the Moscow-Bonn accord. East-West
trade expanded. The European Security Conference brought East and
West together on a grand scale, and negotiations began on the reduction of military forces in Europe. Leonid Brezhnev made a historic
journey—the first by a Soviet leader—to West Germany, then to the
United States, then to France, even though on his way home—unlike
his predecessor Nikita Khrushchev in 1959—he failed to stop in Peking
to brief the Chinese leadership. Indeed, with the possible exception
of the lingering crisis in the Middle East, it was in the danger zone of
the Sino-Soviet borderlands where direct military confrontation could
still threaten the emerging condition of the international system. Elsewhere, the trend toward limited détente was being diligently cultivated.

Or was it? Fallout shelters were still being built in the Soviet Union
and China, and an emergency warning system was still being maintained in the U.S. The military budgets of the major powers were not
expected to decrease in the years ahead. The United States was led by
a man whose rather sudden transition from anti-communism to con-
geniality with the communists could hardly inspire deep confidence.
The Soviet Union was led by a man of Stalinist past, whose troops suppressed the "Prague spring" of 1968 and whose chief delegate at the
European Security Conference was the same Valerian Zorin who had
masterminded the ominous 1948 *coup* in Czechoslovakia. China was
led by a man whose truculent position toward India and Tibet in the
past and toward real or potential domestic adversaries during the more
recent Cultural Revolution would surely fail to qualify him as a peace-
maker.

Under these circumstances, will the era of limited détente last?
What lies beyond the age of the Cold War?

At least three future scenarios can be safely discounted. The achievement of some nebulous "victory" by either the Soviet Union or the
United States, with or without a nuclear encounter, is simply beyond
reach. Given the residue of suspicion, so too is the pursuit by either
side of a policy of turning swords into plowshares, the policy of "diplomacy without deterrence." Thus the resolution of outstanding problems
will not be attained through diplomacy without military strength nor

through military strength without diplomacy. Finally, the once widely discussed economic convergence of the two systems under the impact of modernization is not on the horizon either. However, even if it should evolve over a long period of time, the internal affinity of the two systems would not necessarily guarantee a substantially transformed international environment.

In the coming decade or two, then, the continuation of the pattern of limited détente—*more* cooperation, *some* competition, *no* direct confrontation—is more likely than any other. This conclusion may be supported by the following observations:

(1) In the wake of the war it could not win in Vietnam and of domestic upheaval it could barely control, the *United States* has had to trim its foreign commitments. It is not likely to embark on a different path primarily because more ambitious foreign undertakings require the ability to assume the worst about the adversary's intentions and the skill to mobilize a skeptical public—qualities which are, in periods of relative calm, conspicuously lacking in a democratic society.

(2) In the wake of the Cold War it could not win with the West and of the confrontation it could win but was fearful of provoking with China, and of domestic economic problems it could not eliminate, the *Soviet Union* has had to seek accommodation with the West. It is not likely to embark on a different path primarily because limited détente with the West is on balance more helpful than detrimental in its efforts to contain China, increase its influence in the Indian subcontinent and in the Middle East, and improve its lagging economy.

(3) In the wake of the tumultuous Cultural Revolution generated to uphold the purity of its internal system and of the confrontation with the Soviet Union generated to uphold the purity of the international communist ideal, *China* has also had to trim its often pretentious objectives. It is not likely to embark on a different path primarily because it seems to lack the ability to effect more fundamental changes at home or abroad without the important U.S.-connection.

To paraphrase Metternich, the major antagonists of the international system remain too fearful to fight and too stupid to agree. Accordingly, the promise of the era of limited détente may be only "more of the same," yet this should be a comforting, indeed a bright, prospect for those who have at last emerged from the darkness of the fallout shelter.

CHARLES GATI
East Berne, New York

CAGING THE BEAR:
CONTAINMENT AND THE COLD WAR

PART ONE

THE SETTING, 1947

1

THE POLICY OF CONTAINMENT:
The Truman Doctrine

Mr. President, Mr. Speaker, Members of the Congress of the United States:

The gravity of the situation which confronts the world today necessitates my appearance before a joint session of the Congress.

The foreign policy and the national security of this country are involved.

One aspect of the present situation, which I wish to present to you at this time for your consideration and decision, concerns Greece and Turkey.

The United States has received from the Greek Government an urgent appeal for financial and economic assistance. Preliminary reports from the American Economic Mission now in Greece and reports from the American Ambassador in Greece corroborate the statement of the Greek Government that assistance is imperative if Greece is to survive as a free nation.

I do not believe that the American people and the Congress wish to turn a deaf ear to the appeal of the Greek Government.

Greece is not a rich country. Lack of sufficient natural resources has always forced the Greek people to work hard to make both ends meet. Since 1940 this industrious and peace-loving country has suffered in-

Public Papers of the Presidents of the United States: Harry S Truman, 1947 (Washington: Government Printing Office, 1953), pp. 176–80.

vasion, four years of cruel enemy occupation, and bitter internal strife.

When forces of liberation entered Greece they found that the retreating Germans had destroyed virtually all the railways, roads, port facilities, communications, and merchant marine. More than a thousand villages had been burned. Eighty-five percent of the children were tubercular. Livestock, poultry, and draft animals had almost disappeared. Inflation had wiped out practically all savings.

As a result of these tragic conditions, a militant minority, exploiting human want and misery, was able to create political chaos which, until now, has made economic recovery impossible.

Greece is today without funds to finance the importation of those goods which are essential to bare subsistence. Under these circumstances the people of Greece cannot make progress in solving their problems of reconstruction. Greece is in desperate need of financial and economic assistance to enable it to resume purchases of food, clothing, fuel, and seeds. These are indispensable for the subsistence of its people and are obtainable only from abroad. Greece must have help to import the goods necessary to restore internal order and security so essential for economic and political recovery.

The Greek Government has also asked for the assistance of experienced American administrators, economists, and technicians to insure that the financial and other aid given to Greece shall be used effectively in creating a stable and self-sustaining economy and in improving its public administration.

The very existence of the Greek state is today threatened by the terrorist activities of several thousand armed men, led by Communists, who defy the Government's authority at a number of points, particularly along the northern boundaries. A commission appointed by the United Nations Security Council is at present investigating disturbed conditions in northern Greece and alleged border violations along the frontier between Greece on the one hand and Albania, Bulgaria, and Yugoslavia on the other.

Meanwhile, the Greek Government is unable to cope with the situation. The Greek Army is small and poorly equipped. It needs supplies and equipment if it is to restore authority to the Government throughout Greek territory.

Greece must have assistance if it is to become a self-supporting and self-respecting democracy.

The United States must supply that assistance. We have already extended to Greece certain types of relief and economic aid, but these are inadequate.

There is no other country to which democratic Greece can turn.

No other nation is willing and able to provide the necessary support for a democratic Greek Government.

The British Government, which has been helping Greece, can give no further financial or economic aid after March 31. Great Britain finds itself under the necessity of reducing or liquidating its commitments in several parts of the world, including Greece.

We have considered how the United Nations might assist in this crisis. But the situation is an urgent one requiring immediate action, and the United Nations and its related organizations are not in a position to extend help of the kind that is required.

It is important to note that the Greek Government has asked for our aid in utilizing effectively the financial and other assistance we may give to Greece, and in improving its public administration. It is of the utmost importance that we supervise the use of any funds made available to Greece, in such a manner that each dollar spent will count toward making Greece self-supporting, and will help to build an economy in which a healthy democracy can flourish.

No government is perfect. One of the chief virtues of a democracy, however, is that its defects are always visible and under democratic processes can be pointed out and corrected. The Government of Greece is not perfect. Nevertheless it represents 85 percent of the members of the Greek Parliament who were chosen in an election last year. Foreign observers, including 692 Americans, considered this election to be a fair expression of the views of the Greek people.

The Greek Government has been operating in an atmosphere of chaos and extremism. It has made mistakes. The extension of aid by this country does not mean that the United States condones everything that the Greek Government has done or will do. We have condemned in the past, and we condemn now, extremist measures of the right or the left. We have in the past advised tolerance, and we advise tolerance now.

Greece's neighbor, Turkey, also deserves our attention.

The future of Turkey as an independent and economically sound state is clearly no less important to the freedom-loving peoples of the world than the future of Greece. The circumstances in which Turkey finds itself today are considerably different from those of Greece. Turkey has been spared the disasters that have beset Greece. And during the war the United States and Great Britain furnished Turkey with material aid.

Nevertheless, Turkey now needs our support.

Since the war Turkey has sought additional financial assistance from Great Britain and the United States for the purpose of effecting that modernization necessary for the maintenance of its national integrity.

That integrity is essential to the preservation of order in the Middle East.

The British Government has informed us that, owing to its own difficulties, it can no longer extend financial or economic aid to Turkey.

As in the case of Greece, if Turkey is to have the assistance it needs, the United States must supply it. We are the only country able to provide that help.

I am fully aware of the broad implications involved if the United States extends assistance to Greece and Turkey, and I shall discuss these implications with you at this time.

One of the primary objectives of the foreign policy of the United States is the creation of conditions in which we and other nations will be able to work out a way of life free from coercion. This was a fundamental issue in the war with Germany and Japan. Our victory was won over countries which sought to impose their will, and their way of life, upon other nations.

To insure the peaceful development of nations, free from coercion, the United States has taken a leading part in establishing the United Nations. The United Nations is designed to make possible lasting freedom and independence for all its members. We shall not realize our objectives, however, unless we are willing to help free peoples to maintain their free institutions and their national integrity against aggressive movements that seek to impose upon them totalitarian regimes. This is no more than a frank recognition that totalitarian regimes imposed upon free peoples, by direct or indirect aggression, undermine the foundations of international peace and hence the security of the United States.

The peoples of a number of countries of the world have recently had totalitarian regimes forced upon them against their will. The Government of the United States has made frequent protests against coercion and intimidation, in violation of the Yalta agreement, in Poland, Rumania, and Bulgaria. I must also state that in a number of other countries there have been similar developments.

At the present moment in world history nearly every nation must choose between alternative ways of life. The choice is too often not a free one.

One way of life is based upon the will of the majority, and is distinguished by free institutions, representative government, free elections, guaranties of individual liberty, freedom of speech and religion, and freedom from political oppression.

The second way of life is based upon the will of a minority forcibly imposed upon the majority. It relies upon terror and oppression, a controlled press and radio, fixed elections, and the suppression of personal feedoms.

I believe that it must be the policy of the United States to support free peoples who are resisting attempted subjugation by armed minorities or by outside pressures.

I believe that we must assist free peoples to work out their own destinies in their own way.

I believe that our help should be primarily through economic and financial aid which is essential to economic stability and orderly political processes.

The world is not static, and the *status quo* is not sacred. But we cannot allow changes in the *status quo* in violation of the Charter of the United Nations by such methods as coercion, or by such subterfuges as political infiltration. In helping free and independent nations to maintain their freedom, the United States will be giving effect to the principles of the Charter of the United Nations.

It is necessary only to glance at a map to realize that the survival and integrity of the Greek nation are of grave importance in a much wider situation. If Greece should fall under the control of an armed minority, the effect upon its neighbor, Turkey, would be immediate and serious. Confusion and disorder might well spread throughout the entire Middle East.

Moreover, the disappearance of Greece as an independent state would have a profound effect upon those countries in Europe whose peoples are struggling against great difficulties to maintain their freedoms and their independence while they repair the damages of war.

It would be an unspeakable tragedy if these countries, which have struggled so long against overwhelming odds, should lose that victory for which they sacrificed so much. Collapse of free institutions and loss of independence would be disastrous not only for them but for the world. Discouragement and possibly failure would quickly be the lot of neighboring peoples striving to maintain their freedom and independence.

Should we fail to aid Greece and Turkey in this fateful hour, the effect will be far-reaching to the West as well as to the East.

We must take immediate and resolute action.

I therefore ask the Congress to provide authority for assistance to Greece and Turkey in the amount of $400,000,000 for the period ending June 30, 1948. In requesting these funds, I have taken into consideration the maximum amount of relief assistance which would be furnished to Greece out of the $350,000,000 which I recently requested that the Congress authorize for the prevention of starvation and suffering in countries devastated by the war.

In addition to funds, I ask the Congress to authorize the detail of American civilian and military personnel to Greece and Turkey, at the request of those countries, to assist in the tasks of reconstruction, and for the purpose of supervising the use of such financial and material assistance as may be furnished. I recommend that authority also be provided for the instruction and training of selected Greek and Turkish personnel.

Finally, I ask that the Congess provide authority which will permit the speediest and most effective use, in terms of needed commodities, supplies, and equipment, of such funds as may be authorized.

If further funds, or further authority, should be needed for purposes indicated in this message, I shall not hesitate to bring the situation before the Congress. On this subject the Executive and Legislative branches of the Government must work together.

This is a serious course upon which we embark.

I would not recommend it except that the alternative is much more serious.

The United States contributed $341,000,000,000 toward winning World War II. This is an investment in world freedom and world peace.

The assistance that I am recommending for Greece and Turkey amounts to little more than one-tenth of one percent of this investment. It is only common sense that we should safeguard this investment and make sure that it was not in vain.

The seeds of totalitarian regimes are nurtured by misery and want. They spread and grow in the evil soil of poverty and strife. They reach their full growth when the hope of a people for a better life has died.

We must keep that hope alive.

The free peoples of the world look to us for support in maintaining their freedoms.

If we falter in our leadership, we may endanger the peace of the world—and we shall surely endanger the welfare of our own Nation.

Great responsibilities have been placed upon us by the swift movement of events.

I am confident that the Congress will face these responsibilities squarely.

2

THE IDEOLOGY OF CONTAINMENT:
The X Article

I

The political personality of Soviet power as we know it today is the product of ideology and circumstances: ideology inherited by the present Soviet leaders from the movement in which they had their political origin, and circumstances of the power which they now have exercised for nearly three decades in Russia. There can be few tasks of psychological analysis more difficult than to try to trace the interaction of these two forces and the relative rôle of each in the determination of official Soviet conduct. Yet the attempt must be made if that conduct is to be understood and effectively countered.

It is difficult to summarize the set of ideological concepts with which the Soviet leaders came into power. Marxian ideology, in its Russian-Communist projection, has always been in process of subtle evolution. The materials on which it bases itself are extensive and complex. But the outstanding features of Communist thought as it existed in 1916 may perhaps be summarized as follows: (a) that the central factor in the life of man, the factor which determines the character of public life and the "physiognomy of society," is the system by which material goods are produced and exchanged; (b) that the capitalist system of

Original title: "The Sources of Soviet Conduct." Reprinted by permission of author and publisher from *Foreign Affairs* (July 1947). Copyright © 1947 by Council on Foreign Relations, Inc.

production is a nefarious one which inevitably leads to the exploitation of the working class by the capital-owning class and is incapable of developing adequately the economic resources of society or of distributing fairly the material goods produced by human labor; (c) that capitalism contains the seeds of its own destruction and must, in view of the inability of the capital-owning class to adjust itself to economic change, result eventually and inescapably in a revolutionary transfer of power to the working class; and (d) that imperialism, the final phase of capitalism, leads directly to war and revolution.

The rest may be outlined in Lenin's own words: "Unevenness of economic and political development is the inflexible law of capitalism. It follows from this that the victory of Socialism may come originally in a few capitalist countries or even in a single capitalist country. The victorious proletariat of that country, having expropriated the capitalists and having organized Socialist production at home, would rise against the remaining capitalist world, drawing to itself in the process the oppressed classes of other countries."[1] It must be noted that there was no assumption that capitalism would perish without proletarian revolution. A final push was needed from a revolutionary proletariat movement in order to tip over the tottering structure. But it was regarded as inevitable that sooner or later that push be given.

For 50 years prior to the outbreak of the Revolution, this pattern of thought had exercised great fascination for the members of the Russian revolutionary movement. Frustrated, discontented, hopeless of finding self-expression—or too impatient to seek it—in the confining limits of the Tsarist political system, yet lacking wide popular support for their choice of bloody revolution as a means of social betterment, these revolutionists found in Marxist theory a highly convenient rationalization for their own instinctive desires. It afforded pseudo-scientific justification for their impatience, for their categoric denial of all value in the Tsarist system, for their yearning for power and revenge and for their inclination to cut corners in the pursuit of it. It is therefore no wonder that they had come to believe implicitly in the truth and soundness of the Marxian-Leninist teachings, so congenial to their own impulses and emotions. Their sincerity need not be impugned. This is a phenomenon as old as human nature itself. It has never been more aptly described than by Edward Gibbon, who wrote in "The Decline and Fall of the Roman Empire": "From enthusiasm to imposture the step is perilous and slippery; the demon of Socrates affords a memorable instance how a wise man may deceive himself, how a good man may deceive others, how the conscience may slumber in a mixed and middle

---

[1] "Concerning the Slogans of the United States of Europe," August 1915. Official Soviet edition of Lenin's works.

state between self-illusion and voluntary fraud." And it was with this set of conceptions that the members of the Bolshevik Party entered into power.

Now it must be noted that through all the years of preparation for revolution, the attention of these men, as indeed of Marx himself, had been centered less on the future form which Socialism[2] would take than on the necessary overthrow of rival power which, in their view, had to precede the introduction of Socialism. Their views, therefore, on the positive program to be put into effect, once power was attained, were for the most part nebulous, visionary and impractical. Beyond the nationalization of industry and the expropriation of large private capital holdings there was no agreed program. The treatment of the peasantry, which according to the Marxist formulation was not of the proletariat, had always been a vague spot in the pattern of Communist thought; and it remained an object of controversy and vacillation for the first ten years of Communist power.

The circumstances of the immediate post-revolution period—the existence in Russia of civil war and foreign intervention, together with the obvious fact that the Communists represented only a tiny minority of the Russian people—made the establishment of dictatorial power a necessity. The experiment with "war Communism" and the abrupt attempt to eliminate private production and trade had unfortunate economic consequences and caused further bitterness against the new revolutionary régime. While the temporary relaxation of the effort to communize Russia, represented by the New Economic Policy, alleviated some of this economic distress and thereby served its purpose, it also made it evident that the "capitalistic sector of society" was still prepared to profit at once from any relaxation of governmental pressure, and would, if permitted to continue to exist, always constitute a powerful opposing element to the Soviet régime and a serious rival for influence in the country. Somewhat the same situation prevailed with respect to the individual peasant who, in his own small way, was also a private producer.

Lenin, had he lived, might have proved a great enough man to reconcile these conflicting forces to the ultimate benefit of Russian society, though this is questionable. But be that as it may, Stalin, and those whom he led in the struggle for succession to Lenin's position of leadership, were not the men to tolerate rival political forces in the sphere of power which they coveted. Their sense of insecurity was too great. Their particular brand of fanaticism, unmodified by any of the Anglo-Saxon traditions of compromise, was too fierce and too jealous to

[2] Here and elsewhere in this paper "Socialism" refers to Marxist or Leninist Communism, not to liberal Socialism of the Second International variety.

envisage any permanent sharing of power. From the Russian-Asiatic world out of which they had emerged they carried with them a skepticism as to the possibilities of permanent and peaceful coexistence of rival forces. Easily persuaded of their own doctrinaire "rightness," they insisted on the submission or destruction of all competing power. Outside of the Communist Party, Russian society was to have no rigidity. There were to be no forms of collective human activity or association which would not be dominated by the Party. No other force in Russian society was to be permitted to achieve vitality or integrity. Only the Party was to have structure. All else was to be an amorphous mass.

And within the Party the same principle was to apply. The mass of Party members might go through the motions of election, deliberation, decision and action; but in these motions they were to be animated not by their own individual wills but by the awesome breath of the Party leadership and the overbrooding presence of "the word."

Let it be stressed again that subjectively these men probably did not seek absolutism for its own sake. They doubtless believed—and found it easy to believe—that they alone knew what was good for society and that they would accomplish that good once their power was secure and unchallengeable. But in seeking that security of their own rule they were prepared to recognize no restrictions, either of God or man, on the character of their methods. And until such time as that security might be achieved, they placed far down on their scale of operational priorities the comforts and happiness of the peoples entrusted to their care.

Now the outstanding circumstance concerning the Soviet régime is that down to the present day this process of political consolidation has never been completed and the men in the Kremlin have continued to be predominantly absorbed with the struggle to secure and make absolute the power which they seized in November 1917. They have endeavored to secure it primarily against forces at home, within Soviet society itself. But they have also endeavored to secure it against the outside world. For ideology, as we have seen, taught them that the outside world was hostile and that it was their duty eventually to overthrow the political forces beyond their borders. The powerful hands of Russian history and tradition reached up to sustain them in this feeling. Finally, their own aggressive intransigence with respect to the outside world began to find its own reaction; and they were soon forced, to use another Gibbonesque phrase, "to chastise the contumacy" which they themselves had provoked. It is an undeniable privilege of every man to prove himself right in the thesis that the world is his enemy; for if he reiterates it frequently enough and makes it the background of his conduct he is bound eventually to be right.

Now it lies in the nature of the mental world of the Soviet leaders, as well as in the character of their ideology, that no opposition to them can be officially recognized as having any merit or justification whatsoever. Such opposition can flow in theory, only from the hostile and incorrigible forces of dying capitalism. As long as remnants of capitalism were officially recognized as existing in Russia, it was possible to place on them, as an internal element, part of the blame for the maintenance of a dictatorial form of society. But as these remnants were liquidated, little by little, this justification fell away; and when it was indicated officially that they had been finally destroyed, it disappeared altogether. And this fact created one of the most basic of the compulsions which came to act upon the Soviet régime: since capitalism no longer existed in Russia and since it could not be admitted that there could be serious or widespread opposition to the Kremlin springing spontaneously from the liberated masses under its authority, it became necessary to justify the retention of the dictatorship by stressing the menace of capitalism abroad.

This began at an early date. In 1924 Stalin specifically defended the retention of the "organs of suppression," meaning, among others, the army and the secret police, on the ground that "as long as there is a capitalist encirclement there will be danger of intervention with all the consequences that flow from that danger." In accordance with that theory, and from that time on, all internal opposition forces in Russia have consistently been portrayed as the agents of foreign forces of reaction antagonistic to Soviet power.

By the same token, tremendous emphasis has been placed on the original Communist thesis of a basic antagonism between the capitalist and Socialist worlds. It is clear, from many indications, that this emphasis is not founded in reality. The real facts concerning it have been confused by the existence abroad of genuine resentment provoked by Soviet philosophy and tactics and occasionally by the existence of great centers of military power, notably the Nazi régime in Germany and the Japanese Government of the late 1930's, which did indeed have aggressive designs against the Soviet Union. But there is ample evidence that the stress laid in Moscow on the menace confronting Soviet society from the world outside its borders is founded not in the realities of foreign antagonism but in the necessity of explaining away the maintenance of dictatorial authority at home.

Now the maintenance of this pattern of Soviet power, namely, the pursuit of unlimited authority domestically, accompanied by the cultivation of the semi-myth of implacable foreign hostility, has gone far to shape the actual machinery of Soviet power as we know it today. Internal organs of administration which did not serve this purpose withered on the vine. Organs which did serve this purpose became vastly swollen. The security of Soviet power came to rest on the iron discipline of the Party, on the severity and ubiquity of the secret police, and on the uncompromising economic monopolism of the state. The "organs of suppression," in which the Soviet leaders had sought security from rival forces, became in large measure the masters of those whom they were designed to serve. Today the major part of the structure of Soviet power is committed to the perfection of the dictatorship and to the maintenance of the concept of Russia as in a state of seige, with the enemy lowering beyond the walls. And the millions of human beings who form that part of the structure of power must defend at all costs this concept of Russia's position, for without it they are themselves superfluous.

As things stand today, the rulers can no longer dream of parting with these organs of suppression. The quest for absolute power, pursued now for nearly three decades with a ruthlessness unparalleled (in scope at least) in modern times, has again produced internally, as it did externally, its own reaction. The excesses of the police apparatus have fanned the potential opposition to the régime into something far greater and more dangerous than it could have been before those excesses began.

But least of all can the rulers dispense with the fiction by which the maintenance of dictatorial power has been defended. For this fiction has been canonized in Soviet philosophy by the excesses already committed in its name; and it is now anchored in the Soviet structure of thought by bonds far greater than those of mere ideology.

II

So much for the historical background. What does it spell in terms of the political personality of Soviet power as we know it today?

Of the original ideology, nothing has been officially junked. Belief is maintained in the basic badness of capitalism, in the inevitability of its destruction, in the obligation of the proletariat to assist in that destruction and to take power into its own hands. But stress has come to be laid primarily on those concepts which relate most specifically to the Soviet régime itself: to its position as the sole truly Socialist régime in a dark and misguided world, and to the relationships of power within it.

The first of these concepts is that of the innate antagonism between capitalism and Socialism. We have seen how deeply that concept has become imbedded in foundations of Soviet power. It has profound implications for Russia's conduct as a member of international society.

It means that there can never be on Moscow's side any sincere assumption of a community of aims between the Soviet Union and powers which are regarded as capitalist. It must invariably be assumed in Moscow that the aims of the capitalist world are antagonistic to the Soviet régime, and therefore to the interests of the peoples it controls. If the Soviet Government occasionally sets its signature to documents which would indicate the contrary, this is to be regarded as a tactical manœuvre permissible in dealing with the enemy (who is without honor) and should be taken in the spirit of caveat emptor. Basically, the antagonism remains. It is postulated. And from it flow many of the phenomena which we find disturbing in the Kremlin's conduct of foreign policy: the secretiveness, the lack of frankness, the duplicity, the wary suspiciousness, and the basic unfriendliness of purpose. These phenomena are there to stay, for the foreseeable future. There can be variations of degree and of emphasis. When there is something the Russians want from us, one or the other of these features of their policy may be thrust temporarily into the background; and when that happens there will always be Americans who will leap forward with gleeful announcements that "the Russians have changed," and some who will even try to take credit for having brought about such "changes." But we should not be misled by tactical manœuvres. These characteristics of Soviet policy, like the postulate from which they flow, are basic to the internal nature of Soviet power, and will be with us, whether in the foreground or the background, until the internal nature of Soviet power is changed.

This means that we are going to continue for a long time to find the Russians difficult to deal with. It does not mean that they should be considered as embarked upon a do-or-die program to overthrow our society by a given date. The theory of the inevitability of the eventual fall of capitalism has the fortunate connotation that there is no hurry about it. The forces of progress can take their time in preparing the final coup de grâce. Meanwhile, what is vital is that the "Socialist fatherland"—that oasis of power which has been already won for Socialism in the person of the Soviet Union—should be cherished and defended by all good Communists at home and abroad, its fortunes promoted, its enemies badgered and confounded. The promotion of premature, "adventuristic" revolutionary projects abroad which might embarrass Soviet power in any way would be an inexcusable, even a counter-revolutionary act. The cause of Socialism is the support and promotion of Soviet power, as defined in Moscow.

This brings us to the second of the concepts important to contemporary Soviet outlook. That is the infallibility of the Kremlin. The Soviet concept of power, which permits no focal points of organization outside the Party itself, requires that the Party leadership remain in theory the sole repository of truth. For if truth were to be found elsewhere, there would be justification for its expression in organized activity. But it is precisely that which the Kremlin cannot and will not permit.

The leadership of the Communist Party is therefore always right, and has been always right ever since in 1929 Stalin formalized his personal power by announcing that decisions of the Politburo were being taken unanimously.

On the principle of infallibility there rests the iron discipline of the Communist Party. In fact, the two concepts are mutually self-supporting. Perfect discipline requires recognition of infallibility. Infallibility requires the observance of discipline. And the two together go far to determine the behaviorism of the entire Soviet apparatus of power. But their effect cannot be understood unless a third factor be taken into account: namely, the fact that the leadership is at liberty to put forward for tactical purposes any particular thesis which it finds useful to the cause at any particular moment and to require the faithful and unquestioning acceptance of that thesis by the members of the movement as a whole. This means that truth is not a constant but is actually created, for all intents and purposes, by the Soviet leaders themselves. It may vary from week to week, from month to month. It is nothing absolute and immutable—nothing which flows from objective reality. It is only the most recent manifestation of the wisdom of those in whom the ultimate wisdom is supposed to reside, because they represent the logic of history. The accumulative effect of these factors is to give to the whole subordinate apparatus of Soviet power an unshakable stubbornness and steadfastness in its orientation. This orientation can be changed at will by the Kremlin but by no other power. Once a given party line has been laid down on a given issue of current policy, the whole Soviet governmental machine, including the mechanism of diplomacy, moves inexorably along the prescribed path, like a persistent toy automobile wound up and headed in a given direction, stopping only when it meets with some unanswerable force. The individuals who are the components of this machine are unamenable to argument or reason which comes to them from outside sources. Their whole training has taught them to mistrust and discount the glib persuasiveness of the outside world. Like the white dog before the phonograph, they hear only the "master's voice." And if they are to be called off from the purposes last dictated to them, it is the master who must call them off. Thus the foreign representative cannot hope that his words will make any impression on them. The most that he can hope is that they will be transmitted to those at the top, who are capable of changing the party line. But even those are not likely to be swayed by any normal logic in the words of the bourgeois representative. Since there can be no appeal to common purposes, there can be no appeal to common mental approaches. For this reason, facts speak louder than words to the ears of the Kremlin; and words carry the greatest weight when they have the ring of reflecting, or being backed up by, facts of unchallengeable validity.

But we have seen that the Kremlin is under no ideological compulsion to accomplish its purposes in a hurry. Like the Church, it is dealing in ideological concepts which are of long-term validity, and it can afford to be patient. It has no right to risk the existing achievements of the revolution for the sake of vain baubles of the future. The very teachings of Lenin himself require great caution and flexibility in the pursuit of Communist purposes. Again, these precepts are fortified by the lessons of Russian history: of centuries of obscure battles between nomadic forces over the stretches of a vast unfortified plain. Here caution, circumspection, flexibility and deception are the valuable qualities; and their value finds natural appreciation in the Russian or the oriental mind. Thus the Kremlin has no compunction about retreating in the face of superior force. And being under the compulsion of no timetable, it does not get panicky under the necessity for such retreat. Its political action is a fluid stream which moves constantly, wherever it is permitted to move, toward a given goal. Its main concern is to make sure that it has filled every nook and cranny available to it in the basin of world power. But if it finds unassailable barriers in its path, it accepts these philosophically and accommodates itself to them. The main thing is that there should always be pressure, unceasing constant pressure, toward the desired goal. There is no trace of any feeling in Soviet psychology that that goal must be reached at any given time.

These considerations make Soviet diplomacy at once easier and more difficult to deal with than the diplomacy of individual aggressive leaders like Napoleon and Hitler. On the one hand it is more sensitive to contrary force, more ready to yield on individual sectors of the diplomatic front when that force is felt to be too strong, and thus more rational in the logic and rhetoric of power. On the other hand it cannot be easily defeated or discouraged by a single victory on the part of its opponents. And the patient persistence by which it is animated means that it can be effectively countered not by sporadic acts which represent the momentary whims of democratic opinion but only by intelligent long-range policies on the part of Russia's adversaries—policies no less steady in their purpose, and no less variegated and resourceful in their application, than those of the Soviet Union itself.

In these circumstances it is clear that the main element of any United States policy toward the Soviet Union must be that of a long-term, patient but firm and vigilant containment of Russian expansive tendencies. It is important to note, however, that such a policy has nothing to do with outward histrionics: with threats or blustering or superfluous gestures of outward "toughness." While the Kremlin is basically flexible in its reaction to political realities, it is by no means unamenable to considerations of prestige. Like almost any other government, it can be placed by tactless and threatening gestures in a position where it cannot afford to yield even though this might be dictated by its sense of realism. The Russian leaders are keen judges of human psychology, and as such they are highly conscious that loss of temper and of self-control is never a source of strength in political affairs. They are quick to exploit such evidences of weakness. For these reasons, it is a *sine qua non* of successful dealing with Russia that the foreign government in question should remain at all times cool and collected and that its demands on Russian policy should be put forward in such a manner as to leave the way open for a compliance not too detrimental to Russian prestige.

III

In the light of the above, it will be clearly seen that the Soviet pressure against the free institutions of the western world is something that can be contained by the adroit and vigilant application of counter-force at a series of constantly shifting geographical and political points, corresponding to the shifts and manœuvres of Soviet policy, but which cannot be charmed or talked out of existence. The Russians look forward to a duel of infinite duration, and they see that already they have scored great successes. It must be borne in mind that there was a time when the Communist Party represented far more of a minority in the sphere of Russian national life than Soviet power today represents in the world community.

But if ideology convinces the rulers of Russia that truth is on their side and that they can therefore afford to wait, those of us on whom that ideology has no claim are free to examine objectively the validity of that premise. The Soviet thesis not only implies complete lack of control by the west over its own economic destiny, it likewise assumes Russian unity, discipline and patience over an infinite period. Let us bring this apocalyptic vision down to earth, and suppose that the western world finds the strength and resourcefulness to contain Soviet power over a period of ten to fifteen years. What does that spell for Russia itself?

The Soviet leaders, taking advantage of the contributions of modern technique to the arts of despotism, have solved the question of obedience within the confines of their power. Few challenge their authority; and even those who do are unable to make that challenge valid as against the organs of suppression of the state.

The Kremlin has also proved able to accomplish its purpose of building up in Russia, regardless of the interests of the inhabitants, an industrial foundation of heavy metallurgy, which is, to be sure, not yet complete but which is nevertheless continuing to grow and is approaching those of the other major industrial countries. All of this, however, both the maintenance of internal political security and the building of heavy industry, has been carried out at a terrible cost in human life and in human hopes and energies. It has necessitated the use of forced labor on a scale unprecedented in modern times under conditions of peace. It has involved the neglect or abuse of other phases of Soviet economic life, particularly agriculture, consumers' goods production, housing and transportation.

To all that, the war has added its tremendous toll of destruction, death and human exhaustion. In consequence of this, we have in Russia today a population which is physically and spiritually tired. The mass of the people are disillusioned, skeptical and no longer as accessible as they once were to the magical attraction which Soviet power still radiates to its followers abroad. The avidity with which people seized upon the slight respite accorded to the Church for tactical reasons during the war was eloquent testimony to the fact that their capacity for faith and devotion found little expression in the purposes of the régime.

In these circumstances, there are limits to the physical and nervous strength of people themselves. These limits are absolute ones, and are binding even for the cruelest dictatorship, because beyond them people cannot be driven. The forced labor camps and the other agencies of constraint provide temporary means of compelling people to work longer hours than their own volition or mere economic pressure would dictate; but if people survive them at all they become old before their time and must be considered as human casualties to the demands of dictatorship. In either case their best powers are no longer available to society and can no longer be enlisted in the services of the state.

Here only the younger generation can help. The younger generation, despite all vicissitudes and sufferings, is numerous and vigorous; and the Russians are a talented people. But it still remains to be seen what will be the effects on mature performance of the abnormal emotional strains of childhood which Soviet dictatorship created and which were enormously increased by the war. Such things as normal security and placidity of home environment have practically ceased to exist in the Soviet Union outside of the most remote farms and villages. And observers are not yet sure whether that is not going to leave its mark on the over-all capacity of the generation now coming into maturity.

In addition to this, we have the fact that Soviet economic development, while it can list certain formidable achievements, has been precariously spotty and uneven. Russian Communists who speak of the "uneven development of capitalism" should blush at the contemplation of their own national economy. Here certain branches of economic life, such as the metallurgical and machine industries, have been pushed out of all proportion to other sectors of economy. Here is a nation striving to become in a short period one of the great industrial nations of the world while it still has no highway network worthy of the name and only a relatively primitive network of railways. Much has been done to increase efficiency of labor and to teach primitive peasants something about the operation of machines. But maintenance is still a crying deficiency of all Soviet economy. Construction is hasty and poor in quality. Depreciation must be enormous. And in vast sectors of economic life it has not yet been possible to instill into labor anything like that general culture of production and technical self-respect which characterizes the skilled worker of the west.

It is difficult to see how these deficiencies can be corrected at an early date by a tired and dispirited population working largely under the shadow of fear and compulsion. And as long as they are not overcome, Russia will remain economically a vulnerable, and in a certain sense an impotent, nation, capable of exporting its enthusiasms and of radiating the strange charm of its primitive political vitality but unable to back up those articles of export by the real evidences of material power and prosperity.

Meanwhile, a great uncertainty hangs over the political life of the Soviet Union. That is the uncertainty involved in the transfer of power from one individual or group of individuals to others.

This is, of course, outstandingly the problem of the personal position of Stalin. We must remember that his succession to Lenin's pinnacle of preëminence in the Communist movement was the only such transfer of individual authority which the Soviet Union has experienced. That transfer took 12 years to consolidate. It cost the lives of millions of people and shook the state to its foundations. The attendant tremors were felt all through the international revolutionary movement, to the disadvantage of the Kremlin itself.

It is always possible that another transfer of preëminent power may take place quietly and inconspicuously, with no repercussions anywhere. But again, it is possible that the questions involved may unleash, to use some of Lenin's words, one of those "incredibly swift transitions" from "delicate deceit" to "wild violence" which characterize Russian history, and may shake Soviet power to its foundations.

But this is not only a question of Stalin himself. There has been, since 1938, a dangerous congealment of political life in the higher circles of Soviet power. The All-Union Congress of Soviets, in theory the supreme body of the Party, is supposed to meet not less often than once in three years. It will soon be eight full years since its last meeting. During this period membership in the Party has numerically doubled. Party mortality during the war was enormous; and today well over half of the Party members are persons who have entered since the last Party congress was held. Meanwhile, the same small group of men has carried on at the top through an amazing series of national vicissitudes. Surely there is some reason why the experiences of the war brought basic political changes to every one of the great governments of the west. Surely the causes of that phenomenon are basic enough to be present somewhere in the obscurity of Soviet political life, as well. And yet no recognition has been given to these causes in Russia.

It must be surmised from this that even within so highly disciplined an organization as the Communist Party there must be a growing divergence in age, outlook and interest between the great mass of Party members, only so recently recruited into the movement, and the little self-perpetuating clique of men at the top, whom most of these Party members have never met, with whom they have never conversed, and with whom they can have no political intimacy.

Who can say whether, in these circumstances, the eventual rejuvenation of the higher spheres of authority (which can only be a matter of time) can take place smoothly and peacefully, or whether rivals in the quest for higher power will not eventually reach down into these politically immature and inexperienced masses in order to find support for their respective claims? If this were ever to happen, strange consequences could flow for the Communist Party: for the membership at large has been exercised only in the practices of iron discipline and obedience and not in the arts of compromise and accommodation. And if disunity were ever to seize and paralyze the Party, the chaos and weakness of Russian society would be revealed in forms beyond description. For we have seen that Soviet power is only a crust concealing an amorphous mass of human beings among whom no independent organizational structure is tolerated. In Russia there is not even such a thing as local government. The present generation of Russians have never known spontaneity of collective action. If, consequently, anything were ever to occur to disrupt the unity and efficacy of the Party as a political instrument, Soviet Russia might be changed overnight from one of the strongest to one of the weakest and most pitiable of national societies.

Thus the future of Soviet power may not be by any means as secure as Russian capacity for self-delusion would make it appear to the men in the Kremlin. That they can keep power themselves, they have demonstrated. That they can quietly and easily turn it over to others remains to be proved. Meanwhile, the hardships of their rule and the vicissitudes of international life have taken a heavy toll of the strength and hopes of the great people on whom their power rests. It is curious to note that the ideological power of Soviet authority is strongest today in areas beyond the frontiers of Russia, beyond the reach of its police power. This phenomenon brings to mind a comparison used by Thomas Mann in his great novel "Buddenbrooks." Observing that human institutions often show the greatest outward brilliance at a moment when inner decay is in reality farthest advanced, he compared the Buddenbrook family, in the days of its greatest glamour, to one of those stars whose light shines most brightly on this world when in reality it has long since ceased to exist. And who can say with assurance that the strong light still cast by the Kremlin on the dissatisfied peoples of the western world is not the powerful afterglow of a constellation which is in actuality on the wane? This cannot be proved. And it cannot be disproved. But the possibility remains (and in the opinion of this writer it is a strong one) that Soviet power, like the capitalist world of its conception, bears within it the seeds of its own decay, and that the sprouting of these seeds is well advanced.

IV

It is clear that the United States cannot expect in the foreseeable future to enjoy political intimacy with the Soviet régime. It must continue to regard the Soviet Union as a rival, not a partner, in the political arena. It must continue to expect that Soviet policies will reflect no abstract love of peace and stability, no real faith in the possibility of a permanent happy coexistence of the Socialist and capitalist worlds, but rather a cautious, persistent pressure toward the disruption and weakening of all rival influence and rival power.

Balanced against this are the facts that Russia, as opposed to the western world in general, is still by far the weaker party, that Soviet policy is highly flexible, and that Soviet society may well contain deficiencies which will eventually weaken its own total potential. This would of itself warrant the United States entering with reasonable confidence upon a policy of firm containment, designed to confront the Russians with unalterable counter-force at every point where they show signs of encroaching upon the interests of a peaceful and stable world.

But in actuality the possibilities for American policy are by no means limited to holding the line and hoping for the best. It is entirely possible for the United States to influence by its actions the internal developments, both within Russia and throughout the international Communist movement, by which Russian policy is largely determined. This is not only a question of the modest measure of informational activity which this government can conduct in the Soviet Union and elsewhere, although that, too, is important. It is rather a question of the degree to which the United States can create among the peoples of the world generally the impression of a country which knows what it wants, which is coping successfully with the problems of its internal life and with the responsibilities of a World Power, and which has a spiritual vitality capable of holding its own among the major ideological currents of the time. To the extent that such an impression can be created and maintained, the aims of Russian Communism must appear sterile and quixotic, the hopes and enthusiasm of Moscow's supporters must wane, and added strain must be imposed on the Kremlin's foreign policies. For the palsied decrepitude of the capitalist world is the keystone of Communist philosophy. Even the failure of the United States to experience the early economic depression which the ravens of the Red Square have been predicting with such complacent confidence since hostilities ceased would have deep and important repercussions throughout the Communist world.

By the same token, exhibitions of indecision, disunity and internal disintegration within this country have an exhilarating effect on the whole Communist movement. At each evidence of these tendencies, a thrill of hope and excitement goes through the Communist world; a new jauntiness can be noted in the Moscow tread; new groups of foreign supporters climb on to what they can only view as the band wagon of international politics; and Russian pressure increases all along the line in international affairs.

It would be an exaggeration to say that American behavior unassisted and alone could exercise a power of life and death over the Communist movement and bring about the early fall of Soviet power in Russia. But the United States has it in its power to increase enormously the strains under which Soviet policy must operate, to force upon the Kremlin a far greater degree of moderation and circumspection than it has had to observe in recent years, and in this way to promote tendencies which must eventually find their outlet in either the break-up or the gradual mellowing of Soviet power. For no mystical, Messianic movement—and particularly not that of the Kremlin—can face frustration indefinitely without eventually adjusting itself in one way or another to the logic of that state of affairs.

Thus the decision will really fall in large measure in this country itself. The issue of Soviet-American relations is in essence a test of the over-all worth of the United States as a nation among nations. To avoid destruction the United States need only measure up to its own best traditions and prove itself worthy of preservation as a great nation.

Surely, there was never a fairer test of national quality than this. In the light of these circumstances, the thoughtful observer of Russian-American relations will find no cause for complaint in the Kremlin's challenge to American society. He will rather experience a certain gratitude to a Providence which, by providing the American people with this implacable challenge, has made their entire security as a nation dependent on their pulling themselves together and accepting the responsibilities of moral and political leadership that history plainly intended them to bear.

PART TWO

CONTAINMENT AND ITS ALTERNATIVES

3

MR. X REVISITED:
An Interview With George F. Kennan

In the "X" article you wrote: "Now the outstanding circumstance concerning the Soviet regime is that down to the present day this process of political consolidation has never been completed and the men in the Kremlin have continued to be predominantly absorbed with the struggle to secure and make absolute the power which they seized in November 1917. They have endeavored to secure it primarily against forces at home, within Soviet society itself. But they have also endeavored to secure it against the outside world." And you went on to state that the "characteristics of Soviet policy, like the postulates from which they flow, are basic to the internal nature of Soviet power, and will be with us, whether in the foreground or the background, until the internal nature of Soviet power is changed."

Do you view the principal themes of Soviet policy as essentially the same today as they were in 1947?

No. The conditions to which Soviet policymakers had to address themselves in 1947 have changed drastically over these 25 years.

In 1947, the Soviet Union, though seriously exhausted by the war,

Original title: "Interview with George F. Kennan." Reprinted by permission of author and publisher from *Foreign Policy* (Summer 1972). Copyright © by National Affairs, Inc. Questions posed to Mr. Kennan were prepared by the Editors of *Foreign Policy*, with the assistance of Charles Gati and Richard H. Ullman.

enjoyed great prestige. Stalin's hold on the international Communist movement was monolithic and almost unchallenged. There was still, in the major Western countries and to some extent elsewhere, a strong contingent of pro-Soviet intellectuals and fellow-travellers who were amenable to Soviet influence and could be counted on to give general support to Soviet policies. All around the Soviet frontiers, on the other hand, there was great instability. This applied to East Asia, as well as to Europe and the Middle East. For the Soviet leadership, this presented both opportunity and danger: opportunity for taking advantage of this instability, danger that if they did not do so, others would. Their foreign policy, in these circumstances, was directed to two main objectives: one, the elimination, to the extent possible, of all other great-power influence—and this meant primarily American influence—everywhere on the Eurasian land mass, so that the Soviet Union would overshadow everything that was left, in power and prestige; and, two, the achievement and consolidation of effective strategic glacis in East, South, and West.

Compare that with the situation the present generation of Soviet leaders has before it today. The international Communist movement has broken into several pieces. They retain, beyond the limits of their own military-occupational power, the overt loyalty of only a portion of it. This is a not insignificant portion; but the facade of solidarity can be maintained, today, only by extensive concessions to the real independence of the respective Communist parties. Meanwhile, a great deal of the erstwhile liberal following in other countries, disillusioned by Soviet repressive measures at home and in Eastern Europe, has lost confidence in Soviet leadership. As a military power, the U.S.S.R. has great prestige—greater, in fact, than in 1947—but as a political power it has less than it did then.

The instability in the areas surrounding the Soviet Union has in part disappeared. The Chinese and Japanese have put an end to it in East Asia. Economic recovery, NATO, and the movements towards unification have largely done so in Western Europe, although there are disturbing symptoms of an underlying instability in Western Germany, and a state of semi-chaos in Italy that is only slightly less alarming because it is chronic.

The East Asian glacis was largely taken away from them by the Chinese. The Middle Eastern one they are gradually gaining; but it is precarious, undependable, and expensive to keep. The European one, i.e., the satellite area of Eastern and Central Europe, they continue to hold (Yugoslavia excepted) either by occupying it or by overshadowing it militarily. It is flawed by a certain potential instability in the form of the positions taken by the Rumanians; but it has won acceptance in the

West, and does not appear, at the moment, to be seriously threatened. It may be said, generally, that the southern and western glacis are fulfilling their function, as does the remaining one—Outer Mongolia—in East Asia; and the Soviet leaders undoubtedly derive from this fact a certain heightened sense of security.

The effort to expel American influence and presence from the Eurasian land mass has also been largely successful, though rather by the force of circumstance than as a response to anything the Russians themselves have done. Yet the result is only in part satisfactory from the Soviet point of view. In Northeast Asia, the Americans never did play a role, except in South Korea and Japan; and they have now largely forfeited their influence over the Japanese. On the other hand, Russia now finds herself confronted there by two local great powers—China and Japan—both capable of making more trouble for her in that region than the Americans ever did. In the Middle East, the American presence and influence are pretty well eliminated everywhere except in Israel, Jordan, and Saudi Arabia. As for Western Europe: the American guaranty remains, as does the American military presence. Moscow would still like to eliminate both—just to be on the safe side. But the need for doing so has been reduced by the general Western acceptance of the Soviet hegemony in Eastern Europe. And the agreements concluded with the Brandt government, if ratified, will relieve the Soviet leaders of their greatest single anxiety: that of an association of American military power with a *revanchiste* and revisionist Western Germany.

If, then, today the Soviet leaders have a sense of military insecurity, it is not—for the first time in Russian history—primarily with relation to stronger forces just beyond their land borders, but rather in relation to the nuclear weapons race, which is a subject in itself. Where they really feel most insecure is politically. The Chinese inroads on their international prestige and on their influence in the world Communist movement have really hurt and alarmed them, because they leave them no alternatives except isolation or alliance with capitalist countries, which could undermine the legitimacy of their power at home. They are also insecure at home, because they are dimly conscious, as was the Tsar's regime 70 years ago, that they have lost the confidence of their own intellectuals, and don't know how to recover it. Finally, there is the continuing hostility of the populations in most of Eastern Europe to the Soviet hegemony, a hostility which even with full control of the media over 25 years they have not been able to overcome.

What, in the face of these environmental conditions, are their policies? These no longer represent a unified whole, or reflect any unified concept. The Party priesthood exerts itself mightily to recover ground lost to the Chinese in the foreign Communist communities. The Foreign

Office pursues a policy of detente with France and Germany and Italy in order to prove to the Chinese that Russia has an alternative to good relations with them, and can easily arrange for security on her Western front. The military-industrial complex, as real there as in Washington, struggles to match the United States in the cultivation of nuclear weaponry. The hot-heads in their military establishment appear to be obsessed with the hope of breaking the long-standing supremacy of the Anglo-Americans on the high seas, and this strikes me, incidentally, as the most irresponsible and dangerous, at the moment, of all Soviet undertakings, comparable to the Kaiser's effort to out-balance the British in naval forces before World War I.

These policies present a sharp contrast to those of 1947. The Soviet-American conflict has been largely removed geographically from the Eurasian land mass and relegated to the struggle for the control of the high seas and the fantasy world of nuclear weaponry. A great part of the energy of Soviet foreign policy is today devoted to the effort to "contain," politically, another Socialist state—China. The anti-American propaganda and the competition with the United States for favor and influence in the Third World continue; but this is more of a force of habit than a policy, and the few successes achieved to date have come from American mistakes far more than from Soviet brilliance. "World revolution" has simply faded out of the picture, as a concrete aim of Soviet foreign policy. In general, the situation of the Soviet Union is such that were it not for the dangerous nuclear and naval rivalry, the outside world, and particularly, the United States, would have little more to fear from Russia today than it did in 1910. The ideological factor makes itself felt today almost exclusively in the Soviet relationship to the French and Italian Communist parties, which, if they were to come into power, would easily destroy NATO and upset the power balance in Europe. But these parties are reflections of long-term internal crises within the respective countries, and their influence cannot be treated as primarily a problem of international relations.

In what ways, if any, has "the internal nature of Soviet power" changed so as to affect Soviet policy?

Stalin was well aware that the legitimacy of his ascendancy in the Party had never been wholly accepted by his comrades, that he had killed millions of people and virtually decimated the Party in his effort to crush opposition, that he had thus provoked great potential contumacy, and that his rule rested overwhelmingly on fear. His successors are in a different position. Being largely men brought into the seats of power only towards the close of the Stalin era, they are not saddled with the same sense of guilt. Most surprisingly, furthermore—to us and to them—it turns out that the system itself is now strong enough to bear most of the weight: it does not have to depend on their charisma, as in Lenin's case, or their capacity to terrorize, as in Stalin's. Of course, they oppress the restless intellectuals. These people challenge the sense of orthodoxy that seems, to any Russian governmental mind, essential to the stability of the system. The Soviet leaders are simply acting, here, in established Russian tradition. But they are the first rulers of the Soviet Union who find themselves in the pleasing position of being able to be borne by the system—to ride along on it—instead of having to carry it; and for this reason, they feel more secure than did Lenin, who died before the system was consolidated, or Stalin, who felt it necessary to dominate it by raping it. I think, therefore, that *inner* insecurity plays less of a role in their psychology than it did in that of their predecessors, but there is strong sense of *external* insecurity, particularly with relation to the Chinese. No Leninist-Marxist can endure being outflanked to the Left, and this is what the Chinese have repeatedly done to them.

Would you today continue to emphasize "the internal nature of Soviet power," rather than the international environment, as the most pertinent factor in the making of Soviet foreign policy?

No, for the reasons just given. But an exception must be made for the challenge presented by the Chinese. The position of Moscow as the "third Rome" of international Communism is little short of essential to the carefully-cultivated Soviet image of self. Take it away, and the whole contrived history of Soviet Communism, its whole rationale and sense of legitimacy, is threatened. Moscow must oppose China with real desperation, because China threatens the intactness of its own sense of identity—of the fiction on which it has made itself dependent and without which it would not know how to live.

What are the implications for American policy of these changes in Soviet internal politics and external policies?

What all this means for Soviet-American relations is this: that the United States, having accepted the Soviet domination of Eastern Europe as well as the situation in all of Asia other than its south-eastern extremity, has today, for the first time, no serious territorial-political conflict with the Soviet government, the one exception being the Middle East. But the Middle Eastern situation is, by common agreement, not worth a war between the two powers, and both hope to avoid its leading to one. This means that today the military rivalry, in naval power as in nuclear weaponry, is simply riding along on its own momentum, like an object in space. It has no foundation in real interests—no foundation, in fact, but in fear, and in an essentially irrational fear at that. It is carried not by any reason to believe that the other side *would,* but only by an hypnotic fascination with the fact that it *could.* It is simply an institutionalized force of habit. If someone could suddenly make the two sides realize that it has no purpose and if they were then to desist, the world would presumably go on, in all important respects, just as it is going on today.

There is a Kafkaesque quality to this encounter. We stand like two men who find themselves confronting each other with guns in their hands, neither with any real reason to believe that the other has murderous intentions towards him, but both hypnotized by the uncertainty and the unreasoning fear of the fact that the other is armed. The two armament efforts feed and justify each other.

Admitting that it is unreasonable to expect either side to disarm suddenly and unilaterally, one must still recognize that this curious deadlock, devoid of hope, replete with danger, is unlikely to be resolved just by carefully-negotiated contractual agreements: these latter will have to be supported by reciprocal unilateral steps of restraint in the development of various forms of weaponry.

If one could begin to work this process backward, and eventually reduce the armed establishments of the two countries to something like reasonable dimensions—for both have, of course, ulterior military obligations and commitments as well—then there is no reason why the Soviet Union should be considered a serious threat to American security.

Should this happen, however, the United States would do well not to indulge itself in unreal hopes for intimacy with either the Soviet regime or the Soviet population. There are deeply-rooted traits in Soviet psychology—some of old-Russian origin, some of more recent Soviet provenance—that would rule this out. Chief among these, in my opinion, are the congenital disregard of the truth, the addiction to propagandistic exaggeration, distortion, and falsehood, the habitual foulness of mouth in official utterance. So pernicious has been the effect of 50 years of cynicism about the role of objective truth in political statement that one begins to wonder whether these Soviet leaders have not destroyed in themselves the power to distinguish truth from falsehood. The very vocabulary in which they have taught themselves to speak, politically, with its constant references to the American "imperialists" and "monopolists," is confusing and offensive, and constitutes in itself a barrier to better international understanding. Add to this the hysterical preoccupation with espionage, the continued fear of foreigners and effort to isolate the Soviet population allowed to play in the conduct of Soviet diplomacy, and one is obliged to recognize that it is simply

unrealistic for Americans to look for any great intimacy or even normalcy, as we understand it, of relations with the Soviet Union. As is
also the case with China, though for somewhat different reasons, relations can be reasonably good, but they must also be reasonably distant;
and the more distant they are, in a sense, the better they will be.

**In the "X" article you emphasized the vulnerability of the Soviet sys-
tem, suggesting "that Soviet power, like the capitalist world of its conception, bears within it the seeds of its own decay." In fact, you seem
to have expected "either the break-up or the gradual mellowing of
Soviet power." In retrospect, was this a realistic assessment or wishful
thinking on your part? And, in 1972, would you tend to emphasize the
Soviet system's strengths rather than its weaknesses?**

I think there *has* been a very considerable mellowing of Soviet power.
However little we may like the Soviet regime's internal policies, and
admitting that there has recently been a considerable revival of the role
of the secret police within the system, only someone who had never
known the heyday of Stalin's rule could fail to recognize the enormous
difference between the conditions of his time and this one.

This mellowing, I think, has been a source of strength, rather than
weakness, for the Soviet regime over the short term. But any form of
despotism faces, ultimately, its own dilemmas. One cannot help but
notice how similar is the situation of the Soviet regime of 1972 to that
of the Tsar's government in—say—1912. It has lost the confidence of
the intellectuals. It is faced with a strong hard-line Stalinist opposition,
chauvinistic and anti-Semitic, and comparable to the Tsarist reactionary-
monarchists, which operates from *within* the official establishment; and
it is faced with a liberal-democratic opposition, comparable to the old
Kadet and moderate-socialist parties, which operates essentially from
outside the system. Tsardom dragged along, in essentially this situation,
for several decades, and then fell only when weakened by a long war
and a foolish imperial couple. But the effect of modern communications has been in many respects more revolutionary than the ideas of
Marx and Lenin, and whether this same longevity-by-pure-bureaucratic-
inertia will be granted to the Soviet regime no one can tell. The great
average age of the present Soviet leadership is also a source of potential instability. If I had to guess, I would say that the dangers confronting
these present leaders are considerably greater than they themselves
realize.

**In your *Memoirs* you speak of containment as a political rather than
military undertaking and express regret over the militarization of American foreign policy. Looking at the history of the past 25 years, though,**

wouldn't you agree that American military power has had a great deal to do with the containment of what you once called Soviet aggressive tendencies?

This is an extremely difficult question. That we have taught the Soviet leadership something of our own obsession with military strength—have taught them, that is, to think in American-Pentagon terms—have caused them, too, to be hypnotized by the nuclear weapons race—I do not doubt. We also have to recognize that armaments are powerful not just in their actual use, or in support of overt threats, but also in the shadows they cast—particularly over fearful people. The Western Europeans, in particular, have a *manie d'invasion,* and I suppose it is true that if we had not eventually created some sort of compensatory ground forces, they would—in political terms—have tended ultimately "to commit suicide for fear of death." I concede, therefore, that there was need for the creation of something resembling NATO in Western Europe. But I don't think this was a reason for putting economic recovery and other constructive purposes into the background, nor was it a reason for pretending to ourselves, over two decades, that the Russians were longing to attack Western Europe, and it was only we who were deterring them from this mad purpose. Finally, I do not think the nuclear weapon was at all essential as a factor in the creation of this necessary balance. The thesis that Western Europe could never be defended against Russia by conventional means is so out of accord with all historical, economic, cultural, and demographic realities that it did not deserve to be taken seriously. The nuclear weapon is, as Stalin correctly observed, something with which you frighten people with weak nerves. We have rendered a fearful and historic disservice—to ourselves and to the world at large—by pinning our own concept of our security, and indeed the security of the entire Western world, on this ghastly, sterile, and unusable weapon, which is incapable of serving any coherent political purpose.

The expansion of Soviet influence in world affairs could take three forms: (1) direct military aggression; (2) political expansion through the seizure of power by a Communist party controlled by Moscow; or (3) diplomatic expansion through the increased influence of the U.S.S.R. in other societies by virtue of military and economic assistance, treaties, trade, cultural relations, and the like. Your notion of containment was originally concerned primarily with the possibility of the second type of Soviet expansion, although it was misinterpreted to be directed primarily against the first. In recent years, however, Soviet expansion has primarily taken the diplomatic form: increasing naval deployments in the Mediterranean and Indian Oceans, military and economic assistance

to India and Arab countries, treaties with India and Egypt, expanded trade relations with many Asian and Latin American countries. Should this expansion of Soviet influence be of major concern to the United States? What policies should the United States adopt in relation to this "moving outward" by the Soviet Union?

It seems to me that what you are saying in this question is that Russia is behaving suspiciously like a great power. You list a number of things she is doing: naval deployments in distant oceans, military and economic aid programs, treaties with Egypt and India, expanded trade relations with many countries. Correct. But is there any reason why a country of Russia's size and economic potential should *not* do these things? Are there, in fact, any of them that we do not do—any of them in which we have not set the example?

It seems to me that those who see a danger in these activities are predicating, just as in the case of the weapons race, some underlying political conflict which may not be there at all. I admit that Soviet activities in many of these countries are impregnated with anti-American attitudes, and one of their objectives, if not the leading one, seems to be at least the discrediting and the isolation of the United States—a purpose at which, I must say, we connive with an adeptness little short of genius. As a traditionalist who does not believe that this country is well constituted, anyway, to play a very active role in world affairs, I find myself less frightened than others over the fact that Soviet policies are so inspired.

It would be a very sad and hopeless situation if we were to convince ourselves that the peace of the world depended on the ability of the rest of us to prevent the Soviet Union indefinitely from acting like a great power. Would it not be better to avoid assuming that all Soviet activities are aimed primarily against us—unless, at least, it is proved otherwise—and to see whether there are not some areas of assistance to other nations, and constructive involvement with their affairs, where we and the Russians could work together instead of separately?

In saying these things one must, I suppose, make a certain exception with respect to Soviet policies in the Middle East. In addition to the program of naval expansion and maritime espionage, this seems to me to be the only area of Soviet foreign relations that has been marked both by evident lack of coordination in Moscow and by certain signs of a disturbing adventurism. If one were to be asked to guess at the motives of Soviet policy from the surface appearances, one could only conclude that Soviet policy towards the Arab countries was based on a serious desire to gain total control over this area and to exclude every form of Western influence. Given the existing dependence of Western

Europe on Middle Eastern oil, this represents a serious and even dangerous challenge to the security of Western Europe, and one which seems poorly to accord with the prudence shown in other areas of the Soviet government's foreign relations. Soviet policy-makers might do well to remind themselves that not every fruit that seems about to fall is one which it is desirable to pick.

In *Memoirs: 1925–1950* **you wrote: "What I said in the X-Article was not intended as a doctrine. I am afraid that when I think about foreign policy, I do not think in terms of doctrines. I think in terms of principles." There has been much talk recently about the desirability of the United States following a "balance of power" policy. Do you think this is an appropriate and useful principle to guide U.S. policy-makers in the future? What other principles would you recommend?**

If a "balance of power policy" means using American influence, wherever possible, to assure that the ability to develop military power on the grand scale is divided among several governmental entities and not concentrated entirely in any one of them, then I think that I favor it. But only with two reservations.

First of all, I think it should not be cynically conceived, and it should not, above all, be taken to mean pushing other people into conflict with each other. In this, I am fully in accord with what I understand to be the view of the present Administration.

But secondly, I would not overrate our power to affect these relationships. Twenty-five years ago we did have very considerable power to affect them, particularly in Europe, and this lay behind some of my own views about disengagement, because I thought that a better balance could be created between Russian power and a united Europe than between Russian power and a divided one. Today, except for our role in NATO, and such influence as we might have—or might have had—on the situation in the subcontinent of India-Pakistan, our possibilities are decidedly limited.

A curious balance of power does already exist today in East Asia, as between the Russians, the Chinese, and the Japanese. So long as the Russians remain strong enough to defend their own Far Eastern territories, plus Outer Mongolia, as they are today, this should assure peace along the Russian-Chinese border; and anxiety lest Japanese industrial power be added to the resources of the other party should cause both Russians and Chinese to cultivate good and peaceful relations with the Japanese. This situation is not our doing, and it needs no stimulation from us; but it serves our interests, and we should be careful not to disturb it.

In the "X" article you wrote that the ability of the United States to influence internal developments in the Communist nations, and therefore the policies they pursue, varies according to "the degree to which the United States can create among the peoples of the world generally the impression of a country which knows what it wants, which is coping successfully with the problems of its internal life and with the responsibilities of a World Power, and which has a spiritual vitality capable of holding its own among the major ideological currents of the time." Do you still believe this to be so? Given these criteria, how would you assess the record of the past 25 years?

I do believe this to be so, but it is here that I consider we have failed most miserably. We have simply not faced up successfully to our own internal problems and we have lost, just since World War II, a great deal of our value, and our potential influence, as an example to other peoples. So obvious is this that if, thinking about the worldwide loss of American prestige and influence in recent years, one asks whether the Russians have succeeded in setting us back, one has to give the answer: no—we and the Russians have each defeated ourselves; neither was up to its own pretensions of earlier years.

How well do the Nixon-Kissinger policies for dealing with the Communist nations seem to fit the notions which underlay your own thinking at the time of the "X" article and subsequently?

The Nixon-Kissinger policies fit the conceptions of the "X" article, it seems to me, only indifferently.

Those policies continue to give great attention, geographically, to what I viewed in 1947, and have always viewed, as a secondary area from the standpoint of our interest: Southeast Asia.

While the SALT talks are certainly a significant and welcome step in advance, a great deal of American governmental attention and energy continues to be riveted to the sterile and dangerous effort to excel the Russians in the nuclear arms race. That had no place in my scheme of things.

There is undue emphasis on China, from which we have very little to gain in terms of world policy, and a certain slighting, in my view, of Japan.

You may say that much of this is not responsive to your question, which involved our dealings with the Communist nations, directly. But it has always been true that the secret of successful dealings with Russia itself—and the same now goes for China—is the proper handling of our relations with the remainder of the world that lies between us.

Finally, there is the obvious partiality for summit meetings with Communist leaders, a procedure which may have its domestic-political dividends but which I regard as at best irrevelant, and potentially pernicious, to a sound handling of relations with the great Communist governments.

So far as the Soviet Union itself is concerned, I do not see a great deal that the Nixon Administration could do that it is not now doing. I think—though it may not be of major importance—that we should at once agree to the cessation of underground testing. I think that we could well take certain further unilateral measures of restraint in the development of nuclear weapons and their carriers, with a view to encouraging the others to do likewise. I think we should press talks with the Russians to see whether we could not agree with them on putting a stop to the childish and dangerous mutual shadowing of naval vessels that now goes on all over the high seas. I think we should bend every effort to develop technical collaboration with them—in space activities as well as in international environmental undertakings. We should keep in communication with them—constantly—concerning the situation in the Middle East, with a view to avoiding misunderstandings. Beyond that, there is not much we can do.

In the light of its subsequent misinterpretation, do you regret having written the "X" article?

No—not on balance. I regret having written it exactly the way I did. But it was meant to sound—and did sound, I think, at the time— a hopeful note, urging people to believe that our differences with the Soviet Union of Stalin's day, while serious indeed, were not ones that could be solved only—or indeed, solved at all—by war. Well—we have struggled along for another quarter of a century, and there has been no war—at least not between us and the Russians. And there is even less reason to think one necessary today than there was then.

The importance of the "X" article was of course distorted out of all reasonable proportion by the treatment it received at the hands of the press. The American mass media produce upon any given event an effect analogous to that produced on a man's shadow by the angle of the sun—causing it normally to be either much greater or much less than life-size. In the case of this particular article it was much greater.

But the principle enunciated in it—that our differences with the Russians are not ones which it would take a war to solve—is still sound. What we need mostly to do is to free ourselves from some of our fixations with relation to the military competition—to remind ourselves that there is really no reason why we and the Russians should wish to do frightful things to each other and to the world—and to address ourselves vigorously, and with some degree of boldness, to the enormous danger presented by the very existence in human hands, and above all the proliferation, of weapons such as the nuclear ones. Somewhere between the intimacy we cannot have—either with the Russians or the Chinese—and the war there is no reason for us to fight, there is a middle ground of peaceful, if somewhat distant, coexistence on which our relationship with the great Communist powers could be considerably safer and more pleasant than it now is. We cannot make it so by our own efforts alone; the Russians and Chinese will have to help. But we could do better, in a number of respects, than we have been doing.

4

MR. X REASSESSED:
The Meaning of Containment

I. INTRODUCTION

Like Soviet foreign policy which was one of its main themes, the 1947 "X" article in *Foreign Affairs*—"The Sources of Soviet Conduct"—also turned out to be something of a riddle wrapped in a mystery inside an enigma.[1] Published anonymously, much of this scholarly article, setting forth this country's rationale of and design for containment, almost immediately found its way to the pages of such popular magazines as *Life* and *Reader's Digest*. Sensing its importance, Walter Lippmann devoted 12 critical columns to a rebuttal of its implications in the old *New York Herald Tribune*. Meanwhile, newsmen in Washington and New York, led by Arthur Krock of the *New York Times*, identified Mr. X as George F. Kennan, Director of the Policy Planning Staff of the Department of State.

As the attribution was not denied, part of the initial mystery evaporated. Other, no doubt less sensational, parts of the mystery, however, have remained on the public agenda ever since. To begin with, much of

Original title: "What Containment Meant." Reprinted by permission of author and publisher from *Foreign Policy* (Summer 1972). Copyright © 1972 by National Affairs, Inc.

[1] For their most helpful comments on an earlier draft of this article, I am indebted to Vernon V. Aspaturian, Zbigniew Brzezinski, Bertell Ollman, and Marshall D. Shulman. I also wish to thank Toby Trister for research assistance and for a perceptive critique of the original draft.

what Kennan himself has said and written since 1947, especially since 1950, appears to be in contradistinction to the conclusions of his "X" article; indeed, as soon as the article appeared, Kennan relates in his 1967 *Memoirs,* he thought he had been both misread and misrepresented. Reading Lippmann's severe critique, in particular, he recalls "the feeling of bewilderment and frustration with which—helpless now to reply publicly because of my official position—I read these columns as they appeared and found held against me so many views with which I profoundly agreed."

Many years later, at least some of his readers are still mystified if not confused. At one end of the political spectrum, the otherwise distinguished social scientist Anatol Rapoport finds it possible to liken Kennan's views with those of the apostles of hysterical anti-Communism. He argues that Kennan, this cultivated and sophisticated diplomat, and Fred Schwartz, leader of the Christian Anti-Communist Crusade, have held essentially the same perception of the cold war. At the other end of the political spectrum, William S. Schlamm of the *National Review* attacks Kennan as a "second-rate prophet" who "pathetically lacks" the ability for "abstract conceptions," and John Foster Dulles of course used to label Kennan's notion of containment "negative, futile, and immoral."

Yet bewilderment or obfuscation, controversy, misrepresentations, or the curious circumstances of its appearance do not fully explain the significance and enduring quality of the "X" article. More importantly, the significance of Kennan's observations was in that he provided a relatively simple explanation of the Soviet challenge in world affairs as well as an equally simple prescription for American foreign policy to meet that challenge. His observations came to be reflected in widely held public attitudes, for no other comparable theoretical formula or grand design has emerged since to catch the attention or imagination of the American public. In short—and to Kennan's subsequent dismay —his analysis of Soviet behavior and his prescriptions for Western policy have survived the passage of time and immense changes in international alignments. What Kennan said about the sources of Soviet aggressive tendencies and about the need to contain these tendencies has become ingrained in the American political conscience; "The Sources of Soviet Conduct" has made a lasting, if unfortunate, impression on the American public.

II. THE ANALYSIS OF SOVIET CONDUCT

It is worth noting that Kennan's proposal for "containment" was based on an intensive analysis of *Soviet* behavior. As the title of the article indicates, he dealt at some length with the sources of Soviet conduct, identified as (a) Marxist-Leninist ideology and (b) the "circumstances of power."

As to ideology, Kennan considered relevant to an understanding of the Russian leaders' political mentality their perception of reality, their appraisal of what is to be done. He found the familiar Marxist view of capitalism and the Leninist doctrine of imperialism most germane, concluding that insofar as capitalism was thought to contain the seeds of its own destruction and imperialism was thought to lead directly to war and revolution, Soviet leaders must expect the collapse of the non-Communist world, partly because of its own problems, partly because of the inevitability of a proletarian revolution. At the same time, Kennan noted that Marxists in general and Lenin and Stalin in particular had frequently cautioned against haste and eagerness, expressing wariness over the prospect of revolutionary action in non-revolutionary situations.

Although implying that Marxist-Leninist ideology was one of the two sources of Soviet conduct, Kennan explicitly stated that it served as rationalization for what the Soviet leaders had wanted to do in the first place. Russian "revolutionists found in Marxist theory a highly convenient rationalization for their own instinctive desires," he observed. "It afforded pseudo-scientific justification for their impatience, for their categorical denial of all value in the Tsarist system, for their yearning for power and revenge and for their inclination to cut corners in the pursuit of it. It is therefore no wonder that they had come to believe implicitly in the truth and soundness of the Marxist-Leninist teachings, so congenial to their own impulses and emotions."

Thus, Kennan's perspective of the role of ideology was paradoxical if not blurred. He spoke of the Soviet leaders' "instinctive desires" and "impatience" for power, suggesting that their impulses and emotions could explain their need to obtain, retain and expand power—a broad, general, and rather vague, though not necessarily inaccurate, explanation. What was unclear was Kennan's distinction, if any, between ideology as a motivating force on the one hand and ideology as rationalization on the other.

It is of course plausible to say that Soviet leaders are genuinely motivated by ideology in which case their ultimate (if not short-term) goal must be the realization of its teachings; it is equally plausible to say that they are using ideology to explain to their followers, to their foes, and probably to themselves that which they would intrinsically want to do anyway. In its first meaning, ideology is perceived as a guide for policy-makers. In its second meaning, the function of ideology is drastically different: it is then used to justify policy, to explain it or explain it away, to score points in intra-party or inter-party political debates, and so on. Finally, it is also plausible to say that ideology is *both* a genuine motivating force and a convenient rationalization—that it is one or the other depending on the policy issue, on the individual leaders, perhaps, or on the circumstances at hand. If this is the meaning of ideology for Soviet foreign-policy-makers, then the task is to find out *under what circumstances* ideology is pertinent to a foreign policy situation.

Two additional points should be made. First: aside from "motivation" and "rationalization," ideology performs other distinct functions in the Soviet system as well—it serves as a system of communication; it stands as a symbol of legitimacy and continuity; it provides a prism through which the international system is seen and analyzed. Second: concerning the specific circumstances under which doctrine is pertinent to foreign policy, recent studies indicate, *inter alia,* that the impact of doctrine is generally greater in the Soviet public analysis of long-term policies than in the analysis of short-term policies; that the older members of the Soviet foreign policy elite use doctrinal stereotypes more frequently than their younger colleagues; that those whose main preoccupation is domestic politics (party work or economics) adopt ideological terminology more often than those whose main concern is foreign affairs.[2]

To the extent that such analytical distinctions are neither explicitly raised nor answered by the "X" article, its assessment of the role of ideology in Soviet political life may be regarded, by today's standards at least, as rather unsophisticated—a judgment which is only partially mitigated by the continuing scholarly controversy on the subject.

As to the "circumstances of power," postulated in the "X" article as the second source of Soviet conduct, Kennan spoke of the seemingly endless process of political consolidation in the Soviet Union. He regarded the Soviet system as exceedingly vulnerable in a number of key areas—political succession, the economy (he called it "impotent"), domestic opposition, conflict within the party, generational conflicts. He particularly emphasized the possibility of disruption if and when a younger generation would let itself be heard, and he observed a growing divergence in age, outlook, and interest between leaders and followers within the party itself. Under these circumstances, he concluded, "great uncertainty hangs over the political life of the Soviet Union," and the strong "possibility remains . . . that Soviet power, like the capitalist world of its conception, bears within it the seeds of its own decay, and

---

[2] See, especially, Vernon V. Aspaturian, *Process & Power in Soviet Foreign Policy* (Boston: Little, Brown & Company, 1971) and Jan F. Triska and David D. Finley, *Soviet Foreign Policy* (New York: Macmillan, 1968).

that the sprouting of these seeds is well advanced." Indeed, he specifically forecast the eventual breakup (or gradual mellowing) of Soviet
power.

Thus, Kennan posited the Soviet system's domestic vulnerability as
the other compelling source of a dynamic and aggressive foreign policy.
This again is a central issue that has occupied students of Soviet politics
ever since. Indeed, Kennan's excellent list can now be extended. From
the perspective of the 1970's, we can also speak of the complex problems of modernization, of adaptation to what Zbigniew Brzezinski aptly
called the "technetronic" era, of intellectual dissent, of the nationalities,
or of the immense problem in the post-Stalin era of running a dictatorship by persuasion if possible and by coercion only if necessary. These
and other problems of Soviet life, indeed Kennan's own analysis of
Soviet vulnerability and his emphasis on the relationship between
domestic and foreign policy, raise three rather fundamental questions.
The *first* is whether it was then or is today accurate to speak of not only
the apparent weaknesses but the likely demise of the Soviet system; the
second is whether domestic weakness produces a more belligerent
foreign policy, as Kennan expected or, on the contrary, a more conciliatory one; and the *third* is why the international, as opposed to the
domestic, environment of Soviet foreign policy did not figure more
explicitly in the "X" article.

As to the first question, the Soviet Union surely appeared weaker and
more vulnerable in 1947 that it does in 1972. Devastated by war, de-
ficient in resources for reconstruction, frustrated by the continuing
purges, suspicious and even fearful of foreign adversaries, the Soviet
Union looked like the exhausted giant it was. As Walter Lippmann noted
at the time, though, forecasting its demise represented wishful thinking.
Indeed, the Soviet Union has since recovered, its economy, while ter-
ribly uneven, is hardly "impotent," it has muddled through several
crises of political succession, it has either successfully stifled or has
kept within safe bounds intellectual dissent, and it has managed to miti-
gate generational problems. To suggest, then, that it is a decaying society or one whose socio-economic model is obsolete may be a matter
of interpretation; to forecast its breakup, even in somewhat qualified
terms, is to vastly underestimate both the inherent strengths and
adaptive capacity of the Soviet system, demonstrated time and again
since 1917.

Yet even if one were to accept Kennan's view of Soviet vulnerability
or subscribe to the still prevalent popular belief that "dictatorships cannot last," the relevance of his analysis to *foreign* policy is still doubtful,
i.e., his supposition that, when confronted with acute domestic problems, the Soviet leadership will be belligerent abroad—either in order

to prove the system's viability or to draw attention away from the domestic scene. In fact, what evidence there is (and was in 1947) seems to point in a different direction. As Alexander Dallin points out, Soviet response to foreign threats in the 1920's and 1930's, when Stalin was certainly aware of the Soviet Union's weak international position, was often one of "reluctant accommodation, retrenchment, and even appeasement." Although Dallin emphasizes that "perceived weakness need not always produce a conciliatory mood in Moscow" and that Soviet willingness to seek a detente or compromise need not stem from weakness alone,[3] a conclusion more plausible than Kennan's is that perceived *strength,* rather than weakness, vis-à-vis its adversaries is likely to encourage the Soviet leadership to pursue a more hostile and aggressive foreign policy.

As to the third question, Kennan of course recognized, albeit implicitly, Soviet interest in the international distribution of power. He thought the United States could very well influence internal developments in the Soviet Union. In what was held to be one of his most important conclusions, Kennan suggested that the United States could "increase enormously the strains under which Soviet policy must operate, to force upon the Kremlin a far greater degree of moderation and circumspection than it [had] observe[d] in recent years, and in this way promote tendencies which must eventually find their outlet in either the breakup or the gradual mellowing of Soviet power."

Thus, while the gist of the Kennan article is that Soviet conduct springs from internal sources, he also concludes that Soviet policy is basically reactive to and perhaps even dependent on the external environment. In this respect, the "X" article anticipated a still persistent division between Western specialists of Soviet behavior: between those who explain Soviet policy primarily in terms of *internal needs* and those who explain it primarily in terms of *external possibilities.* Although we are hardly dealing with an either/or proposition, there is reason to emphasize the primacy of the external environment in the Soviet foreign-policy-making process.[4] While explaining Soviet foreign policy primarily in terms of the international system gives us no magic "key" to Soviet behavior, it does modify the basic question about that behavior from "what *must* the Soviet Union do?" to "what do the Soviet leaders think the Soviet Union *can* do?" and thus it underlines the reactive nature of Soviet foreign policy.

[3] Alexander Dallin, "Soviet Foreign Policy and Domestic Politics: A Framework for Analysis," *Journal of International Affairs,* vol. XXIII, no. 2, 1969, pp. 250–265.

[4] See, especially, Marshall D. Shulman, *Stalin's Foreign Policy Reappraised* (Cambridge: Harvard University Press, 1963) and William Zimmerman, "Elite Perspectives and the Explanation of Soviet Foreign Policy," *Journal of International Affairs,* vol. XXIV, no. 1, 1970, pp. 84–98.

III. PRESCRIPTIONS FOR AMERICAN CONDUCT

Prescriptions for American actions constituted the more controversial parts of the "X" article. Unlike Kennan's analysis of Soviet society which received little attention, his notion of containment obtained immediate, thorough, and systematic criticism—notably from Walter Lippmann and Hans Morgenthau.[5] Essentially, both Lippmann and Morgenthau objected to the sweeping implications of the containment formula. They thought that formula entailed commitments without proper limits by assigning to the United States, in Kennan's own words, the task of a "long-term, patient but firm and vigilant containment of Russian expansive tendencies." They objected, in particular, to Kennan's assumption that the Soviet Union could be "contained by the adroit and vigilant application of counterforce at a series of constantly shifting geographical and political points, corresponding to the shifts and maneuvers of Soviet policy." Indeed, Morgenthau appealed to the American public to forget "the crusading notion that any nation, however virtuous and powerful, can have the mission to make the world over in its own image," and to remember "that no nation's power is without limits, and hence that its policies must respect the power and interests of others."[6]

In addition to objecting to Kennan's low estimate of Soviet strength ("Soviet power bears within itself the seeds of its own decay" and "Soviet Russia might be changed overnight from one of the strongest to one of the weakest and most pitiable of national societies"), Walter Lippmann's detailed critique included the following four major points:

1. Lippmann anticipated the Republican critics of the 1950's who were to regard containment as too negative. He, too, thought the Kennan formula would deprive the United States and the West in general of foreign policy initiatives. Alluding to Kennan's assertion that history has chosen the United States to carry the burden of leadership vis-à-vis the Soviet Union, Lippmann argued that leadership should require something more than mere adaptation to the maneuvers of Soviet foreign policy at shifting points around the world. As Lippmann saw it, the policy of containment conceded the strategic initiative to the Soviet leadership.

2. Lippmann raised the issue of priorities. By his standards, the essential factor in the international politics of the postwar era was the presence of the Soviet army in the heart of Europe, and he contended

---

[5] Walter Lippmann, *The Cold War: A Study in U.S. Foreign Policy* (New York: Harper & Row, 1947); Hans J. Morgenthau, *In Defense of the National Interest* (New York: Alfred A. Knopf, Inc., 1951).

[6] Morgenthau, *Defense of National Interest*, pp. 241–242.

that all other Soviet activities and pressures, as in the Middle East or Asia, must be regarded as secondary and subsidiary to that paramount factor. For this reason, a correctly conceived foreign policy should concentrate on Europe and on the eventual and peaceful removal of the Soviet army from Europe. Thus Lippmann sought to limit the American commitment—a familiar theme since the 1960's—with priority given to the problems created by the presence of Soviet power in Europe.

Lippmann saw two advantages to his definition of limited American objectives: first, the United States would in this way clarify the "real issue" between the Soviet Union and the United States and thus work toward a specific, though exceedingly difficult, objective—that of settling the postwar conflict in Europe; and conversely, we would free ourselves of obligations and liabilities around the world implied in the containment formula.

3. Lippmann severely criticized what he regarded as the root of Kennan's perspective and his major analytical shortcoming, namely, Kennan's "disbelief in the possibility of a settlement of the issue raised by [the] war."[7] While agreeing with Kennan's observation that the Soviet Union could no longer be considered a partner but a rival of the United States in the world and therefore "political intimacy" should not be expected, Lippmann nonetheless maintained that rivals had often obtained agreements in history. "There would be little for diplomats to do," he argued, "if the world consisted of partners enjoying political intimacy, and responding to common appeals."[8]

4. Lippmann addressed himself to domestic problems raised by the extravagant spectacle of world-wide containment, i.e., the relationship of such foreign policy to our domestic, political, and economic structure. Anticipating, in this case, the executive-legislative conflicts of the 1960's and 1970's—indeed, the end of bipartisanship in foreign affairs —he wondered if Congress was going to be asked "for a blank check on the Treasury and for a blank authorization to use the armed forces."[9] The policy of global containment, he noted, might well be suited to the centralized Soviet system of politics and economics, it was certainly not suited to ours.

Lippmann's critique of containment was both devastating and somewhat sweeping; he eloquently explained what he did not like and want, without saying enough about what he did. He asked some analytically perceptive questions, but failed to put forth his own vision of a world order and America's proper role to bring it about. Yet his reading of the meaning and implications of containment, as outlined in the "X"

---

[7] Lippmann, The Cold War, p. 60.
[8] Ibid.
[9] Ibid., p. 15.

article, was widely shared both in the United States and abroad. The "X" article—especially when read together with the Truman Doctrine —was clearly understood to have signalled the assumption of a global or universal task by the United States: the task of opposing Communist power everywhere. "I believe it must be the policy of the United States," declared President Truman, "to support free peoples who are resisting subjugation by armed minorities or by outside pressures." The United States should confront the Russians, echoed Kennan, "with unalterable counterforce at every point where they show signs of encroaching upon the interests of a peaceful world."

Perhaps the only person who held a different understanding of the meaning of the "X" article and of its similarity to the Truman Doctrine was Kennan himself. He was deeply troubled when the various interpretations appeared; he was soon to fall ill with ulcers. Specifically, Kennan claims to have been misunderstood on two issues: on the global nature of containment and on the military nature of containment.

His reference in the "X" article to the need to confront the Soviet Union "at every point where they show signs of encroaching upon the interests of a peaceful world" was taken to mean that containment was to be applied without geographic limits. On the other hand, however, even before his article appeared in *Foreign Affairs* and thus well before the publication of Lippmann's critique, some of Kennan's views on this subject had apparently undergone some modification. Probably more than anything else, his reading of a draft of the Truman Doctrine seems to have altered the perspective he had put forth in the "X" article and, prior to that, in his 1945–46 diplomatic dispatches. The following detailed account by Joseph Marion Jones in his *The Fifteen Weeks* describes Kennan's reaction to the draft:

> George Kennan, often regarded as the mastermind of the policy of containment, came over to the State Department from the War College on the afternoon of March 6 to find out how things were going and was shown a copy of the [Truman] message that had been drafted. To say that he found objections to it is to put it mildly. He objected strongly both to the tone of the message and the specific action proposed. He was in favor of economic aid to Greece, but he had hoped that military aid to Greece would be kept small, and he was opposed to aid of any kind to Turkey. It was nevertheless to the tone and ideological content of the message, the portraying of two opposing ways of life, and the open-end commitment to aid free peoples that he objected most. The Russians might even reply by declaring war! Kennan voiced his objections to a number of people, including, finally, Acheson. It

was too late. The decisions had already been taken and widely approved.

Disappointed as he was by the wording of the Truman Doctrine, Kennan was said to have stated privately that it had "amounted to a promise to intervene everywhere in the world where people were threatened by Communism, quite regardless of the prospects for success of any efforts that we may make on their behalf."[10] At about the same time, in the semi-public atmosphere of the National War College, he lectured on the main criteria for extending American assistance abroad. We should provide such assistance, he maintained, only when the "problem at hand is one within our economic, technical, and financial capabilities"; when, in the absence of action, "the resulting situation might redound very decidedly to the advantage of our political adversaries"; and when, if we do provide assistance, we can expect that "the favorable consequences will carry far beyond" the specific country itself.

After recovery from ulcers, Kennan made several public speeches as well, some of which almost literally repeated Lippmann's earlier points. In May 1950, for example, in Milwaukee, he spoke on the subject of American policy and the Chinese civil war and argued, by implication at least, against the global containment of Communism. "I can conceive of no more ghastly and fateful mistake," he said on this occasion, "and nothing more calculated to confuse the issues in this world today, than for us to go into another great country and try to uphold by force of our own blood and treasures a regime which had clearly lost the confidence of its own people. . . . I look back with pride on the fact that people in our Government, in the State Department and elsewhere, had the good sense and the courage to resist the flamboyant and emotional appeals for action in this direction."

The substantial difference between the "X" article and Kennan's diplomatic dispatches, on the one hand, and his private reactions to the Truman Doctrine as well as his subsequent speeches, on the other, is clear: in the "X" article he put forth a general formula for American foreign policy, according to which the purpose of the United States was to be the global containment of Communism; hence the origins of what was to be called American "globalism" in the 1960's must be traced to this article. On the other hand, Kennan's subsequent views expounded the notion of "limitationism": a more restrictive conception of foreign policy goals, the essence of which was the rule of priorities, choice, and discrimination in the use of national power. In

[10] As quoted in Marcus G. Raskin and Bernard R. Fall (eds.), The Viet-Nam Reader (New York: Random House, 1965), p. 17.

terms of geography, then, his position was clearly globalist in the "X" article itself, while in his private reactions and semipublic lectures at the time and in his public speeches by 1950 or so he revealed a limitationist frame of mind.

His other disclaimer, noted in his 1967 *Memoirs*, seems less convincing, i.e., the argument that what he was proposing was "not containment by military means of a military threat, but the political containment of a political threat." In point of fact, his distinction between political and military containment did not find its way into the "X" article; on the contrary, his recommendation for the "adroit and vigilant application of counterforce" surely entailed the use of military power. Moreover, Kennan kept emphasizing the importance of the military for years to come—as in the following remarks made as late as September of 1949:

> It is clear that in this coming phase of international life there can be no relaxation of the vigilance and energy with which the foreign affairs of this government must be conducted. . . . So long as things remain this way, there can be no normal peace, and world stability will have to rest on a number of factors which would otherwise not have to bear so large a part of this burden. Prominent among these factors is the maintenance by this country of a powerful and impressive armed forces establishment, commensurate with the great responsibilities we are being forced to assume in the life of of the world community.

All in all, some of the mystery surrounding the "X" article remains unresolved. If he did not perceive containment in military terms, how are we to account for his 1949 speech which so persuasively argued for a strong military establishment? Why did Kennan advocate such an undiscriminating stance toward the Soviet Union both in his diplomatic essays and in the "X" article when his private criticism of the Truman Doctrine on the same point was so unequivocal? Why did he submit his article to State Department officials for clearance on March 13, 1947 and then to the editors of *Foreign Affairs* for publication on April 8 when, as Jones recounts, on March 6 he had voiced his objections to the essentially same views contained in the Truman message?

It may be that the mystery stems not so much from the discrepancy between what Kennan said and what he thought he said, or between his perception of what the article proposed and what his readers read into it; it may be, instead, that there was a subtle yet important difference between *what* Kennan said and *how* he said it—for, perhaps, the gentle music of his language was not always in harmony with the tough song itself. Thus, to a reader who was also a listener, the tone of the article could have conveyed a less encompassing, indeed limitationist, notion of containment than the text itself did.

IV. POSTSCRIPT: BEYOND CONTAINMENT

In this writer's view, limitationism rather than globalism turned out to be the guideline for the *actual conduct* of American foreign policy throughout the postwar era, with the notable exception of Vietnam. Indeed, it is worth noting that American might was considerably restrained in Korea, East Berlin, Hungary, Cuba, Czechoslovakia, Chile, and elsewhere. Declarations of policy intentions to the contrary notwithstanding, American foreign policy quite consistently avoided extravagant or overambitious undertakings, manifesting a sense of balance and proportion. What blurred our vision has been the discrepancy between our words and deeds, for in and out of political campaigns, particularly in the 1950's, political talk still centered on the "rollback" of Soviet power, "liberation" of the satellites, and the like. Consequently, *undiscriminating verbal anti-Communism overshadowed actual restraint in the public mind,* creating in turn pressure for a more "dynamic" foreign policy. In part but in a very real sense, Vietnam was then the price the United States paid for that misleading rhetoric; implicitly, and probably unconsciously, we were drawn into this unnecessary and "globalist" war in Vietnam to satisfy that disappointed, bitter, morally indignant, solution-hungry, and vocal public which had taken political talk at face value and pressed for the implementation of a universally applied policy of containment. Thus, the "X" article launched almost a generation of cold war rhetoric; but United States behavior followed the more limitationist approach advocated by Lippmann and, indeed, Kennan later on.

Ironically, it was left for President Nixon, whose utterances on global anti-Communism had always been excessive, to both reduce American commitments in Vietnam and elsewhere and narrow the discrepancy between word and deed in the American political discourse on foreign policy. Prodded by a partly limitationist, partly isolationist Senate, Nixon's foreign policy can thus be said to follow a middle-of-the-road course between globalism and isolationism, a nationalist and conservative foreign policy whose features appear to be our disinterest in the developing world, including Latin America, and the pursuit of a traditional, great-power diplomacy with both Russia and China, including important efforts toward the limitation of strategic arms and eventually partial disarmament.

This turn in American foreign policy, with concurrent declarations of reduced objectives accompanying it (i.e., the "Nixon Doctrine"), indicates the beginning of an official revision of Kennan's early assessment of both Soviet power and America's role in the world. The underlying assumptions of the Nixon-Kissinger foreign policy appear to be the following:

1. The Soviet political system, in substantially unaltered form, is here to stay;

2. the long-term ideological aims of Soviet foreign policy should not obscure more limited, short-term Soviet objectives, defined largely, if not exclusively, in terms of configurations in the international system, i.e., more in terms of what is possible than what is desirable;

3. while Soviet foreign policy is persistent and ambitious, it is also stable and steady, and for this reason the United States can treat Russia as a state rather than the center of a revolutionary movement;

4. the conflict between the Soviet Union and China is of a traditional rather than merely ideological nature, involving divergent outlooks, interests, and personalities, and for this reason the United States should have limited cooperation with both in order to obtain increased leverage in the international system; and

5. the possible future extension of Soviet influence (outside of Europe) might represent such acute problems for the Soviet Union as the extension of American influence has for the United States, and for this reason the United States should be attentive to but not overly anxious about such possibilities, i.e., the United States should not *necessarily* counter every Soviet attempt in this direction.

With the exception of the Sino-Soviet rift, an issue not yet on the political horizon at the time, these assumptions bear remarkable similarity to the views expounded not by Kennan in the "X" article, but by Walter Lippmann. As early as 1943, Lippmann put forth what he called the principle of maximizing the equilibrium between input and output in foreign policy: "The nation must maintain its objectives and its power in equilibrium," he wrote, "its purposes within means and its means equal to its purposes, its commitments related to its resources and its resources adequate to its commitments."[11] Then and later, Lippmann's outlook on foreign policy always rested on the notion of solvency, i.e., the United States should seek to do no more than what is economically and politically possible, what is, in other words, *domestically feasible.*

Domestic feasibility and awareness of what is thought to be the legitimate interests of the Soviet Union and China constitute foreign policy considerations far different from those developed by Kennan in the "X" article. They represent the first steps toward the formulation of

[11] Walter Lippmann, *U.S. Foreign Policy: Shield of the Republic* (Boston: Little, Brown and Company, 1943), p. 7.

a post-containment doctrine for American foreign policy. Whether these considerations, and the policies based on them, provide an adequate and coherent response to the needs of the American temper and of the international community in the 1970's is far less clear so far.

What remains unclear is the meaning of reduced American objectives. Does it mean that the United States no longer cares about the ultimate outcome of the war in Southeast Asia? Does it mean that the new understanding of the American interest excludes participation or active concern about conflict in South Asia? Does it still matter to us what kinds of political systems emerge in Italy or Brazil? If the answer to these questions is positive, if we are concerned, then what instruments of foreign policy are we prepared to use to bring about our objectives?

If, however, the answer to these questions is negative, if we are indeed disinterested in much of the world beyond our borders, then what remains of America's role in the international system? For it is one thing to applaud in general terms the Nixon-Kissinger (and Lippmann!) trend toward both verbal and actual limitationism, approve of the notion of solvency between domestic capability and international obligations, welcome our new approach to China, or indeed recognize the end of an era in postwar world politics; it is, however, something else to embrace a policy whose goals are undefined and whose consequences are unforeseeable.

What is urgently needed in the 1970's, then, is (a) a more precise conceptual definition of this country's international role, a definition that both delineates, at least in general terms, the American sphere of influence and specifies the kinds of foreign policy instruments to be used under various circumstances and at various areas of the world, and (b) a vigorous intellectual and political campaign to explain its meaning to the American people as well as to our friends and adversaries abroad. In the absence of such undertakings, this potentially promising trend in American foreign policy can easily lead us astray—either to the dangerous alternative of isolationism or the obsolete alternative of undiscriminating containment.

5

THE TRUMAN DOCTRINE RECONSIDERED:
From Greece to Vietnam

For reasons still not wholly known and understood, the grand alliance of the Second World War broke up almost as soon as victory was won, and the powers that had called themselves "the United Nations" fell into the pattern of hostility, periodic crisis, and "limited" war that has characterized world politics for the last twenty-five years. At Yalta in February, 1945, the United States, Great Britain, and the Soviet Union pledged to maintain and strengthen in peace the "unity of purpose and of action" that was bringing victory in war. Just over two years later, on March 12, 1947, President Truman proclaimed the doctrine that came to be recognized as the basic rationale, from the American standpoint, for the Cold War. President Truman based the appeal he made to Congress for support of Greece and Turkey not primarily on the specific circumstances of those two countries at that time but on a general formulation of the American national interest which held that "totalitarian regimes imposed on free peoples, by direct or indirect aggression, undermine the foundations of international peace and hence the security of the United States." President Truman went on to say that at

Original title: "Reflections: In Thrall to Fear." From *The Crippled Giant*, by J. William Fulbright. Copyright © 1972 by J. William Fulbright. Reprinted by permission of author and of Random House, Inc. A portion of this book originally appeared in *The New Yorker* in somewhat different form.

that moment in world history "nearly every nation must choose between alternative ways of life"—the one based on democratic institutions, like our own, and the other based on "terror and oppression," for which the model, of course, was the Soviet Union.

Most of us thought we knew how and why this great transition—from "unity of purpose and of action" to Truman's declaration of ideological warfare—had come about in so short a time. The cause was Soviet Communist aggression, limited at the outset to Stalin's subjugation of Eastern Europe but shown by Marxist-Leninist doctrine to be universal in design, aimed at nothing less than the Communization of the world. American policy and opinion were profoundly influenced in the early postwar period by the thesis that George Kennan, signing himself "X," set forth in *Foreign Affairs* for July, 1947, which depicted Soviet policy as relentlessly expansionist, committed by a fanatical ideology to filling "every nook and cranny available . . . in the basin of world power," and "stopping only when it meets with some unanswerable force." Warning against bluster and excessive reliance on military force, Kennan nonetheless called for an American policy of "unalterable counter force," of "firm and vigilant containment," which he anticipated would "increase enormously the strains under which Soviet policy must operate," and encourage changes within Russia leading to "either the breakup or the gradual mellowing of Soviet power."

From Korea to Berlin to Cuba to Vietnam, the Truman Doctrine governed America's response to the Communist world. Tactics changed —from "massive retaliation" to "limited war" and "counterinsurgency" —but these were variations on a classic formulation based on assumptions that few really questioned. Sustained by an inert Congress, the policymakers of the forties, fifties, and early sixties were never compelled to reëxamine the premises of the Truman Doctrine, or even to defend them in constructive adversary proceedings.

Change has come not from wisdom but from disaster. The calamitous failure of American policy in Vietnam has induced on the part of scholars, journalists, and politicians a belated willingness to reëxamine the basic assumptions of American postwar policy. Induced by the agitations of the present moment, this new look at old events may well result in an excess of revision, or of emotion, but the corrective is much needed if we are to profit from experience and recast our policies. It cannot be said that the assumptions underlying the Truman Doctrine were wholly false, especially for their time and place. But there is a powerful presumptive case against their subsequent universal application—the case deriving from the disaster of our policy in Asia—and it seems appropriate to look back and try to discover how and why the promise of the

United Nations Charter gave way so quickly to ideological warfare
between East and West.

Until fairly recently, I accepted the conventional view that the United
States had acted in good faith to make the United Nations work but that
the Charter was undermined by the Soviet veto. In retrospect, this seems
less certain, and one suspects now that, like the League of Nations before it, the United Nations was orphaned at birth. Whereas Woodrow
Wilson's great creation was abandoned to skeptical Europeans, Franklin
Roosevelt's project was consigned to the care of unsympathetic men of
his own country. President Roosevelt died only two weeks before the
opening of the meeting in San Francisco at which the United Nations
was organized. Truman, as a new and inexperienced President, was
naturally more dependent on his advisers than President Roosevelt had
been; among these, so far as I know, none was a strong supporter of the
plan for a world organization, as Cordell Hull had been. The Under-
Secretary of State, Dean Acheson, was assigned to lobby for Senate
approval of the United Nations Charter, and he recalled later that "I did
my duty faithfully and successfully, but always believed that the Charter
was impractical." And, with even greater asperity and candor, he told
an interviewer in 1970, "I never thought the United Nations was worth
a damn. To a lot of people it was a Holy Grail, and those who set store
by it had the misfortune to believe their own bunk."

Disdaining the United Nations, the framers of the Truman Doctrine
also nurtured an intense hostility toward Communism and the Soviet
Union. Stalin, of course, did much to earn this hostility, with his paranoiac suspiciousness, the imposition of Soviet domination in Eastern
Europe, and the use of Western Communist parties as instruments of
Soviet policy. All this is well known. Less well known, far more puzzling,
and also more pertinent to our position in the world today is the eagerness with which we seized upon postwar Soviet provocations and
plunged into the Cold War. If it be granted that Stalin started the Cold
War, it must also be recognized that the Truman Administration seemed
to welcome it.

By early 1947—a year and a half after the founding of the United
Nations—the assumptions of the Cold War were all but unchallenged
within the United States government. It was *assumed* that the object of
Soviet policy was the Communization of the world; if Soviet behavior in
Europe and northern China were not proof enough, the design was
spelled out in the writings of Lenin and Marx, which our policymakers
chose to read not as a body of political philosophy but as the field
manual of Soviet strategy. It is true, of course, that by 1947, with the
United States virtually disarmed and Western Europe in a condition of

economic paralysis, the Soviet Union might plausibly have tried to take over Western Europe through the manipulation of Communist parties, through military intimidation, through economic strangulation, and possibly even through direct military action. The fact that Stalin could have done this, and might well have tried but for timely American counteraction through the Marshall Plan and the formation of NATO, was quickly and uncritically taken as proof of a design for unlimited conquest comparable to that of Nazi Germany. Neither in the executive branch of our government nor in Congress were more than a few, isolated voices raised to suggest the possibility that Soviet policy in Europe might be motivated by morbid fears for the security of the Soviet Union rather than by a design for world conquest. Virtually no one in a position of power was receptive to the hypothesis that Soviet truculence reflected weakness rather than strength, intensified by memories of 1919, when the Western powers had intervened in an effort—however halfhearted—to strangle the Bolshevik "monster" in its cradle. Our own policy was formed without the benefit of constructive adversary proceedings. A few brave individuals, like former Vice-President Henry Wallace, offered dissenting counsel—and paid dear for it.

When Great Britain informed the United States in February, 1947, that is was no longer able to provide military support for Greece, the American government was ready with a policy and a world view. The latter was an early version of the domino theory. Knowing, as we thought we did, that Russian support for Communist insurgents in Greece was part of a grand design for the takeover first of Greece, then of Turkey, the Middle East, and so forth, we were not content simply to assume the British role of providing arms to a beleaguered government; instead, we chose to issue a declaration of ideological warfare in the form of the Truman Doctrine. It may well be true that the grand phrases were motivated in part by a desire to arouse this nation's combative spirit, and so to build congressional support for the funds involved, but it is also true—at least, according to Joseph Jones, the State Department official who drafted President Truman's appeal to Congress, under Acheson's direction—that the new policy was conceived not just as a practical measure to bolster the Greeks and Turks but as a historic summons of the United States to world leadership. "*All* barriers to bold action were indeed down," as Jones has written. Among the State Department policymakers, Jones reports, it was felt that "a new chapter in world history had opened, and they were the most privileged of men, participants in a drama such as rarely occurs even in the long life of a great nation."

The Truman Doctrine, which may have made sense for its time and place, was followed by the Marshall Plan and NATO, which surely did make sense for their time and place. But as a charter for twenty-five years of global ideological warfare and unilateral military intervention against Communist insurgencies the Truman Doctrine has a different set of implications altogether. It represents a view of Communism, of the world, and of our role in the world that has had much to do with the disaster of our policy in Asia. Even in the country to which it was first applied, President Truman's basic formulation—that "we shall not realize our objectives . . . unless we are willing to help free peoples to maintain their free institutions"—has been reduced to a mockery. But who remembers now (surely not Mr. Agnew) that the Truman Doctrine was initially designed to preserve democracy in Greece?

Acheson, who prided himself on being a realist, may not have taken all that ideological claptrap seriously, but his successors Dulles and Rusk certainly did, and they framed their policies accordingly. Whatever merit the Truman Doctrine may have had in the circumstances of early-postwar Europe, the bond with reality became more and more strained as the Doctrine came to be applied at times and in places increasingly remote from the Greek civil war. Operating on a set of assumptions that defined reality for them—that as a social system Communism was deeply immoral, that as a political movement it was a conspiracy for world conquest—our leaders became liberated from the normal rules of evidence and inference when it came to dealing with Communism. After all, who ever heard of giving the Devil a fair shake? Since we know what he has in mind, it is pedantry to split hairs over what he is actually doing.

Political pressures at home intensified the virulence of the anti-Communist ideology. In retrospect, the surprise Democratic victory in the election of 1948 was probably a misfortune for the country. The Republicans, frustrated and enraged by their fifth successive defeat, became desperate in their search for a winning issue. They found their issue in the threat of Communism, at home and abroad, and they seized upon it with uncommon ferocity. They blamed the Truman Administration for Chiang Kai-shek's defeat in the Chinese civil war; they attacked President Truman for the bloody stalemate in Korea, although they had strongly supported his initial commitment; and they tolerated and in many cases encouraged Senator Joseph R. McCarthy's attacks on reputable, and even eminent, Americans. Every American President since that time has been under intense pressure to demonstrate his anti-Communist orthodxy.

More by far than any other factor, the anti-Communism of the Truman Doctrine has been the guiding spirit of American foreign policy since the Second World War. Stalin and Mao Tse-tung and even Ho Chi Minh replaced Hitler in our minds as the sources of all evil in the world. We came to see the hand of "Moscow Communism" in every disruption that occurred anywhere. First, there was the conception of Communism as an international conspiracy—as an octopus with its body in Moscow and its tentacles reaching out to the farthest corners of the world. Later, after the Sino-Soviet break, sophisticated foreign-policy analysts disavowed the conspiracy thesis, but at the same time they disavowed it they said things that showed that the faith lingered on. Secretary Rusk and his associates professed to be scornful of the conspiracy thesis, but still they defended the Vietnam war with references to a world "cut in two by Asian Communism," the only difference between the earlier view and the later one being that where once we had seen one octopus we now saw two.

If you accepted the premise, the rest followed. If Moscow and Peking represented centers of great power implacably hostile to the United States, and if every local crisis, from Cuba to the Congo to Vietnam, had the Communist mark upon it, then it followed logically that every crisis posed a threat to the security of the United States. The effect of the anti-Communist ideology was to spare us the task of taking cognizance of the specific facts of specific situations. Our "faith" liberated us, like the believers of old, from the requirements of empirical thinking, from the necessity of observing and evaluating the actual behavior of the nations and leaders with whom we were dealing. Like medieval theologians, we had a philosophy that explained everything to us in advance, and everything that did not fit could be readily identified as a fraud or a lie or an illusion. The fact that in some respects the behavior of the Soviet Union and of China and North Vietnam lived up to our ideological expectations made it all the easier to ignore the instances in which it did not. What we are now, belatedly, discovering is not that the Communist states have never really been hostile to us but that they have been neither consistent nor united in hostility to us; that their hostility has by no means been wholly unprovoked; and that they have been willing from time to time to do business or come to terms with us. Our ideological blinders concealed these instances from us, robbing us of useful information and of promising opportunities. The perniciousness of the anti-Communist ideology of the Truman Doctrine arises not from any patent falsehood but from its distortion and simplification of reality, from its universalization and its elevation to the status of a revealed truth.

Psychologists tell us that there is often a great difference between what one person says and what another hears, or, in variation of the old adage, that the evil may be in the ear of the hearer. When Khrushchev said, "We will bury you," Americans heard the statement as a threat of nuclear war and were outraged accordingly. The matter was raised when Chairman Khrushchev visited the United States in 1959, and he replied with some anger that he had been talking about economic competition. "I am deeply concerned over these conscious distortions of my thoughts," he said. "I've never mentioned any rockets."

We will never know, of course, but it is possible that an opportunity for a stable peace was lost during the years of Khrushchev's power. As we look back now on the many things he said regarding peaceful co-existence, the words have a different ring. At the time, we did not believe them: at best, they were Communist propaganda; at worst, outright lies. I recalled recently, for example, the visit of Chairman Khrushchev to the Senate Foreign Relations Committee on September 16, 1959. Suggesting that we lay aside the polemics of the past, Mr. Khrushchev said:

> We must face the future more and have wisdom enough to secure peace for our countries and for the whole world. We have always had great respect for the American people. We have also been somewhat envious of your achievements in the economic field, and for that reason we are doing our best to try to catch up with you in that field, to compete with you, and when we do catch up to move further ahead. I should say that future generations would be grateful to us if we managed to switch our efforts from stock-piling and perfecting weapons and concentrated those efforts fully on competition in the economic field.

Now, in retrospect, one wonders: why were we so sure that Khrushchev didn't mean what he said about peace? The answer lies in part, I believe, in our anti-Communist obsession—in the distortions it created in our perception of Soviet behavior, and in the extraordinary sense of threat we experienced when the Russians proclaimed their desire to catch up and overtake us economically. In our own national value system, competition has always been prized; why, then, should we have been so alarmed by a challenge to compete? Perhaps our national tendency to extoll competition rather than coöperation as a social virtue and our preoccupation with our own primacy—with being the "biggest," the "greatest" nation—suggest an underlying lack of confidence in ourselves, a supposition that unless we are "No. 1" we will be nothing: worthless and despised, and deservedly so. I am convinced that the real reason we squandered twenty billion dollars or more getting men to the moon in the decade of the sixties was our fear of something like horrible humiliation if the Russians got men there first. All this suggests that slogans about competition and our own primacy in that competition are largely hot air—sincerely believed, no doubt, but nonetheless masking an exaggerated fear of failure, which, in turn, lends a quality of desperation to our competitive endeavors. One detects this cast of mind in President Johnson's determination that he would not be "the first

American President to lose a war," and also in President Nixon's spectre of America as "a pitiful, helpless giant."

This kind of thinking robs a nation's policymakers of objectivity and drives them to irresponsible behavior. The distortion of priorities involved in going to the moon is a relatively benign example. The perpetuation of the Vietnam war is the most terrible and fateful manifestation of the determination to prove that we are "No. 1." Assistant Secretary of Defense for International Security Affairs John T. McNaughton, as quoted in the Pentagon Papers, measured the American interest in Vietnam and found that "to permit the people of South Vietnam to enjoy a better, freer way of life" accounted for a mere ten percent and "to avoid a humiliating U.S. defeat" for up to seventy percent. McNaughton's statistical metaphor suggests a nation in thrall to fear; it suggests a policymaking élite unable to distinguish between the national interest and their own personal pride.

Perhaps if we had been less proud and less fearful, we would have responded in a more positive way to the earthy, unorthodox Khrushchev. Whatever his faults and excesses, Khrushchev is recognized in retrospect as the Communist leader who repudiated the Marxist dogma of the "inevitability" of war between Socialist and capitalist states. Understanding the insanity of war with nuclear weapons, Khrushchev became the advocate of "goulash" Communism, of peaceful economic competition with the West. During his period in office, some amenities were restored in East-West relations; the Berlin issue was stirred up but finally defused, and, most important, the limited-nuclear-test-ban treaty was concluded. These were solid achievements, though meagre in proportion to mankind's need for peace, and meagre, too, it now appears, in proportion to the opportunity that may then have existed. One wonders how much more might have been accomplished—particularly in the field of disarmament—if Americans had not still been caught up in the prideful, fearful spirit of the Truman Doctrine.

Even the crises look different in retrospect, especially when one takes into account the internal workings of the Communist world. A leading British authority on Soviet affairs, Victor Zorza, has traced the beginning of the Vietnam war to a "fatal misreading" by President Kennedy of Khrushchev's endorsement of "wars of national liberation." The Kennedy Administration interpreted Khrushchev's statement as a declaration that the Soviet Union intended to sponsor subversion, guerrilla warfare, and rebellion all over the world. Accordingly, the Administration attached enormous significance to Soviet material support for the Laotian Communists, as if the issue in that remote and backward land were directly pertinent to the world balance of power. It was judged that Khrushchev must be shown that he could not get away with it. We had taught Stalin that "direct" aggression did not pay; now we must teach Khrushchev—and the Chinese—that "indirect" aggression did not pay. In Zorza's view, Khrushchev's talk of "wars of national liberation" was not a serious plan for worldwide subversion but a response to Communist China, whose leaders were then accusing Khrushchev of selling out the cause of revolution and making a deal with the United States.

In the spirit of the Truman Doctrine, the Kennedy Administration read the Soviet endorsement of "wars of national liberation" as a direct challenge to the United States. Speaking of Russia and China, President Kennedy said in his first State of the Union Message, "We must never be lulled into believing that either power has yielded its ambitions for world domination—ambitions which they forcefully restated only a short time ago." I do not recall these words for purposes of reproach; they represented an assessment of Communist intentions that most of us shared at that time, an assessment that had been held by every Administration and most members of Congress since the Second World War, an assessment that had scarcely—if at all—been brought up for critical examination in the executive branch, in congressional committees, in the proliferating "think tanks," or in the universities. Perhaps no better assessment could have been made on the basis of the information available at that time, but I doubt it. I think it more likely that we simply chose to ignore evidence that did not fit our preconceptions, or—as is more often the case—when the facts lent themselves to several possible interpretations we chose to seize upon the one with which we were most familiar: the Communist drive for world domination.

In the amplified form it acquired during the Johnson years, the conception of "wars of national liberation" as part of the Communist design for world domination became the basic rationale for the Vietnam war. All the other excuses—defending freedom, honoring our "commitments," demonstrating America's resolution—are secondary in importance and are easily shown to be fallacious and contradictory. But no one can *prove* that Mao Tse-tung and Brezhnev and Kosygin—or Khrushchev, for that matter—have not harbored secret ambitions to conquer the world. Who can prove that the desire or the intention was never in their minds? The truly remarkable thing about this Cold War psychology is the totally illogical transfer of the burden of proof from those who make charges to those who question them. In this frame of reference, Communists are guilty until proved innocent—or simply by definition. The Cold Warriors, instead of having to say how they knew that Vietnam was part of a plan for the Communization of the world, so manipulated the terms of public discussion as to be able to demand that the skeptics prove that it was not. If the skeptics could not, then the war must go on—to end it would be recklessly risking the national security. We come to the ultimate illogic: war is the course of prudence and sobriety until the case for peace is proved under impossible rules of evidence—or until the enemy surrenders.

Rational men cannot deal with each other on this basis. Recognizing their inability to know with anything like certainty what is going on in other men's minds, they do not try to deal with others on the basis of their presumed intentions. Instead, rational men respond to others on the basis of their actual, observable behavior, and they place the burden of proof where it belongs—on those who assert and accuse rather than on those who question or deny. The departure from these elementary rules for the ascertainment of truth is the essence of the Cold War way of thinking; its weakened but still formidable hold on our minds is indicative of the surviving tyranny of the Truman Doctrine.

In a decade's perspective—and without the blinders of the Truman Doctrine—it even seems possible that the Cuban missile crisis of 1962 was not so enormous a crisis as it then seemed. Khrushchev in the early sixties was engaged in an internal struggle with the Soviet military, who, not unlike our own generals, were constantly lobbying for more funds for ever more colossal weapons systems. Khrushchev had been cutting back on conventional forces and, largely for purposes of appeasing his unhappy generals, was talking a great deal about the power of Soviet missiles. President Kennedy, however, was applying pressure from another direction: unnerved by Khrushchev's endorsement of "wars of national liberation," he was undertaking to build up American conventional forces at the same time that he was greatly expanding the American nuclear-missile force, even though by this time the United States had an enormous strategic superiority. Khrushchev's effort to resist the pressures from his generals was, of course, undermined by the American buildup. It exposed him to pressures within the Kremlin from a hostile coalition of thwarted generals and politicians who opposed his de-Stalinization policies. In the view of a number of specialists in the Soviet field, the placement of missiles in Cuba was motivated largely, if not primarily, by Khrushchev's need to deal with these domestic pressures; it was meant to close or narrow the Soviet "missile gap" in relation to the United States without forcing Khrushchev to concentrate all available resources on a ruinous arms race.

Lacking an expert knowledge of my own on these matters, I commend this interpretation of Khrushchev's purpose not as necessarily true but as highly plausible. As far as I know, however, none of the American officials who participated in the decisions relating to the Cuban missile crisis seriously considered the possibility that Khrushchev might be acting defensively or in response to domestic pressures. It was universally assumed that the installation of Soviet missiles in Cuba was an aggressive strategic move against the United States—that, and nothing more. Assuming Khrushchev's aggressive intent, we imposed on the Soviet Union a resounding defeat, for which Khrushchev was naturally held responsible. In this way, we helped to strengthen the military and political conservatives within the Soviet Union, who were to overthrow Khrushchev two years later. If we had been willing to consider the possibility that Khrushchev was acting on internal considerations, we would still have wished to secure the removal of the missiles from Cuba, but it might have been accomplished by means less embarrassing to Khrushchev, such as a *quid pro quo* under which we would have removed our Jupiter missiles from Turkey.

Khrushchev had paid dear for his "softness on capitalism" in an earlier encounter with President Eisenhower. After his visit to the United States in 1959, Khrushchev apparently tried to persuade his skeptical, hard-line colleagues that Americans were not such monsters as they supposed and that President Eisenhower was a reasonable man. This heretical theory—heretical from the Soviet point of view—was shot out of the sky along with the American U-2 spy plane in May, 1960. When President Eisenhower subsequently declined the opportunity Khrushchev offered him to disclaim personal responsibility, Khrushchev felt compelled to break up the Paris summit meeting. The U-2 incident was later cited by Khrushchev himself as a critical moment in his loss of power at home. It shattered his plans for President Eisenhower to pay a visit to the Soviet Union—for which, it is said, he had already had a golf course secretly constructed in the Crimea.

There were, of course, other factors in Khrushchev's fall, and perhaps more important ones; nor is it suggested that his intentions toward the West were necessarily benevolent. The point that must emerge, however—more for the sake of the future than for history's sake—is that if we had not been wearing ideological blinders, if our judgment had not been clouded by fear and hostility, we might have perceived in Khrushchev a world statesman with whom constructive business could be done. When he fell, his successors put an end to de-Stalinization, began the military buildup that has brought the Soviet Union to a rough strategic parity with the United States, and greatly stepped up their aid to Communist forces in Vietnam.

While our response to Soviet Communism has been marked by hostility, tensions, and fear, our response to Communism in Asia has been marked by all these and, in addition, by a profound sense of injury and betrayal. Russia never was a country for which we had much affection anyway; it was the bleak and terrible land of the czars, which, when it went to the Communist devils, was merely trading one tyranny for another. But China had a special place in our hearts. We had favored her with our merchants and missionaries and our "open door" policy; we had even given back the Boxer indemnity so that Chinese students could study in America. In the Second World War, we fought shoulder to shoulder with "free" China; we were filled with admiration for its fighting Generalissimo Chiang Kai-shek, and utterly charmed by his Wellesley-educated wife.

When the Chinese darlings of our patronizing hearts went to Communist perdition, we could only assume that they had been sold or betrayed into bondage. It was inconceivable that our star pupils in the East could actually have willed this calamity; it had to be the work of Chinese traitors, abetted by disloyal Americans, joined in an unholy alliance to sell out China to those quintessential bad people, the Russians. A white paper on China was issued in 1949, and Secretary of State Acheson's letter of transmittal recounted accurately the intense but futile American effort to salvage a Kuomintang regime whose officials and soldiers had "sunk into corruption, into a scramble for place and power, and into reliance on the United States to win the war for them and to preserve their own domestic supremacy." Then, having exonerated the United States from responsibility for the loss of China, Secretary Acheson wrote:

> The heart of China is in Communist hands. The Communist leaders have forsworn their Chinese heritage and have publicly announced their subservience to a foreign power, Russia, which during the last 50 years, under czars and Communists alike, has been most assiduous in its efforts to extend its control in the Far East. . . . The foreign domination has been masked behind the facade of a vast crusading movement which apparently has seemed to many Chinese to be wholly indigenous and national. . . .
>
> However tragic may be the immediate future of China and however ruthlessly a major portion of this great people may be exploited by a party in the interest of a foreign imperialism, ultimately the profound civilization and the democratic individualism of China will reassert themselves and she will throw off the foreign yoke. I consider that we should encourage all developments in China which now and in the future work toward this end.

In these words, the United States government enunciated what became its Truman Doctrine for Asia. By the end of 1950, we were at war with China in Korea, but even then our belief in Moscow's control of the "Communist conspiracy" or our sentimental unwillingness to

believe that China of its own free will would make war on the United
States, or some combination of the two, made it difficult for us to believe that the Chinese Communists had intervened in Korea for reasons
directly related to their own national interest. The fact that General
MacArthur's sweep to the Yalu was bringing American ground forces
within striking distance of China's industrial heartland in Manchuria
was not at that time widely thought to be a factor in China's intervention
in the war. The view of Dean Rusk, then the Assistant Secretary of State
for Far Eastern Affairs, was that "the peace and security of China are
being sacrificed to the ambitions of the Communist conspiracy," and
that "China has been driven by foreign masters into an adventure of
foreign aggression which cuts across the most fundamental national
interests of the Chinese people." Mr. Rusk went on to say, "We do not
recognize the authorities in Peiping for what they pretend to be. The
Peiping régime may be a colonial Russian government—a Slavic Manchukuo on a larger scale. It is not the government of China."

Nonetheless, for the first time in our history we were coming to
regard China as our enemy, departing from a half century's policy of
supporting a strong, independent China. One of our leading young
China scholars, Warren I. Cohen, has provided this summary in his
recent book, "America's Response to China":

> The great aberration in American policy began in 1950, as the
> people and their leaders were blinded by fear of Communism and
> forgot the sound geopolitical, economic, and ethical basis of their
> historic desire for China's well-being. Having always assumed that
> China would be friendly, Americans were further bewildered by
> the hostility of Mao's China, leading them to forsake their tradi-
> tional support of Asian nationalism, not only in China, but wher-
> ever Marxist leadership threatened to enlarge the apparent Com-
> munist monolith. With the full support of the American people,
> Truman and his advisors committed the United States to a policy
> of containing Communism in Asia as well as in Europe—and in
> practice this policy became increasingly anti-Chinese, an unprece-
> dented campaign of opposition to the development of a strong,
> modern China. There was no longer any question of whether the
> United States would interpose itself between China and her ene-
> mies, for the United States had become China's principal enemy.

Over the years, the notion of a "Slavic Manchukuo" gave way to
a recognition of the Chinese Communists as the authors of their own
deviltry. This was not a fundamental change of outlook toward "international Communism" but an accommodation to a fact that had become obvious to all save the most fanatical and self-deluded Cold

Warriors: that, far from being an instrument in Moscow's hands, the Chinese Communist leaders had become defiant and hostile toward Soviet leadership of the Communist world. Now, from the American viewpoint, there were two "Communist conspiracies," and of the two great Communist states China was judged to be the more virulent and aggressive. The Chinese had withdrawn their troops from Korea in 1958, limited themselves to a border adjustment with India in 1962 (when they could have detached a large area after defeating the Indian Army), and assumed no direct combat role in the developing conflict in Vietnam. But these facts were judged to be less important than the fact that they were Communists, who openly advocated subversion and "wars of national liberation." Communist China was not judged to be aggressive on the basis of its actions; it was presumed to be aggressive because it was Communist.

In much the same way that Khrushchev terrified us with his talk of "burying" us, the Chinese sent us into a panic with their doctrine of "wars of national liberation." While the Russians had become relatively benign, contained by America's nuclear deterrent, China claimed to be impervious to the horrors of nuclear war and was still intensely revolutionary itself, committed to the promotion and support of "wars of national liberation" throughout the world. The Kennedy and Johnson Administrations concluded that still another gauntlet had been flung down before the United States. To meet this presumed threat, our military planners invented the strategy of "counterinsurgency," which they undertook to put into effect in Vietnam.

None of this is meant to suggest that China would have been friendly to us if we ourselves had not been hostile. I do not know whether the Chinese Communists would have been friendly or not; nor, I think, does anyone else know, since we never tried to find out. Most probably, in the turmoil of revolutionary change, the Chinese Communists would have been deeply suspicious and verbally abusive of the citadel of capitalism and the leader of the Western "imperialist camp" even if the United States had been willing to come to terms with them. Be that as it may, an objective observer must admit that on the basis of their actual behavior the Chinese Communists have never proved the Hitlerian menace we have taken them to be. They have not tried to conquer and subjugate their neighbors. Nor, upon examination, does the doctrine of "wars of national liberation," as set forth by Lin Piao, constitute a charter of Chinese aggression. It stresses self-reliance and the limitations of external support. Lin Piao wrote:

In order to make a revolution and to fight a people's war and be victorious, it is imperative to adhere to the policy of self-reliance, rely on the strength of the masses in one's own country and prepare to carry on the fight independently even when all material aid from outside is cut off. If one does not operate by one's own efforts, does not independently ponder and solve the problems of the revolution in one's own country, and does not rely on the strength of the masses, but leans wholly on foreign aid —even though this be aid from Socialist countries which persist in revolution—no victory can be won, or be consolidated even if it is won.

The sudden reversal of American policy toward China in 1971 necessarily invites our attention back to the basic causes of these two decades of conflict between the United States and the Communist countries of Asia. In the course of these two decades, we have engaged in armed conflict with all three of these countries—with Communist China, North Korea, and North Vietnam—but we have never fought a war with the Soviet Union, which is the only Communist power capable of posing a direct strategic threat to the United States. Although it was assumed from the outset of the Cold War that our real strategic interests lay in Europe rather than in Asia, it has been in Asia that we have thought it necessary to fight two wars to enforce the Truman Doctrine. Looking back, one is bound to ask whether these conflicts were inescapable. Having avoided war in the region we judged more important, and with the power we judged the greater threat, why have we found it necessary to fight in Asia, at such enormous cost in lives and money and in the internal cohesion of our own society? Is it possible that if Mao Tse-tung and Ho Chi Minh had not borne the title of "Communist" but otherwise had done exactly what they have done in their two countries, we would have accepted their victories over their domestic rivals and lived with them in peace? I think it quite possible that we would have come to terms with both. Apart from the North Korean invasion of South Korea, which was a direct violation of the United Nations Charter, the Communist countries of Asia have done nothing that has threatened the security of the United States and little, if anything, that has impaired our legitimate interests. We intervened in the Chinese and Vietnamese civil wars only because the stronger side in each case was the Communist side and we assumed that, as Communists, they were parties to a conspiracy for world domination, and were therefore our enemies. We intervened against them not for what they *did* but for what they *were* and for what we assumed to be their purpose.

There were Americans in official positions who provided a more objective, less ideologically colored view of the Chinese Communists

back in the days before they won their civil war. These wartime observers in China, who included John S. Service, John Paton Davies, and
Colonel David D. Barrett, were themselves sympathetic to the National
government of Chiang Kai-shek, at least to the extent of urging it to
make the reforms that might have allowed it to survive. Nonetheless,
they reported objectively on the weakness and corruption of the Kuomintang and on the organization and discipline of the Communists in
their headquarters in Yenan. They also provided information suggesting
that at that time Mao Tse-tung and his associates had no intention whatever of becoming subservient to the Soviet Union and hoped to coöperate with the United States. Not only did the observations of these
men go unheeded; they themselves were subsequently denounced and
persecuted. Colonel Barrett did not attain the promotion to brigadier
general that his service in the Army merited, and Service and Davies
were hounded out of the Foreign Service, charged with advocacy of,
and even responsibility for, the Chinese Communist victory that they
had foreseen. The nation was deprived thereafter of their accurate observations and valuable insights, and, what is more, their surviving colleagues in the bureaucracy got the unmistakable message that it was
unhealthy to deviate from the anti-Communist line. To survive and get
ahead, it was necessary to see the world as the world was defined by the
Truman Doctrine.

Having been thoroughly educated in the catechism of the Cold War,
we look back now with astonishment on the reports of Service, Barrett,
and others from China in 1944. Barrett and Service came to know the
Chinese Communist leaders well through the Dixie Mission, which was
the name given to the mission of the United States Army Observer
Group, headed by Colonel Barrett, at Chinese Communist headquarters
in Yenan in late 1944 and early 1945. Their assignment was to assess the
potential contribution of the Chinese Communists to a final assault
against Japanese forces in China. They came to know and respect the
Communists, not for their ideology but for their discipline, organization, fighting skills, and morale.

In his recent book "Dixie Mission," Colonel Barrett comments,
"The Chinese Communists are our bitter enemies now, but they were
certainly 'good guys' then, particularly to the airmen who received their
help." Colonel Barrett found that as sources of information about the
Japanese the Communists were "all we had hoped they would be and
even more"—among other reasons, because they "could almost always
count on the coöperation and support of a local population." American
observers sent out into the countryside from Yenan "all expressed the
belief that the Communists were being supported by the entire civil
population." In retrospect, Colonel Barrett felt that he had been "over-

sold" on the Communists in Yenan, but nonetheless he comments, "The overall look of things there was one which most Americans were inclined to regard with favor." American observers were impressed by the absence of sentries around the leaders, in contrast with the Nationalist capital in Chungking, where there were "police and sentries everywhere;" by the tough, well-nourished, and well-dressed troops, in contrast with the poorly nourished, shabbily uniformed Kuomintang soldiers; and by the general atmosphere of roughhewn equality and shared sacrifice. "As a whole," Colonel Barrett comments, "the Communist outlook on life was old-fashioned and conservative."

Even the flamboyant and volatile General Patrick J. Hurley—Roosevelt's special emissary and, later, Ambassador to Chungking—was at first favorably impressed by the Chinese Communists' terms for a settlement with Chiang Kai-shek. In November, 1944, Hurley flew to Yenan, where he signed an agreement with Mao Tse-tung calling for a coalition government; Hurley pronounced the agreement eminently fair, and even told Mao—in Barrett's hearing—that the terms did not go far enough in the Communists' favor. Chiang Kai-shek rejected Hurley's plan out of hand; nonetheless, Hurley thereafter supported Chiang as the sole leader of China and publicly blamed the failure of his mediation on his Embassy staff, whom he accused, in effect, of being pro-Communist. Although he contended in November, 1944, that "if there is a breakdown in the parleys it will be the fault of the Government and not the Communists," and although he told President Truman in May, 1945, that the Communists were holding back "in my opinion with some degree of reasonableness," Hurley still backed the Nationalist regime to the hilt, and in the spring of 1945 even reimposed the ban on nonmilitary travel by Americans to the Communist headquarters in Yenan. Thus began the process, culminating in the failure of the mission undertaken in 1946 by General George C. Marshall through which, without having ascertained their attitudes and intentions toward us, the United States government came to identify the Chinese Communists as enemies of the United States—presaging the policy of isolation and containment that was to endure at least until 1971.

This was not at the outset the result of decisions made at the highest level. President Roosevelt wrote to a friend on November 15, 1944, "I am hoping and praying for a real working out of the situation with the so-called Communists." And in March, 1945, in reply to a question from Edgar Snow about whether we could work with two governments in China for purposes of prosecuting the war with Japan, Roosevelt said, "Well, I've been working with two governments there. I intend to go on doing so until we can get them together." Within a few weeks after that interview, Roosevelt was dead and the conduct of American foreign policy had passed into the hands of the inexperienced President Truman. Neither Roosevelt nor Truman, however, seems in the last days of the Second World War to have given serious and sustained thought to the internal problems of China. Both Presidents were preoccupied with the defeat of Japan, and it had been clear for some time that China was unlikely to play a decisive role in bringing that about.

There was no lack of information available to the United States government in 1944 and 1945 about either the weakness and corruption of the Kuomintang or the strength and aspirations of the Chinese Communists. The views of the professional diplomats were rejected, however, and their reports ignored—that is, until the witchhunters in the State Department and Congress got hold of them. In June, 1944, for example, a warning was conveyed to Washington in a memorandum written principally by John Service:

> The situation in China is rapidly becoming critical. . . . There is a progressive internal breakdown. . . . The fundamental cause of this suicidal trend is that the Kuomintang, steadily losing popular support . . . is concentrating more and more on putting the preservation of its shrinking power above all other considerations.
>
> These policies, unless checked by the internal opposition they evoke and by friendly foreign influence, seem certain to bring about a collapse which will be harmful to the war and our long-term interests in the Far East.

At the same time that American observers in China were reporting the enfeeblement of the Kuomintang, they were providing detailed accounts of the growing military and political strength of the Communists. Service summed up the importance of these circumstances for the United States.

> From the basic fact that the Communists have built up popular support of a magnitude and depth which makes their elimination impossible, we must draw the conclusion that the Communists will have a certain and important share in China's future.

His colleague John Paton Davies put it even more succinctly:

> The Communists are in China to stay. And China's destiny is not Chiang's but theirs.

The Communists were not only strong but—at least, so they said —willing and eager to coöperate with the United States. In his recent book "The Amerasia Papers: Some Problems in the History of U.S.-

China Relations," Service reports on a long conversation he had with
Mao Tse-tung in Yenan on August 23, 1944, in which Mao emphasized
that the Chinese Communists were "first of all Chinese," and appealed
for American help for China after the war. "The Russians," Mao said,
"have suffered greatly in the war and will have their hands full with
their own job of rebuilding. We do not expect Russian help." America,
he thought, could help China, and he told Service:

> China must industrialize. This can be done—in China—only
> by free enterprise and with the aid of foreign capital. Chinese and
> American interests are correlated and similar. They fit together,
> economically and politically. We can and must work together.
> The United States would find us more coöperative than the
> Kuomintang. We will not be afraid of democratic American influ-
> ence—we will welcome it. We have no silly ideas of taking only
> Western mechanical techniques. . . .
> America does not need to fear that we will not be coöperative.
> We must coöperate and we must have American help. This is why
> it is so important to us Communists to know what you Americans
> are thinking and planning. We cannot risk crossing you—cannot
> risk any conflict with you.

We do not know, of course, whether Mao was sincere in his repeated
appeals for American friendship. The reason we do not know is that we
never tried to find out. In our postwar anti-Communist hysteria, we
assumed that the Chinese Communists were hostile simply because
they were Communists, and we also assumed, despite impressive evidence to the contrary, that they were subservient to the Soviet Union.
We thereupon made our fateful commitment to the losing side in the
Chinese civil war—the side of whose weakness and probable defeat
full warning had been provided by our own highly competent observers. From these events followed two wars and a quarter century of
bitter hostility, which might have been avoided if we had remained
neutral in the Chinese civil war.

This is not to say that Mao might have been expected to put Sino-
American relations back on their prewar basis. He most assuredly would
not have done that. Certainly our pretentions to a benevolent pater-
nalism toward China would have been given short shrift; the age of
missionaries and the "open door" was at an end. But whatever our
relations might have been if we had not intervened in the civil war,
they would at least have been initiated on a more realistic and more
promising basis. We might have long ago established a working relationship at least as tolerable, and as peaceful, as the one we have
had with the Soviet Union: the sort of relationship toward which—be-

latedly but most commendably—the Nixon Administration now seems to be working.

The anti-Communist spirit that governed our relations with China after the Second World War also shaped—and distorted—our involvement in Vietnam. Our interest in China's civil war, though tragic in consequence, was attenuated and limited in time. Vietnam was less fortunate. In a test application of the new science of "counterinsurgency," it has been subjected to prolonged, though inconclusive, devastation. But for the American intervention, the Vietnamese civil war would have ended long ago—at infinitely less cost in lives, money, and property—in a nationalist Communist victory under the leadership of Ho Chi Minh.

In retrospect, it is difficult to understand how we could have accepted the "loss" of China but not the "loss" of the small, undeveloped countries on China's southern border. Only in the context of the assumptions of the Truman Doctrine could the Vietnamese war ever have been rationalized as having something to do with American security or American interests. Looking through our anti-communist prism, we saw Ho Chi Minh not as a Vietnamese nationalist who was also a Communist but as a spear-carrier for the international Communist conspiracy, the driving force for a "world cut in two by Asian Communism." The Johnson Administration, as Mr. Johnson's memoirs show clearly, believed itself to be acting on President Truman's doctrine that "totalitarian regimes imposed on free peoples, by direct or indirect aggression, undermine the foundations of international peace and hence the security of the United States." President Johnson and his advisers believed this despite a set of facts that did not fit the formula: the fact that the issue was not between a "free people" and a "totalitarian regime" but between rival totalitarian regimes; the fact that the war was not one of international aggression, "direct" or otherwise, but an anti-colonial war and then a civil war; and the fact that, in any case, the country was too small and the issue too indigenous to Vietnam to pose anything resembling a threat to "the foundations of international peace," much less to "the security of the United States." In practice, the issue had resolved itself into a corruption of the Truman Doctrine—into the fear of a "humiliating" defeat at the hands of Communists. It was not so much that we needed to win, or that there was anything for us to win, as that our leaders felt—for reasons of prestige abroad and political standing at home—that they could not afford to "lose." President Johnson said soon after he took office, "I am not going to be the President who saw Southeast Asia go the way China went."

The notion that a country is "lost" or "gone" when it becomes Communist is a peculiarly revealing one. How can we have "lost" a country unless it was ours to begin with—unless it was some part of an unacknowledged American imperium? To my eye, China under Mao is in the same place on the map that it was in the days of Chiang. Where, then, has it "gone"? To the moon? Or to the devil? The "lost" and "gone" concept is indicative of a virulent sanctimoniousness that is only now beginning to abate. In October, 1971, members of the Senate gave President Tito of Yugoslavia a cordial reception at an afternoon tea. In September, 1959, a similar reception was held for Chairman Khrushchev, but one senator refused to sit in the room with him—for fear, apparently, of ideological contamination. As the President now moves toward lifting the "quarantine" of China, as we recognize at long last that there really still is a China, Communist though it may be, the tragic irrationality of the Vietnam war is thrown once again into high relief. All that bloodletting—not just for ourselves but for the Vietnamese—could have been avoided by an awareness that Communism is not a contagious disease but a political movement and a way of organizing a society.

In the case of Ho Chi Minh, as in the case of Mao Tse-tung, we might have come to this awareness twenty-five years—and two wars—ago. Ho, in fact, was a lifelong admirer of the American Revolution, of Lincoln, and of Wilson and his Fourteen Points. As a young man, in 1919, he went to the Versailles Peace Conference to appeal for self-determination for his country in accordance with President Wilson's principles, but no attention was paid to him, and Vietnam remained within the French empire. In 1945, Ho Chi Minh started his declaration of independence for Vietnam with words taken from our own: "All men are created equal." In 1945 and 1946, Ho addressed a series of letters to the United States government asking for its mediation toward a compromise with France, but none of these letters were ever answered, because Ho was, in Dean Acheson's words, "an outright Commie."

President Roosevelt, during the Second World War, had favored independence for Indo-China, or a trusteeship, but in any event he was opposed to letting the French recover Indo-China for their colonial empire. Roosevelt's attitude was spelled out in a memorandum to Secretary of State Hull dated January 24, 1944, which appears in the Pentagon Papers:

> I saw Halifax last week and told him quite frankly that it was perfectly true that I had, for over a year, expressed the opinion that Indo-China should not go back to France but that it should

be administered by an international trusteeship. France has had the country—thirty million inhabitants—for nearly one hundred years, and the people are worse off than they were at the beginning.

As a matter of interest, I am wholeheartedly supported in this view by Generalissimo Chiang Kai-shek and by Marshal Stalin. I see no reason to play in with the British Foreign Office in this matter. The only reason they seem to oppose it is that they fear the effect it would have on their own possessions and those of the Dutch. They have never liked the idea of trusteeship because it is, in some instances, aimed at future independence. This is true in the case of Indo-China.

Each case must, of course, stand on its own feet, but the case of Indo-China is perfectly clear. France has milked it for one hundred years. The people of Indo-China are entitled to something better than that.

British intransigence and the requirements of military strategy prevented Roosevelt from acting on his anti-colonialist preference, which was so wholly in keeping with the traditional American outlook. When the Truman Administration took office, American policy was changed, and the French were officially assured by our State Department that the United States had never questioned, "even by implication, French sovereignty over Indo-China." The United States would advocate reforms but would leave it to the French to decide when, or even whether, the people of Indo-China were to be given independence: "Such decisions would preclude the establishment of a trusteeship in Indo-China except with the consent of the French Government."

Whether this initial commitment to France—and therefore against Ho—was the result of growing anti-Communist sentiment within the Truman Administration or of friendly feelings toward the colonial powers on the part of President Truman's old-line advisers, or both, American policy was constant and firm from that time on. Later, when Acheson and his colleagues were attempting to build up France as the centerpiece of the anti-Communist coalition in Europe, the commitment to France's position in Indo-China became stronger than ever. By 1951, the United States was paying forty percent of the cost of France's war against the Vietminh, and by 1954 eighty percent. After the Geneva settlement, American military aid to South Vietnam averaged about two hundred million dollars a year between 1955 and 1961. By 1963, South Vietnam ranked first among the recipients of our military assistance, and only India and Pakistan received more in economic assistance. In this way, foreign aid served as a vehicle of commitment, from our initial support of French colonial rule in Indo-China to sending an American force of over half a million men to fight in a war that is still going on.

As with China, it might have been different. The Pentagon Papers show that between October, 1945, and February, 1946, Ho Chi Minh addressed at least eight communications to the President of the United States or to the Secretary of State asking America to intervene for Vietnamese independence. Earlier, in the summer of 1945, Ho had asked that Vietnam be accorded "the same status as the Phillipines" —a period of tutelage to be followed by independence. Following the outbreak of hostilities in Vietnam in the early fall of 1945, Ho made his appeals to President Truman on the basis of the Atlantic Charter, the United Nations Charter, and Mr. Truman's Navy Day speech of October 27, 1945, in which the President expressed the American belief that "all peoples who are prepared for self-government should be permitted to choose their own form of government by their own freely expressed choice, without interference from any foreign source." In November, 1945, Ho wrote to the Secretary of State requesting the initiation of cultural relations through the sending of fifty Vietnamese students to the United States. On February 16, 1946, in a letter to President Truman, Ho referred to American "complicity" with the French, but he still appealed to the Americans "as guardians and champions of world justice" to "take a decisive step" in support of Vietnamese independence, and pointed out that he was asking only what had been "graciously granted to the Philippines." On September 11, 1946, Ho communicated directly with the United States government for the last time, expressing to an American Embassy official in Paris his own admiration for the United States and the Vietnamese people's respect and affection for President Roosevelt; again he referred to America's granting of independence to the Philippines.

As far as the record shows, neither President Truman nor any of his subordinates replied to any of Ho Chi Minh's appeals. He got his answer nonetheless, clearly and unmistakably. By late 1946, with the first Vietnam war under way, American military equipment was being used by the French against the Vietnamese. As far as the United States government was concerned, Vietnam was a sideshow to the real struggle against Communism, in Europe. If the price of French support in that struggle was American support of French colonialism in Southeast Asia—and we seem never to have questioned that it was—the Truman Administration was ready to pay that price. Ho, after all, was just another "Commie." In a cable to the United States representative in Hanoi in May, 1949, Acheson said:

QUESTION WHETHER HO AS MUCH NATIONALIST AS COM-
MIE IS IRRELEVANT. ALL STALINISTS IN COLONIAL AREAS ARE
NATIONALISTS. WITH ACHIEVEMENT NAT'L AIMS (I.E., INDE-
PENDENCE) THEIR OBJECTIVE NECESSARILY BECOMES SUB-
ORDINATION STATE TO COMMIE PURPOSES.

In February, 1950, the recognition of Ho Chi Minh's government
by the Communist powers moved Secretary Acheson to declare that
this recognition "should remove any illusion as to the nationalist character of Ho Chi Minh's aims and reveals Ho in his true colors as the
mortal enemy of native independence in Indochina."

As with China under Mao Tse-tung, we might have got along toler-
ably well—maybe even quite well—with a unified, independent Vietnam under Ho Chi Minh if our leaders' minds had not been hopelessly
locked in by the imprisoning theory of the international Communist
conspiracy. Ho was an authentic Vietnamese patriot, revered by his
countrymen. He had led the resistance to the Japanese within Vietnam
and had welcomed the Allies as liberators. His unwillingness to submit
to foreign domination was clear—or should have been clear—from
the outset: But if the evidence of Ho Chi Minh's Vietnamese nationalism ever reached the American policymakers, it certainly did not persuade them. Acting Secretary of State Acheson instructed an American
diplomat in Hanoi in December, 1946, "KEEP IN MIND HO'S CLEAR
RECORD AS AGENT INTERNATIONAL COMMUNISM." In February,
1947, by which time the war between France and the Vietminh was
well under way, Secretary of State Marshall conceded, in another cable,
that colonial empires were rapidly becoming a thing of the past but,
as to Vietnam,

WE DO NOT LOSE SIGHT FACT THAT HO CHI MINH HAS DI-
RECT COMMUNIST CONNECTIONS, AND IT SHOULD BE OBVI-
OUS THAT WE ARE NOT INTERESTED IN SEEING COLONIAL
EMPIRE ADMINISTRATIONS SUPPLANTED BY PHILOSOPHY
AND POLITICAL ORGANIZATIONS EMANATING FROM AND
CONTROLLED BY KREMLIN.

General Marshall's words were prophetic of what became a guiding
principle—or, more accurately, a guiding abberation—of American foreign policy for at least two decades: where Communists were involved,
the United States would depart from its traditional anti-colonialism and
support the imperial power. Assuming as we did that Communists by
definition were agents of an international conspiracy, we further assumed that a Communist leader could not be an authentic patriot no

matter what he said or did. If the choice was to be—as we then rationalized it—between the old imperialism of the West and the new imperialism of the Kremlin, we would side with the former. Where possible, we told ourselves, we would support or nurture "third forces" —genuine independence movements that were neither colonialist nor Communist—and where such movements existed, as in India, we did support and welcome independence. Where they did not exist, as in Vietnam and Cuba and the Dominican Republic, we intervened, making these countries the great crisis areas of postwar American foreign policy and, in the process, earning for the United States the reputation of foremost imperialist power.

The role is one to which we are unsuited by temperament and tradition. Until a generation ago, America was regarded throughout the world—and deservedly so—as the one great nation that was authentically anti-imperialist. It was Woodrow Wilson who introduced into international relations the revolutionary principle of "justice to all peoples and nationalities, and their right to live on equal terms of liberty and safety with one another, whether they be strong or weak." Perhaps it was a utopian dream, but Americans meant it at the time, and the world believed we meant it, and we had plans for realizing it: first the Covenant of the League of Nations and then the United Nations Charter, both purporting to introduce the rule of law into international relations, both purporting to supplant the old imperialist anarchy with the principle of trusteeship for the weak and the poor, both purporting to supplant the old balance of power with a new community of power.

The dismay and disillusion that have overtaken so many of us in America are the result, I believe, of our departure from these traditional American values. The corrosive, consuming fear of Communism has driven us into a role in the world which suits us badly and which we deeply dislike. I think that the American people have sensed this all along and are moving now to an active, conscious awareness of their own real preferences. It is no easy matter for us to knock over the household gods we have been taught for a generation to worship, but I think the American people have all along had an uneasy awareness that the dictators and warlords with whom we have been in league for so long are not really our kind of people. I suspect, too, that if Khrushchev and Mao and Ho had not had the name of "Communist" we might have recognized them as men we could respect: tough and sometimes ruthless, but patriots nonetheless; committed to an ideology we would not want for ourselves, but also committed to the well-being of their own people. With China's entry into the United Nations and the President's imminent trip to Peking, we may find that we can do business with the Chinese, just as we have done with the Russians. We may even find it possible to be cordial, as we have been with the Yugoslavs. Eventually (who knows?), we may even kick over the household gods once and for all and become friends. Huck Finn, when he helped Jim escape, knew it was a sin and knew he was going to go to Hell for it, but he liked Jim, so he did it anyway.

History is filled with turning points that are not easily identified until long after the event. It seems almost inevitable that Vietnam will prove to have been a watershed in American foreign policy, but it is by no means clear what kind. Before it can represent anything of a lasting historical nature, the war, of course, will have to be ended—not just scaled down but ended, and not just for Americans but for the tortured Vietnamese as well. One assumes that it will be ended—if not by our present leaders, then by their successors—and that when at last it is, the American people will once again in their history have the opportunity and the responsibility of deciding where they want to go in the world, of deciding what kind of role they want their country to play, of deciding what kind of country they want America to be.

The Truman Doctrine, which made limited sense for a limited time in a particular place, has led us in its universalized form to disaster in Southeast Asia and demoralization at home. In view of all that has happened, it seems unlikely that we will wish to resume the anti-Communist crusade of the early postwar years. Yet it is not impossible: memories will fade, controversies may recur, pride may once again be challenged and competitive instincts aroused. The Truman Doctrine is frayed and tattered, but it is still an influence upon our policy and outlook.

I do not think we are going to return to isolationism. I will go further: I do not think there is or ever has been the slightest chance of the United States' returning to the isolationism of the prewar years. It will not happen because it cannot happen: we are inextricably involved with the world politically, economically, militarily, and—in case anyone cares—legally. We could not get loose if we wanted to. And no one wants to. The people who are called "neo-isolationists" are no such thing; the word is an invention of people who confuse internationalism with an intrusive American unilateralism, with a quasi-imperialism. Those of us who are accused of "neo-isolationism" are, I believe, the opposite: internationalists in the classic sense of that term —in the sense in which it was brought into American usage by Woodrow Wilson and Franklin Roosevelt. We believe in international coöperation through international institutions. We would like to try to keep the peace through the United Nations, and we would like to try to assist the poor countries through institutions like the World Bank. We do not think the United Nations is a failure; we think it has never been tried.

In the aftermath of Vietnam, it is America's option—not its "destiny," because there is no such thing—to return to the practical idealism of the United Nations Charter. It is, I believe, consistent with our national tradition and congenial to our national character, and is therefore the most natural course for us to follow. It is also the most logical, in terms of our interests and the interests of all other nations living in a diverse and crowded but interdependent world in the age of nuclear weapons.

The essence of any community—local, national, or international—is some degree of acceptance of the principle that the good of the whole must take precedence over the good of the parts. I do not believe that the United States (or any of the other big countries) has ever accepted that principle with respect to the United Nations. Like the Soviet Union and other great powers, we have treated the United Nations as an instrument of our policy, to be used when it is helpful but otherwise ignored. Orphaned at birth by the passing from the political scene of those who understood its potential real usefulness, the United Nations has never been treated as a potential world-security community—as an institution to be developed and strengthened for the long-term purpose of protecting humanity from the destructiveness of unrestrained nationalism. The immediate, short-term advantage of the leading members has invariably been given precedence over the needs of the collectivity. That is why the United Nations has not worked. There is no mystery about it, no fatal shortcoming in the Charter. Our own federal government would soon collapse if the states and the people had no loyalty to it. The reason that the United Nations has not functioned as a peace-keeping organization is that its members, including the United States, have not wished it to; if they had wanted it to work, it could have—and it still can. Acheson and his colleagues were wholly justified in their expectation of the United Nations' failure; their own cynicism, along with Stalin's cynicism, assured that failure.

Our shortsighted, self-serving, and sanctimonious view of the United Nations was put on vivid display in the reaction to the General Assembly's vote to take in mainland China and expel Nationalist China. Mr. Nixon expressed unctuous indignation, not at the loss of the vote but at the "shocking demonstration" of "undisguised glee" shown by the winners, especially those among the winners to whom the United States had been "quite generous"—as the President's press secretary was at pains to add. Mr. Agnew at least spared us the pomposities, denouncing the United Nations as a "paper tiger" and a "sounding board for the left," whose only value for the United States was that "it's good to be in the other guy's huddle." The Senate Minority Leader was equally candid: "I think we are going to wipe off some of the smiles from the faces we saw on television during the United Nations voting." The revelations are striking. Having controlled the United Nations for many years as tightly and as easily as a big-city boss controls his party machine, we had got used to the idea that the United Nations was a place where we could work our will; Communists could delay and disrupt the proceedings and could exercise the Soviet veto in the Security Council, but they certainly were not supposed to be able to win votes. When they did, we were naturally shocked—all the more because, as one European diplomat commented, our unrestrained arm-twisting had turned the issue into a "worldwide plebiscite for or against the United States," and had thereby made it difficult for many nations to judge the question of Chinese representation on its merits. When the vote went against us nonetheless, the right-wingers among us saw that as proof of what they had always contended—that the United Nations was a nest of Red vipers.

The test of devotion to the law is not how people behave when it goes their way but how they behave when it goes against them. During these years of internal dissension over the war in Vietnam, our leaders have pointed out frequently—and correctly—that citizens, however little they may like it, have a duty to obey the law. The same principle applies on the international level. *"Pacta sunt servanda,"* the international lawyers say: "The law must be obeyed." The China vote in the General Assembly may well have been unwise, and it may have shown a certain vindictiveness toward the United States, but it was a legal vote, wholly consistent with the procedures spelled out in the Charter.

The old balance-of-power system is a discredited failure, having broken down in two world wars in the twentieth century. The human race managed to survive those conflicts; it is by no means certain that it would survive another. This being the case, it is myopic to dismiss the idea of an effective world peace-keeping organization as a visionary ideal—or as anything, indeed, but an immediate, practical necessity.

With the coöperation of the major powers—and there is no reason in terms of their own national interests for them not to coöperate—the conflict in the Middle East could be resolved on the basis of the Security Council resolution of 1967, to which all the principal parties have agreed, calling for a settlement based upon, among other things, the principle of "the inadmissibility of the acquisition of territory by war." Similarly, I believe that the Security Council should have interceded to prevent war between India and Pakistan. This proved impossible largely because of the self-seeking of the great powers, each of which perceived and acted upon the situation not on its merits, and certainly not in terms of human cost, but in terms of its own shortsighted geopolitical interests. Moreover, the Security Council waited until war had actually broken out and an Indian victory seemed certain before attempting to intervene. The time for the United Nations to act on the crisis in East Pakistan was many months earlier, when the Bengalis were brutally suppressed by the armed forces of the Pakistani government. The United Nations, it is true, is proscribed by Article 2 of the Charter from intervention in "matters which are essentially within the domestic jurisdiction of any state," but Article 2 also states that "the principle shall not prejudice the application of enforcement measures" under the peace-enforcement provisions of the Charter. By any reasonable standard of judgment, the mass killing of East Bengalis and the flight of ten million refugees across the Indian border constituted a "threat to the peace" as that term is used in the Charter, warranting United Nations intervention. I do not think it likely under present circumstances that the United Nations could play a mediating role in the war in Indo-China, the disabling circumstance being that the belligerents, including the United States, almost certainly would not permit it. But, looking ahead to the time when the Vietnam war is finally ended, I think it would be feasible for the United Nations to oversee and police a general peace settlement, through a revived International Control Commission, and perhaps through the assignment of peace-keeping forces.

When a conflict presents what Article 39 of the Charter calls a "threat to the peace, breach of the peace, or act of aggression," it makes no sense to leave the issue to the caprices of the belligerents. I have never understood why it is so widely regarded as outrageous or immoral for external parties to impose a solution to a dangerous conflict. Under the United Nations Charter, the Security Council has full authority—possibly even an obligation—to impose a settlement upon warring parties that fail to make peace on their own. The very premise of the Charter is that warring nations can no longer be permitted immunity from a world police power. As far as the United States is concerned, it is worth recalling that the United Nations Charter is a valid and binding obligation upon us, ratified as a treaty with the advice and consent of the Senate. And as far as the parties to various conflicts are concerned—Arabs and Israelis, Indians and Pakistanis— it needs to be recognized that they, too, are signatories to the Charter and are therefore obligated, under Article 25, "to accept and carry out the decisions of the Security Council in accordance with the present Charter."

In this century of conflict, the United States led in the conception and formulation of plans for an international peace-keeping organization. We did not invent the idea, nor have we been its only proponents, but without our leadership the ideal embodied in the Covenant of the League of Nations and the United Nations Charter would not have attained even the meagre degree of realization it has attained. It is this idea of world organization—rather than our democratic ideology, or our capitalist economy, or our power and the responsibilities it is supposed to have thrust upon us—that entitles the United States to claim to have made a valuable and unique contribution to the progress of international relations. Coming as we did on the international scene as a new and inexperienced participant, with a special historical experience that had sheltered us from the normal pressures of world politics, we Americans pursued our conception of a rational world order with uncritical optimism and excessive fervor. As a consequence, the first encounter with disappointment, in the form of Stalin and his ambitions in Eastern Europe, sent us reeling back from Wilsonian idealism. And from the practical idealism of the United Nations Charter we reverted to the unrealistic "realism" of the Truman Doctrine in its universalized application. We made the conversion from Wilson to Machiavelli with zeal.

At no point, of course, did the leading architects of Vietnam or the Bay of Pigs or the participants in the Cuban missile crisis conceive of themselves as power brokers pure and simple. Having themselves been reared in the tenets of Wilson-Roosevelt internationalism, and having lived through the disaster of appeasement in the inter-war years, they came to regard themselves as "tough-minded idealists," as "realists with vision," and, above all, as practitioners of collective security against aggression. What the United Nations could not do the United States could and would do, with allies if possible, alone if necessary. We, after all, were the ones who bore the burden of the "responsibilities of power." It was up to us, if all else failed, to curb aggression at its outset, to accept whatever sacrifices had to be made in order to defend the "free world" against the new Communist predator. We, in effect, were the successors to an enfeebled United Nations, and were forced by fate and circumstance to endure the glory and agony of power.

In this heady frame of reference, Vietnam and its consequences might be conceived as the ripe harvest of the American era of romantic "realism." Primarily, no doubt, because of its military failures, the war in Vietnam has brought many Americans to an awareness of the sham idealism of the "responsibilities of power," and of the inadequacies of the new "realism" once it is stripped of its romantic façade. Many young Americans, and some older ones, are appalled not only by the

horrors of the Vietnam war but by the deterministic philosophy, es-
poused by the intellectuals who came into government in the sixties,
of a permanent, purposeless struggle for power and advantage. We
seem to be discovering once again that without a moral purpose and
frame of reference there can be no such thing as "advantage."

America may be coming near to the closing of a circle. Having
begun the postwar period with the idealism of the United Nations
Charter, we retreated in disillusion to the "realism" of the Cold War,
to the Truman Doctrine and its consummation in Vietnam, easing the
transition by telling ourselves that we were not really abandoning the
old values at all but simply applying them in more practical ways. Now,
having failed most dismally and shockingly, we are beginning to cast
about for a new set of values. The American people, if not their leaders,
have come near to recognizing the failure of romantic, aggressive "realism," although a new idealism has yet to take its place. Perhaps we will
settle for an old idealism—the one we conceived and commended to
the world but have never tried.

WILLIAM ZIMMERMAN

6

CHOICES IN THE POSTWAR WORLD (1):
Containment and the Soviet Union

I

The puzzles of why states behave as they do and how it is possible to influence state behavior represent key theoretical issues in the study of comparative foreign policy. The question of how states behave, moreover, has what the Russians would call *aktual'nost*. It is relevant theoretically and at the same time important practically. Knowledge, however putative, is power and used as power. Theories, models, or images which decision makers and their advisors entertain about the elements which explain other states' behavior have a significant impact on the ways in which those who act in the name of states attempt to influence other states' behavior. The effectiveness of efforts to produce intended effects on others may be shaped by the quality and nature of one's image of the actor one is attempting to influence.

For the United States, the central issue in its foreign policy since the last days of World War II has been the question of influencing Soviet behavior. Thus, theoreticians, policy makers, and plain people

Copyright © 1974 by William Zimmerman. The research assistance of Ms. Valerie Bunce and Ms. Gretchen Fei is gratefully acknowledged. A previous draft of this study was presented under the title, "The Sources of Soviet Conduct: A Reconsideration," at the National Convention of the American Political Science Association on September 5, 1972 in Washington, D.C.

in the United States have been intrigued with hypotheses about the sources of Soviet conduct—to use the title of George F. Kennan's famous "X" article.[1] The purpose of this essay is to depict the conventional wisdom about Soviet foreign policy under Stalin, to summarize the emerging consensus in the United States as to the elements which explain post-Stalinist Soviet foreign policy, and then re-examine the assumptions which informed the orthodox approaches to Stalin's foreign policy for the period immediately after World War II up to his death in 1953.

The issue of influencing Soviet foreign policy obviously presupposes a prior question: What changes are we trying to accomplish in Soviet behavior? If, for instance, the change sought is the fundamental restructuring of the Soviet regime, then clearly the magnitude of change required is of a different order than that for efforts to produce modest changes in foreign policy behavior. Similarly, if it is presupposed that at a given time the Soviet Union already constitutes a threat to core values of the United States, then the likelihood of successful influence attempts will be less than if the issue is whether or not extension of Soviet and/or communist influence constitutes a threat to American interests. Likewise, it matters whether or not it is assumed that augmenting Soviet and/or communist influence *anywhere* represents a threat to U.S. interests or, in more limited fashion, whether or not Soviet predominance, control, or absolute dominance of specific areas of the globe poses a danger to U.S. interests. Sometimes the possible influence attempts may not be directed toward containing—to use a word almost unavoidable in this discussion—Soviet influence within or to a specific area but rather might be defined in terms of affecting the style (in the most generic sense) of Soviet foreign policy, specifically to shaping the rules of the game for the conduct of the Soviet-American dyadic relationship.

In the context of the containment dialogue, all the above have been seriously entertained by persons striving to contribute insights as to how one affects or influences Soviet foreign policy. There have been those in the United States who have advocated policies which entailed altering the nature of the Soviet regime. For those who have thought that Soviet behavior was so ineluctably tied up with what the Russians are or what the Soviet regime is, the change envisaged obviously has been fundamental—just as for some Soviet leaders (to wit, Stalin in the early fifties) the world which they sought to establish

[1] "The Sources of Soviet Conduct," *Foreign Affairs* XXIV, no. 4 (July 1947): 566–82 and reproduced in this volume (Chapter 2). My views in many ways parallel those of Gati in Chapter 4 of this volume. See especially pp. 41–44.

was incompatible with the continued existence of the United States as it was—or is presently—constituted. (The most extreme expression of this viewpoint in the Soviet context was the argument that capitalist encirclement was not a geographical but a political concept: As long as any capitalist great power existed, Soviet security was threatened.)[2] Many have argued that the extension of the Soviet Union into Eastern Europe represented a threat to core American values. Long before World War II had been settled, Nicholas J. Spykman wrote that a "Russian state from the Urals to the North Sea can be no great improvement over a German state from the North Sea to the Urals."[3]

In the 1940s and early 1950s, critics of American foreign policy, largely from the right, attacked containment because in their view the aim of American foreign policy should be the expulsion of Soviet influence from Eastern Europe. In the 1960s and 1970s, critics, largely on the left, have ascribed such an *intent* to American policy makers. It has been asked, for instance, "Why did the United States after 1939 permit the conquest of Eastern Europe by Nazi forces, presumably forever, with scarcely a stir, but refused after 1944 to acknowledge any primary Russian interest or right of hegemony in the same region on the heels of a closely won Russian victory against the German invader?" And it has been contended that "When scholars have answered that question fully the historical debate over the Cold War origins will be largely resolved."[4] Christopher Lasch speaks of the "failure, the enormously costly failure, of American efforts to dominate Eastern Europe at the end of World War II."[5] William A. Williams has similarly seen the origins of the Cold War in the efforts by the United States to secure an open door for American trade in Eastern Europe.[6] The thread common to both critiques was the assumption that the United States had vital interests in Eastern Europe which either ostensibly did prompt it to act to deny Soviet influence there or should have caused it to act in such a manner.

In the "X" article and in Kennan's other relevant writings at the end

[2] For a discussion on this point, see Robert C. Tucker, *The Soviet Political Mind* (New York: Frederick A. Praeger, 1963), pp. 20–35.

[3] *America's Strategy in World Politics* (New York: Harcourt, Brace and Co., 1942), p. 460.

[4] Norman A. Graebner, "Cold War Origins and the Continuing Debate: A Review of the Literature," *Journal of Conflict Resolution* XIII, no. 1 (March 1969): 123–32 as reproduced in Erik P. Hoffmann and Frederic J. Fleron, Jr., eds., *The Conduct of Soviet Foreign Policy* (Chicago: Aldine-Atherton, 1971), pp. 217–27 at p. 226.

[5] "The Cold War, Revisited and Re-Visioned" in ibid., pp. 262–74 at p. 274.

[6] This is one of the less telling points of the "Cold War revisionists." As Arthur Schlesinger, Jr. has remarked, it was Henry Wallace who was the most prominent advocate of the Open Door for Eastern Europe.

of, and immediately after, World War II,[7] one can find passages which seem to indicate that he regarded, as he candidly acknowledged subsequently,[8] the extension of Soviet and/or Communist influence anywhere as constituting a threat to U.S. interests. Hence, the references to "the adroit and vigilant application of counter-force at a series of constantly shifting geographical and political points,"[9] "a policy of firm containment, designed to confront the Russians with unalterable counter-force at every point where they show signs of encroaching upon the interests of a peaceful and stable world."[10] Hence, too, Kennan's assumption that "any success of a local Communist party, any advance of Communist power anywhere, had to be regarded as an extension in reality of the political orbit, or at least, the dominant influence of the Kremlin."[11]

In other remarks, by contrast, Kennan gave vent to a view which emphasized the importance of denying certain areas to Soviet and/or Communist influence. In his *Memoirs,* Kennan observes:

> My objection to the Truman Doctrine message revolved largely around its failure to draw [a distinction between various geographic areas]. Repeatedly at that time and in ensuing years, I expressed in talks and lectures the view that there were only five regions in the world—the United States, the United Kingdom, the Rhine valley with adjacent industrial areas, the Soviet Union, and Japan where the sinews of modern strength could be produced in quantity; I pointed out that only one of these was under Communist control; and I defined the main task of containment, accordingly, as one of seeing to it that none of the remaining ones fell under such control.

"Why this was not made clear in the "X" article is, again, a mystery."[12] From the "X" article one could even glean the impression that what really offended Kennan was the matter of Soviet style. In one passage it seems *almost* that what Kennan found most offensive about Soviet

[7] Since the focus, descriptively, of this paper is primarily on the period 1945–47 and since the "X" article was published in 1947 it behooves me to stress that Kennan himself in his *Memoirs, 1925–1950* (New York: Bantam, 1969) declares that the views expressed in the "X" article "were ones arrived at not in the anxieties and disillusionments of 1947, when they first became publicly known, but rather in the impressions of wartime service in Moscow itself, and in the effort to look ahead from that vantage point, on the heels of the Allied victory, into the uncertain future of Russia's relationship to the West" (p. 264).

[8] One of Kennan's most endearing attributes is his candor. For his *samokritika* of the containment argument see especially ibid., pp. 272–82.

[9] Chapter 2 of this volume, p. 18.

[10] Ibid., p. 22.

[11] Kennan, *Memoirs,* p. 385.

[12] Ibid., p. 378.

foreign policy was "the Kremlin's conduct of foreign policy: the secretiveness, the lack of frankness, the duplicity, the wary suspiciousness, and the basic unfriendliness of purpose"[13]—and *not* Soviet expansionist aspirations.

There exist, of course, other options. Goals of containing or "rolling back" Soviet influence or altering the means employed by the Soviet Union in the conduct of its foreign policy are not the only directions in which one might conceivably try to influence the USSR. Immediately after World War II, it might have been thought desirable to increase Soviet influence in order to deal with a possible resurgent Germany; in the 1960s and 1970s certainly many have thought it desirable to direct Soviet expansionist aspirations in such a way as to curb an ostensible Chinese menace. In the 1960s and 1970s, American decision makers came to recognize an interest in influencing Soviet foreign policy so as to facilitate either directly or indirectly the pursuit of U.S. goals. It was realized that it was possible to encourage the Soviet Union to pursue policies which simultaneously increased its security and that of the United States. Beyond that, the United States in the seventies has found itself in the curious position of attempting to expand trade with the Soviet Union (and Eastern Europe) in part as a way to alter its balance of payments, while buying from the USSR the rare metals necessary for heat-resistant steel alloys for supersonic fighter-bombers. Moreover, American policy makers were intrigued by the availability of Soviet natural-gas deposits, as a viable way of dealing with an incipient resource crisis in the United States. Thus, the question of altering Soviet behavior depends to a large degree on what behavioral change one is attempting to accomplish; it depends on whether accomplishing that change requires the implementation of a new policy, a shift in the composition of the ruling group, or—more drastically—a change in the nature of the regime.

II

The changes sought are in part a function of the explanation of Soviet foreign policy imparted by the analyst. If we ask what causes Soviet foreign policy behavior, it is possible to frame an answer in terms of the origins of the inputs which explain Soviet foreign policy. In the study of Soviet foreign policy, as in the more general study of comparative foreign policy and world politics, analysts have generally opted for one of two major orientations. In explaining the behavior of those who act in the name of states, the macroanalytic tradition

---

[13] Chapter 2 of this volume, p. 15.

tends to disregard the internal dynamics of a state's behavior—such factors as the particular political structure of the country, the perspectives and personalities of the decision makers, the articulations of desires on the part of the citizenry. Instead, in the name of analytic parsimony, those in this tradition treat the state as a unitary rational decision maker whose behavior is explained largely in response to the anarchic quality of politics in the absence of an overarching government, to changes in the structure of the international system, or to calculated moves by rival states.

Microanalytic approaches have tended, by contrast, to see foreign policy as an output which in some sense of the phrase represents the continuation of domestic political processes. Foreign policy is seen as a resultant of internal political processes or of the interplay of phenomena particular to the state in question. These explanations stem from an attention to environmental factors: a country's geographic position or its natural resource endowment. Microanalytic approaches also focus on domestic societal forces such as national character, model personality, political culture, the belief systems and ideologies of elites and masses, and social structure. In the same vein are those major strands of political analysis which emphasize the relationship of the institutional structure of the state to foreign policy, a rubric which may subsume such classic explanatory categorizations as the open-closed polity dichotomy, as well as the more contemporary attention to the impact of information flows within bureaucratic structures on policy outputs. Finally, the foreign policy attributes thought to matter for those in the microanalytic tradition may originate in the personalities and even idiosyncracies of the key decision makers—their anxieties, aspirations, and perceptions.[14]

Of the two, the dominant tradition in Western analysis of Soviet foreign policy has been microanalytic. There are several possible explanations for this phenomenon. The Cold War created an atmosphere conducive to stressing the differences between Soviet foreign-policy behavior and the behavior of other states. Soviet studies for a considerable period remained divorced conceptually and methodologically from the mainstream of comparative politics and international-relations inquiry. More importantly, though, most scholars, myself included, concluded that there was compelling evidence to suggest that Soviet foreign policy did diverge from that of other states and that the explanation for the unique in Soviet policies, goals, and instrumentalities was to be found in the radical transformation of the Russian polity and Russian society by the Bolshevik seizure of power in 1917.

[14] The above two paragraphs draw heavily on my "Elite Perspectives and the Explanation of Soviet Foreign Policy," *Journal of International Affairs*, XXIV, no. 1 (1970): 84–85.

One can look, however, at the explanation of foreign policy from a somewhat different perspective. For the purposes of the question "How does one influence Soviet foreign policy," it makes more sense to categorize approaches to Soviet foreign policy along a continuum reflecting the determinism or voluntarism informing the analyst's explanation. As William T. R. Fox wrote in 1959

> Whether one views world politics from the desk of a great-power foreign minister at a critical moment of choice, or from the desk of a scholar in a university during an inter-crisis period of peace, there must almost inevitably be a restless search for the variables in the situation which one can modify and which, if modified, would result in a more efficient protection or promotion of whatever the viewer, whether policy-maker or theorist, regards as valuable.[15]

Variables external to the Soviet Union are more easily modified (at least directly) by the Western policy makers than are those within the Soviet Union. Consequently, the source of the analyst's explanation and the extent of his determinism are likely to be highly correlated. High determinism and heavy attention to microanalytic variables will *generally* go hand in hand, as will an attention to international systemic variables—specifically, the policies of other states—and high voluntarism.

Using the degree of determinism as a criterion, three major approaches to the explanation of Soviet foreign policy may be discerned among Western students: (a) an essentialist, (b) a mechanistic, and (c) an organismic or cybernetic conception. Each approach reifies the Soviet Union in some manner. There are indications in the literature of the emergence of a fourth approach which would question the utility of treating the Soviet Union as an entity.[16]

Generally, the essentialist approach is almost entirely microanalytic in its explanatory orientation, describing Soviet foreign policy behavior as flowing logically from the nature of totalitarianism, just as its Soviet high-Stalinist counterpart explains American foreign policy as flowing logically from the nature of imperialism. In both cases it is not what the country in question *does* but what it *is* which is the source of conflict. Each is concerned to depict what William Welch has described

---

[15] William T. R. Fox, ed., *Theoretical Aspects of International Relations* (Notre Dame: University of Notre Dame Press, 1959), p. 46.

[16] In the Soviet case, see particularly Franklyn Griffiths, "Images, Politics, Arms Control: Aspects and Implications of Postwar Soviet Policy toward the United States" (New York: Columbia University dissertation, 1972). Such a conception is, of course, widespread in the burgeoning literature of comparative foreign policy and is especially prominent in the work of Graham Allison and Morton Halperin.

as "Truth with a capital 'T', Truth about essences."[17] One Russian source, for instance, charges that for Henry Kissinger

> The existence of states with a domestic structure different from the "legitimate", that is, the capitalist structure is in itself a potential reason for counterrevolutionary wars. For confirmation of his idea, Kissinger turns to 18th-century English philosopher Edmund Burke. . . . Burke [said of] . . . the French revolution of 1789: "I never thought we could make peace with the system because it was not for the sake of an object pursued in rivalry with each other but with the system itself that we were at war." The state of war, Burke stressed, was determined by the very fact that a *system foreign to us existed, regardless of its actions.*[18]

More appropriately, the characterization may be ascribed to those students of Soviet foreign policy whom Welch describes as "Ultra-Hard," and whose view of the nature of the Soviet beast Welch likens to the Great Beast of the Apocalypse. Welch has in mind, in particular, Elliot R. Goodman, Robert Strausz-Hupé, and Bertram Wolfe; Welch thus correctly summarizes Wolfe's posture as being that "only when Russia is democratic once more . . . will the outside world be safe and regain its hope of genuine, just, and enduring peace."[19]

The essentialist position is highly determinist. Given the particular attributes of the Soviet political system, which render it peculiarly insusceptible to change, there is virtually no way that American behavior can have an impact on Soviet foreign policy. Thus Wolfe's interpretation of Soviet foreign policy is described by Welch as "ultra-hard and change-resistant because it is the outer extension or shell . . . of a kind of system that is in essence Ultra-Hard and change-resistant."[20] A similarly essentialist stance is reflected in Arthur Schlesinger's summary statement on the origins of the Cold War:

> Stalin and his associates, whatever Roosevelt or Truman did or failed to do, were bound to regard the United States as the enemy, not because of this deed or that, but because of the primordial fact that America was the leading capitalist power and thus, by Leninist syllogism, unappeasably hostile, driven by the logic of its system to oppose, encircle, and destroy Soviet Russia. *Nothing the United States could have done in 1944–45 would have abol-*

17 *American Images of Soviet Foreign Policy* (New Haven: Yale University Press, 1970), p. 300.
18 A. Kunina, "American Dictate Behind the Mask of 'World Community,' " *International Affairs* (Moscow) (June 1971): 51–52.
19 Welch, *American Images,* p. 91.
20 Ibid.

ished this mistrust, required and sanctified as it was by Marxist gospel—nothing short of the conversion of the United States into a Stalinist despotism; and even this would not have sufficed, as the experience of Yugoslavia and China soon showed, unless it were accompanied by total subservience to Moscow. So long as the United States remained a capitalist democracy, no American policy, given Moscow's theology, could hope to win basic Soviet confidence, and every American action was poisoned from the source. So long as the Soviet Union remained a messianic state, ideology compelled a steady expansion of communist power.[21]

Kennan's "X" article qualifies as archetypically representative of the second, mechanistic approach. He speaks of Soviet expansionism in almost Newtonian fashion: The Kremlin's "political action is a fluid stream which moves constantly, wherever it is permitted to move, toward a given goal. Its main concern is to make sure that it has filled every nook and cranny available to it in the basin of world power. But if it finds unassailable barriers in its path, it accepts these philosophically and accommodates itself to them." The "X" article's Soviet Union is like Mao's imperialism: "Make trouble, fail, make trouble again, fail again . . . to their doom, that is the logic of the imperialists and all reactionaries the world over . . . and they will never go against this logic." The machine imagery permeates the article. Kennan describes "the whole Soviet governmental machine, including the mechanism of diplomacy," as moving "inexorably along the prescribed path, like a persistent toy automobile wound up and headed in a given direction, stopping only when it meets with some unanswerable force." He adverts to "individuals who are the components of this machine"; and compares them to "the white dog before the phonograph," who hears "only the 'master's voice.' "[22]

In treating "the iron discipline of the Communist party" Kennan, moreover, accepted Stalin's image of Stalin's Russia—a Soviet Union which was monolithic in outlook, highly cohesive, and accepting the principle of infallibility. With the important exception of succession crises to which Kennan gives great attention,[23] elite politics are absent in the image revealed in the "X" article. Kennan does detect a growing gap both between the regime and society and between the leadership

---

[21] "Origins of the Cold War," *Foreign Affairs* XLVI (October 1967) as reproduced in Hoffmann and Fleron, eds., *Conduct of Soviet Foreign Policy*, pp. 228–54 at p. 249.

[22] These citations from the "X" article can be found in Chapter 2 of this volume, pp. 16–17.

[23] Kennan was not alone in thinking that a succession crisis might produce chaos in the Soviet Union; witness the famous statement by Stalin's heirs on his death urging the populace "not to panic."

and the party masses but sees this as of little relevance in the short run to the conduct of Soviet foreign policy unless a succession crisis cannot be resolved. "The whole subordinate apparatus of Soviet power [has] an unshakable stubbornness and steadfastness in its orientation."[24] Persons within the apparatus do not hold views; they merely accept unquestioningly whatever the leadership declares to be the truth at a given juncture: "Truth is not a constant but is actually created, for all intents and purposes, by the Soviet leaders themselves."[25] Consequently, "the leadership is at liberty to put forward for tactical purposes any particular thesis which it finds useful to the cause at any particular moment and to require the faithful and unquestioning acceptance of that thesis by the members of the movement as a whole."[26] The "X" article makes no mention of non-Soviet Communist parties. Nevertheless, other essays written at the time reveal a strong sense that the world-Communist movement throughout the period 1945–53 was to be seen in the same manner: solely as an instrumentality of Soviet foreign policy. The famous "long telegram" (February 22, 1946) assumed that the dissolution of the Comintern in 1943 had been a charade. There exists, he declared, "an inner central core of Communist parties in other countries" constituting "a concealed Comintern tightly coordinated and directed by Moscow."[27]

The impermeability of the Soviet Union (to outside influence) was an equally important part of Kennan's mechanistic image. Kennan emphasizes the utter self-sufficiency of the Soviet Union. By his own cognizance he was extremely hard-lined on the issue of continuing lend lease. Even in his *Memoirs,* he aligns himself firmly with those advocating its early termination. Indeed, Kennan probably would have terminated it earlier—at the time of the Warsaw rising. He was disposed not to engage in major trade with the Soviet Union. Given his pessimism about Soviet intentions, as early as December 3, 1945, he was advocating what amounted to a blockade posture, fearing that "in furthering the military industrialization of the Soviet Union during the post-hostilities period, we will . . . again, as in the cases of Germany and Japan, be creating military strength which might some day be used to our disadvantage."[28] The notion of impermeability applied equally to Kennan's assessment in the "X" article of the receptivity of Soviet minds to suasion or, for that matter, to generous American acts. In Soviet doctrine, the image of the enemy must be unquestioned. "It must invariably be assumed in Moscow that the aims of the cap-

[24] Chapter 2 of this volume, p. 16.
[25] Ibid.
[26] Ibid.
[27] Kennan, *Memoirs,* p. 591.
[28] Ibid., p. 282.

italist world are antagonistic to the Soviet regime,"[29] Kennan writes. Likewise, he laments the fact that "the individuals who are components of this [Soviet government] machine are unamenable to argument or to reason which comes to them from outside sources."[30]

It was Soviet doctrine, moreover, which in the imagery of the "X" article fueled the Soviet machine. It set Soviet goals, molded Soviet expectations, and shaped Soviet perceptions. Soviet foreign and domestic goals were inextricably linked: with the passing of capitalist "remnants," "it became necessary to justify the retention of the dictatorship by stressing the menace of capitalism abroad."[31] Doctrine imbued Moscow with a sense of patience. "The theory of the inevitability of the eventual fall of capitalism has the fortunate connotation that there is no hurry about it;"[32] this expectation led Kennan to stress the nonadventuristic quality of Soviet foreign policy. Finally, doctrine in Kennan's view produced incredible misperception of the outside world, most notably of the hostility of the West. Repeatedly, in his papers written in 1945–47, in the "X" article itself, and in his *Memoirs* he attests to the inaccuracy of Soviet perceptions. In a famous passage in "The Sources of Soviet Conduct," Kennan observed, "It is an undeniable privilege of every man to prove himself right in the thesis that the world is his enemy; for if he reiterates it frequently enough and makes it the background of his conduct he is bound eventually to be right"[33] and in the "long telegram," he wonders "Who, if anyone, in this great land actually receives accurate and unbiased information about [the] outside world. . . . It is hard to believe that Stalin himself receives anything like an accurate picture of [the] outside world."[34]

The second, mechanistic, approach has been a major trend in the analysis of Soviet foreign policy, especially of the Stalin period. Like the essentialist position, it sees doctrine, as institutionalized in Soviet totalitarianism, as the mainspring of Soviet behavior. However, it is less concerned with essences than with behavior. As exemplified by Kennan[35] in the "X" article, there was (at least by implication) a greater reactive quality attached to Soviet foreign policy than in an essentialist

[29] Chapter 2 of this volume, p. 15.
[30] Ibid., p. 16.
[31] Ibid., p. 13.
[32] Ibid., p. 15.
[33] Ibid., p. 12.
[34] Kennan, *Memoirs*, p. 538.
[35] The major analytic element which distinguishes Kennan from the essentialist posture is that he recognizes both the possibility of "the break-up" and the "gradual mellowing of Soviet power"—thus recognizing that *communist* alternatives to his image of the Soviet Union might evolve which would not behave as depicted in the "X" article. Without such an assumption, Kennan, who argued that the "characteristics of Soviet policy . . . will be with us . . . until the internal nature of Soviet power is changed," would have to be classified an essentialist.

posture. The analysis was more optimistic in that, while stressing the duplicitous intent of tactical changes, it foresaw the possibility of fundamental changes in Soviet behavior within a historically short time frame (for Kennan, ten to fifteen years). For the essentialist, the Soviet Union is a self-maintaining system insulated from the forces of history; but in the mechanistic approach, the Soviet Union—like the toy automobile—can either blow up or run down. Hence, containment successfully applied will "promote tendencies which must eventually find their outlet in either the breakup or the gradual mellowing of Soviet power. For no mystical, Messianic movement—and particularly not that of the Kremlin—can face frustration indefinitely without eventually adjusting itself in one way or another to the logic of that state of affairs."[36]

A third approach to Soviet foreign policy has emerged in the last decade which has been applied primarily to the description of post-Stalinist Soviet foreign policy. It is appreciably more voluntaristic in its explanatory orientation than the mechanistic or essentialist approach. The variables which make for foreign-policy conduct are seen to be ones over which the external world, or Soviet decision makers themselves, have some control. Basically, the image is organismic or cybernetic.

In this imagery, Soviet foreign policy is seen to be highly reactive, not only (as was the mechanistic imagery) to the "logic of force," but also to specific moves by other states and to the general level of threat. Were the emphasis only on the reactive quality of Soviet foreign-policy behavior, it would be possible to describe this evolving consensus merely as a movement away from internally oriented explanations to external stimulus-response conceptions. Certainly with respect to the arms race, this emerging consensus emphasizes the extent to which Soviet decisions are prompted by other states, most notably the United States and China. It reflects a calculus, as I have argued elsewhere,[37] that one ought to accord as much weight to international-system level explanations of Soviet foreign policy as one would for other states, and a conclusion that a model of Soviet foreign policy is analytically incomplete, if in assessing the impact of the international system on Soviet conduct it focuses only on Moscow's likely tactical policy change in response to alterations in the global power configuration.

What largely differentiates this approach from its mechanistic counterparts is its premise that the Soviet Union not only reacts, it *learns*—learning being used to the straight-forward everyday sense,

36 Chapter 2 of this volume, p. 23.
37 "Elite Perspectives . . . ," pp. 95–96.

and as social learning in the cybernetic sense.[38] Not only do attitude changes take place in response to the behavior of other states, but internal organizational changes, a function largely of adapting in order to compete, also occur.

In addition, the mechanistic presumption of unity is also absent from the dominant strand in thinking about post-Stalinist Soviet foreign policy. I reveal no trade secrets in stating that what we used to call the world-Communist movement is no longer unified. There is scarcely a non-Communist country in the world which does not have two or more Communist parties. All are agreed that the days when "Soviet" and "Communist" could be used interchangeably are long since past. Students of Soviet internal politics have abandoned a monarchic-monolithic conception of the Soviet policy process. The image of the Soviet political process is now at minimum oligarchic and perhaps even polyarchic—though presumably those who would argue that in many respects the Soviet Union is polyarchic would recognize that (to quote Alexander Dallin) "of all sectors of public policy, foreign affairs are least susceptible to direct involvement by broader strata of the population."[39] The traditional sharp dichotomy is no longer made between a nonpolitical Soviet Union once a succession crisis is resolved and an extremely political Soviet Union when the right to rule is at stake. Students of the post-Stalin period recognize that the fact that the right to rule may not be at stake does not imply the absence of politics concerning such crucial questions as who gets what, where, and why (or by what rules of the game shall the political process be conducted).

In part, such conceptions of Soviet politics presume the persistence of conflict. Equally significant is an underlying assumption about the stated views and hidden thoughts of Soviet decision makers and the Soviet attentive public. There is much greater recognition of the persistence of attitude differences—a view of the psychology of Soviet public figures which contrasts strikingly with the automaton-like imagery in the mechanistic model. Whether the issue pertains to the nature of the threat or lack thereof by the United States, the nature of the political process in the U.S. or other capitalist countries, the possibility of social progress within capitalist societies, the nature of politics and social change in the third world, or a preference between control over and influence in socialist countries, divergent views are entertained and expressed. There have been, for instance, enduring strands

[38] See especially my chapter in Steven L. Spiegel and Kenneth N. Waltz, eds., *Conflict in World Politics* (Cambridge: Winthrop, 1971), pp. 49–51 and Griffiths, "Images, Politics, Arms Control," passim.

[39] "Soviet Foreign Policy and Domestic Politics: A Framework for Analysis," *Journal of International Affairs* XXIII, no. 2 (1969), as reproduced in Hoffmann and Fleron, *Conduct of Soviet Foreign Policy*, pp. 36–49 at p. 38.

of "leftist" thought within the Soviet Union that have emphasized the uniqueness of communism. Such strands have been goal oriented and optimistic and have stressed, as Alexander Dallin has noted, monolithism, the dialectic, violence, and the inevitability of conflict; they have preferred partisanship ("red") over expertise and have advocated narrow alliance strategies. Equally prevalent have been advocates of "rightist" orientations, who have emphasized the universality of communism. They have tended to be pessimistic about the ripeness of revolutionary advance at a given juncture and have been task-oriented; they have been "linear" in orientation (and thus seeing change for the better within non-communist systems as constituting historical progression), have stressed the avoidability of conflict and non-inevitability of war, and have recognized the role of expertise. And they have advocated coalition strategies which embrace large noncommunist elements.[40]

The emphasis on divergent perspectives rather than unified doctrine is but one aspect of a general rethinking of the role of ideology.[41] Contrary to expectations, the maintenance of *élan* domestically through the retention of doctrinal purity internationally has been sacrificed consistently to the rational and efficient pursuit of foreign policy goals. The doctrine of capitalist encirclement which has been the main prop of the Stalinist contention—the notion that as the Soviet Union advanced toward the building of communism there would not be a slackening but rather an intensification of class struggle—was questioned and ultimately repudiated during the late fifties. Except for the argument that internal consumer needs must be foregone because of the external military threat, the linkage of regime-society relations and the regime's relations with the outside world largely has been severed. The tendency to autarky has been much revised. Doctrine has not proved an impediment to the acquisition of data or of particular insights. It has remained the language of legitimacy and the language of politics, but only to a limited extent has it remained the language of analysis. Rather than a unified, impermeable, doctrinally inspired machine, the Soviet Union is seen as a reactive, penetrable, conflict-ridden organism, governed by elites whose perspectives cannot be predicted by assumptions about how Communists or even Soviet Communists think; indeed, their perspectives are formed out of diverging values, career backgrounds, and political roles.

In short, for the essentialist, no shift in American foreign policy has policy implications for the analysis of Soviet behavior. For the mechan-

---

[40] The above paragraph draws heavily on ibid., p. 45.
[41] See in particular my *Soviet Perspectives on International Relations, 1956–67* (Princeton: Princeton University Press, 1969), pp. 282–94.

ist, it rarely influences the Soviet propensity for expansionist tactics—at least in the short and intermediate run. In the cybernetic or organismic conception of Soviet foreign policy, the policy the United States undertakes is assumed to matter considerably. Moscow, in this approach, *qua* unitary purposive actor, reacts; Moscow, *qua* organism, learns; U.S. acts influence the context of policy debates in a conflict-ridden, oligarchic Kremlin and the propensity for effective interest articulation by various "tendencies" in a somewhat polyarchic Soviet Union.

III

Are we then talking about two Soviet Unions? The conventional wisdom has been to differentiate between radically Stalinist and post-Stalinist foreign policy. Given Stalin's impact on Soviet internal development, doctrine, foreign policy vis-à-vis the West, and on Soviet relations with other socialist states, this obviously is not a foolhardy notion. Nevertheless, what I hope to do in this last section is muster some evidence which indicates that it is now appropriate for us to think further on the nature of Stalinist Soviet foreign policy in the postwar years, and to suggest that the notions implied by the "X" article about Soviet and Communist reality, 1945–53, need to be brought more in line with the organismic or cybernetic imagery which we have applied to post-Stalinist foreign policy.[42] Marshall Shulman in *Stalin's Foreign Policy Reappraised*[43] led the way ten years ago by emphasizing the importance of Western moves as an explanation for Soviet moves. An even more profoundly reactive explanation is presented in the recent study of William Gamson and Andre Modigliani, *Untangling the Cold War*.[44] A cybernetic or organismic imagery of a state's foreign policy, however, not only (a) presupposes a reactive propensity on the part of those who act in the name of the state. It also presupposes that (b) external events have an impact on attitudes and produce structural adaptation and that (c) attitudinal divergence and political conflict are persistent attributes of the political process even within rigidly hierarchical command systems.

The "X" article, as we have seen, describes Soviet perspectives on the outside world as highly distorted, warped by the doctrinally de-

---

[42] In his essay (Chapter 8 of this volume) Professor Spanier asserts that "policy makers need some conceptual foundation on which to base policy" (p. 133), an argument which in effect implies that whether Kennan (who obviously knew something about the Soviet Union) was correct or not was irrelevant. One wonders how far Professor Spanier is seriously willing to carry that contention.

[43] (Cambridge: Harvard University Press, 1963).

[44] (Boston: Little, Brown and Company, 1971).

rived postulate of implacable capitalist hostility. It depicts a command system characterized by the unquestioned acceptance of the leadership's pronouncements (the "master's voice"). It conveys the impression of a singleness of purpose and view within official Moscow such as to imply the absence of high politics—until successful U.S. containment engenders fissiparous tendencies or until the onset of a succession crisis. Other writings by Kennan in the period extended the monolithic unitary purposive actor image to include the non-ruling Communist parties.

These notions, it should be stressed, were not at complete variance with the entire period from the end of the war to Stalin's death in 1953. Nevertheless, it is not possible to describe the entire period as a single piece nor to entertain some elements for the mechanistic conception for the entire period.

The "X" article and other essays by Kennan *are* notably at variance with Soviet and Communist experience, 1945–47, relevant to Soviet conduct in world affairs. Within the world-Communist movement, the conventional wisdom (as exemplified by Kennan's reference in the "long telegram" to a "concealed Comintern") would have it that Jacques Duclos' 1945 article was a "tocsin of the cold war"[45] and that the non-ruling Western Communist parties were simply instrumentalities of Soviet foreign policy. (In Joseph Starobin's words, Duclos' article, based on "data . . . available only in Moscow," had declared heretical the ideas of "peaceful co-existence and Europe's reconstruction on a bourgeois-democratic basis"). Starobin's study of the world-Communist movement at the end of World War II calls the conventional wisdom fundamentally into question. For Starobin, polycentrism was, as a result of World War II, an incipient reality, a reality cut short with the onset of the Cold War, the establishment of the Cominform in 1947, and the consolidation of the Soviet bloc, 1948–53. The years 1946 and early 1947 represent a different kind of communist movement than the monolith which we are accustomed to imagining for the Stalinist period. The attack on "Browderism" by Duclos proves to have been a strange event. Duclos was attacking Browder for advocating the reconstruction of Europe on a "bourgeois-democratic" basis. As Starobin remarks, "the curious thing is that most of the communist parties continued to operate on Browder's assumptions—including the party led by Duclos."[46] For Starobin, the Duclos article is

45 Joseph Starobin, "Origins of the Cold War," *Foreign Affairs* XLVII, no. 4 (July 1969) and reproduced in Hoffmann and Fleron, *Conduct of Soviet Foreign Policy*, pp. 275–88 at p. 284.
46 Ibid.

. . . one of the elements of communism's incoherence. By the close of 1946, only the Yugoslavs and William Z. Foster, who had ousted Browder in the United States, were convinced that even the 'temporary stabilization' of capitalism was unlikely. . . . It is not generally known that when Browder's successor [Foster] visited Europe in March 1947 he was amazed to find that few communist leaders agreed with his views.[47]

Further complications to our image of world communism in 1946 are provided by Starobin's depiction of Asian Communist developments.

During the recent Great Proletarian Cultural Revolution, Chinese historians blamed this coalition strategy [with Chiang Kai-shek] on the now-disgraced Liu Shao-chi, alleging that he was under the influence of "Browder, Togliatti, Thorez and other renegades to the proletariat." But the official Chinese Communist documents show that at the time Mao Tse-tung took credit for it and was himself viewed as a "revisionist"—by the Indian Communists, for example. In those same months, Ho Chi Minh led a coalition delegation to Paris, trying to work out the terms of membership in the French Union; it is a curious but revealing detail that Ho had the previous winter dissolved his own creation, the Communist party of Indochina, in favor of an Association of Marxist Studies without, however, receiving a rebuke from Jacques Duclos.[48]

With respect to Eastern Europe, a similar situation prevailed. Zbigniew Brzezinski, in his definitive The Soviet Bloc,[49] reminds us of Joseph Révai's statement in 1949 about Hungary's political evolution. Commenting on the immediate postwar period, Révai observes "the party didn't possess a united, clarified, elaborated attitude in respect to the character of the People's Democracy and its future development" and implies, as Brzezinski notes, that "Stalin was not very helpful before the autumn of 1947" in determining the character of the Hungarian People's Democracy. In Poland, Wladislaw Gomulka was explicitly referring to "the lengthy" struggle necessary prior to the establishment of socialism and warning against "gross over-simplifications" to the effect that Poland could pass through the transitional stage rapidly. Paul Zinner in his discussion of Communist Strategy and Tactics in Czechoslovakia, 1918–48[50] heads his treatment of the period,

47 Ibid.
48 Ibid., pp. 284–85.
49 (Cambridge: Harvard University Press, 1960), p. 30.
50 (New York: Praeger, 1963), p. 186.

1946 to early 1947, "revolution recedes" and observes that "the revolution, however, had definitely come to a stop." He reports further that the Czech party was repeatedly "subjected to severe criticism from Marshal Tito" who "urged a more rapid pace toward political monolithism and socialism." From 1945 through early 1947, "domesticism" and polycentrism characterized Soviet relations with Communist parties outside the Soviet Union.

Within the Soviet Union there was clear evidence of the continuation of the wartime "honeymoon" between the Soviet Union and its Western allies. As we know from the "Varga controversy," a reasonably accurate, relatively benign, rightist, and in some ways revisionist view of world politics, adumbrating in several major dimensions the views we have come to associate with the Khrushchev and post-Khrushchev era, dominated the postwar period.[51] Eugene Varga himself was a Hungarian who had spent many years as a major figure in the Comintern and who, in 1946, as head of the Institute of World Economy and World Politics, had been one of the leading Soviet economists and theoreticians. Precisely how closely Varga was connected with Stalin and other major Soviet figures (specifically Malenkov) is not within my ken. There seems little reason to doubt Robert Conquest's observation that "Varga had long been closely connected with Stalin."[52] The Varga controversy focused on a book written by Varga at the end of the war and published in late 1946,[53] as well as several articles written by him and published in 1946 and early 1947. Varga's rightist orientation permeates all these writings. His book concludes that "the capitalist countries' attitude toward the Soviet Union will not be what it was in pre-war times. The democratic forces in all countries will aspire to a policy of coöperation with the Soviet Union, toward joint struggle with the Soviet Union against the revival of fascism and aggression in any form." He adds that: "Although reactionary forces will seek to carry out a policy of inflaming contradictions between the two systems, the governments, reckoning with the forces of democracy and with the might of the Soviet Union as demonstrated in the Second World War, will not likely decide to take to armed conflict."[54] Incremental change for the better within non-communist countries was seen to represent distinct improvement; it constituted an historic advance.

[51] My failure to recognize the degree of continuity between this phenomenon in the post-Twentieth C.P.S.U. Congress period and the Varga orientation of 1945–47 is a weakness of *Soviet Perspectives*. . . .

[52] *Power and Policy in the U.S.S.R.* (New York: St. Martin's Press, 1961), p. 88.

[53] *Izmeneniia v ekonomike kapitalizma v itoge vtoroi mirovoi voiny* [Changes in the capitalist economy as a result of the Second World War] (Moscow: Gosizdat, 1946).

[54] Ibid., p. 319.

Moreover, Varga was rather pessimistic about the immediate prospects for revolutionary advance. He treated "people's democracy" as part of the capitalist world and contemplated the possible reconstruction of the United States economy. He regarded as fundamental the change of the relationship between metropole and colony, specifically between Great Britain and India, produced by the war. Similarly in May, 1947, in defending himself against the criticism of several economists in a public meeting called to assess his conclusions, he continued to expound articulately his rightist orientation. Substantively, he corrected himself somewhat with respect to the people's democracies but continued to stress that, "It is wrong to consider all [the people's democracies] as perfectly identical; for the situation in Yugoslavia and Bulgaria is one thing and the situation in Hungary and Rumania another."[55] He stood by his conclusion that the state would play "a greater role by comparison with prewar times" and attacked the "orthodox" posture that "empires have remained empires, the colonies have remained colonies, everything has remained as it was before the war."[56] Methodologically, he aligned himself with the experts' orientation to Marxism-Leninism: "It is not a matter of simply enumerating all the facts so that they lead inevitably to the former conclusions of Marxism-Leninism, but to use the Marxist-Leninist method in studying these facts. The world changes and the content of our work must change also."[57]

It is open to question whether there is a greater disparity between the "X" article's depiction of warped, hostile Soviet assessments of the outside world and the views of Varga (and other members of his institute) or between the image of absolute compliance and the resistance of Varga and his cohorts to the pressure of leftist critics. Re-reading the first major public discussion of Varga's book is not to read a scenario of the kind one associates with the controlled exercise of kritika i samokritika. Varga's defense of his writing has already been adverted to; the resistance of his colleagues to the charge that he and they were in effect "soft on capitalism" was also impressive. I. A. Trachtenberg declared that Varga's study is "a great theoretical work." M. I. Rubinshtein had no hesitation in defending Varga's book against "the speeches for the prosecution." S. G. Strumilin interrupts K. V. Ostrovityanov (who had

[55] Leo Gruliow, trans., Soviet Views on the Post-War World Economy (Washington: Public Affairs Press, 1948), p. 117.

[56] Ibid., p. 7.

[57] Ibid., p. 5. This statement should be compared with Anastas Mikoyan's statement at the Twentieth C.P.S.U. Congress, that it was "not enough" for specialists merely to affirm that "the course of history indicates that in the present stage of imperialism . . . all Marxism-Leninism's basic tenets are invariably confirmed." Rather, according to Mikoyan, they should study "when, where, to what degree, and how this takes place."

charged that politics was invisible in Varga's book) and declares it "invisible to the blind."[58] Even in subsequent years against the ominous backdrop of the *Zhdanovshchina*—the campaign spurred on by Andrei Zhdanov against Soviet citizens from virtually all groups (including people in philosophy, physics, social science) suspected of harboring the views of their Western counterparts—and later the doctors' plot, there were examples of clever dissimulation, courageous silence, and courageous outspokeness by persons in the Varga institute (as well as elsewhere) who were being charged, correctly in a sense, with "bourgeois objectivism."[59] Effectively shouted down, Varga would not be muffled completely: We find him in 1951 at the meeting called to discuss the textbook on political economy raising the issue "whether or not the theories of V. I. Lenin on *the inevitability of wars between imperialist states* remains correct under contemporary conditions of the existence of two worlds, socialist and capitalist, in conditions of cold war and the threat of nuclear war."[60]

The point of all this, of course, is not to suggest that there was no *Zhdanovshchina*, nor to imply that Varga was in error when later on he described 1951 as a time when "dogmatism reigned and for someone other than I. V. Stalin to express something or other new was not considered allowable."[61] Rather, it is to emphasize the persistence of real attitudes throughout the period 1945–53 which were at variance with the official line and to remind us that the *Zhdanovshchina* did not begin in 1945 and was not really in full swing until 1947.

This observation in turn leads to the issue of high politics in the period 1945–53. As M. A. Arzhanov noted during the May, 1947, discussion of Varga's book, "I do not know—I say this in all sincerity—perhaps there are considerations of another order [other than the timing of the writing]. Perhaps in this book, Comrade Varga, *who is not only* (and quite deservedly) *a major authority* among us on these questions, *but also more than an economist*—perhaps here other circumstances were taken into account."[62] The challenge to Varga's policy and institutional position seems to have been a facet of the gradual assertion of primacy by Zhdanov over Malenkov. It is not inconceivable that Malenkov shared much of Varga's rightist orientation, and the attack on Varga

[58] Ibid., pp. 28, 44, 111.

[59] A particularly heroic story is that of V. I. Kaplan, who was criticized in *Bolshevik* in 1948 for bourgeois objectivism in his treatment of the United States between the wars. To my knowledge, he never recanted nor did he publish anything until 1964, when he published *The U.S. in the War and Post-War Years* which has 1585 footnotes including one reference to Lenin, one to Marx alone, and one to Marx and Engels.

[60] Eugen Varga, *Ocherki po problemam politekonomii kapitalizma* (Moscow: Politizdat, 1964), p. 78, italics in original.

[61] Ibid.

[62] Gruliow, trans., *Soviet Views*, p. 62, italics added.

is probably best seen in this light. As it became clear that the wartime alliance would not endure, the rightist policies—those doctrinal formulations which were chiefly Varga's responsibility—were abandoned, and the left-oriented members of the Communist world (primarily Zhdanov and Tito) came rapidly to the fore. Rather than a unitary Moscow engaging in a tactical shift, it appears more likely that the position of those who advocated going slowly because they were pessimistic about going too rapidly and also because they were content with social reforms in Europe within the capitalist context, was, in effect, discredited, and those who advocated rapid revolutionary transformation and a sharp distinction between friend and foe, such as Zhdanov and Tito, came to constitute the dominant force.

Zhdanov's pre-eminence, ironically, was very brief. In 1948 Stalin broke with Tito; by June, 1948, Malenkov had redeemed much of his previous influence. When Zhdanov died on August 31, Malenkov had already been signing messages in the name of the Central Committee for a month.[63] For the next two or three years, Malenkov stood out as Stalin's heir apparent. It has long been assumed that even while Stalin lived, Malenkov had differed with him on the degree of intensity of the outside threat. Several scholars, most notably Robert C. Tucker, have pointed to the discrepancy between Malenkov's 1949 statement that "never before in all its history has our country been surrounded with neighboring countries so friendly to our state"[64] and Zhdanov's 1947 statement at the founding of the Cominform, as well as with the insistence of various ideologues (presumably close to Stalin) in 1952–53 that the doctrine of capitalist encirclement remained in force. Specialists similarly have pointed to Malenkov's remarks in 1954 (a year after Stalin's death) that a new world war would be calamitous to civilization and wondered whether Malenkov was among those "some comrades" Stalin was criticizing for denying the continued validity of the doctrine of inter-imperialist wars. What we have failed to emphasize is the difference between Stalin's view (as expressed in *Economic Problems of Socialism in the USSR*—the major doctrinal document for the Nineteenth Party Congress) that wars between capitalist states remain inevitable and Malenkov's pointed observation (at the same Congress) that the inter-imperialist contradictions which "are now rending the imperialist camp, *may* lead to a war of one capitalist state against another."[65] The implication, it would appear, can only be that Malenkov,

[63] Conquest, *Power and Policy*, p. 93.
[64] Tucker, *Soviet Political Mind*, pp. 27–28.
[65] Leo Gruliow, ed., *Current Soviet Policies I* (New York: Praeger, 1953), p. 105, italics added. Shulman, careful scholar that he is, notes the difference between Stalin's and Malenkov's statements without however emphasizing the implications of the divergent stances. Shulman, *Stalin's Foreign Policy Reappraised*, p. 245.

Stalin's heir apparent, was publicly dissociating himself from Stalin. If this is so, it probably also means that Malenkov was one of those Stalin had in mind to purge; it also implies that, as in the case of the succession crisis at the time of Lenin's death, the succession crisis began while Stalin lived.[66]

It may be objected by those who accept the calculus about the sources of Soviet conduct which permeates the "X" article that an episode such as this and even Zhdanov's political reduction in 1948 (prior to his death) merely lends further credence to the argument that containment had engendered fissiparous tendencies within the Soviet ruling group. While persuasive in some respects, it seems to obscure a more general observation, namely, that political controversy over doctrinal matters having a direct bearing on foreign policy was an enduring theme throughout the early postwar period. If this is so, the argument that containment engendered conflict fails for the simple reason that the conflict preceded containment and very likely was muted in the onset of the Cold War.

What I have been suggesting in this section is not that the mechanistic image of Soviet foreign policy was completely invalid for the last years of Stalin's rule but that its determinist impetus needs to be called into question. What seemed at the onset of the Cold War to be a phenomenon structurally determined by the nature of the Soviet system was rather a product of the policies and beliefs of individuals, individuals whose postures were reinforced by the cumulative impact of the Cold War's beginnings.

IV

It would follow, therefore, that what the United States did after World War II made a difference and that the image of the Soviet Union advanced in the "X" article to explain the sources of Soviet conduct was itself in part a product of the Cold War. It is at least possible that a somewhat different relationship could have emerged after World War II. We know now—or at least have Khrushchev's testimony to this effect[67]— that the Soviet Union demobilized almost as rapidly as did the United States and that the myth of 260 or 175 divisions was exactly that: a myth. (It was a myth, we must add, in part perpetrated for political purposes by Stalin in much the same way Khrushchev was later to perpetrate the

---

[66] It has frequently been stated on the basis of skimpy evidence (N=2) that the Soviet leader, like the Tsar, dies in office. On the basis of half again as much evidence (N=3) we may now confidently declare that succession crises always begin while the dictator is alive.

[67] *Pravda*, January 15, 1960. Khrushchev's figures for the demobilization and re-remobilization of the Soviet armed forces are: May 1945, 11,365,000; 1948, 2,874,000; 1955, 5,763,000.

myth of the missile gap. In both instances the result was an enormous American military build-up.) Containment and what seems, in Kennan's analysis, to have been its logical corollary, the constriction of trade with the Soviet Union, reinforced the already considerable propensity within the Soviet Union for going it alone, for economic autarky, for the siege mentality which characterized the Soviet Union during the Zhdanovshchina and the days of the putative doctors' plot. It reinforced Stalin's disposition to imagine an implacable and encircling West and furthered his sense that there would be a direct confrontation between the United States and the Soviet Union. It complicated the position of the rightists in the ruling group and among the Soviet counterpart of the "attentive public." At least it is conceivable that had U.S. actions reinforced the most favorable Soviet image of American foreign policy, that which we associate with Varga and his institute and with Khrushchev and the successors to Varga's Institute,[68] events might have taken a somewhat different course.

To act in such a manner the United States would have had (a) to reinforce the pessimistic assessment of the immediacy of revolutionary advance in Europe, while at the same time (b) to encourage the assumption that social and political progress within capitalism was possible and the rightist disposition to increase Soviet foreign trade and to be receptive to foreign investment in the Soviet Union. At best, such a strategy might have resulted in the limited adversary relationship between the United States and the Soviet Union of the 1960s and 1970s rather than the total adversary relationship of the Cold War.[69] It is even possible that the polycentrism within the Communist movement, the pronounced rightist orientation, and the oligarchic high politics so much in evidence in the 1960s and 1970s—the same phenomena sometimes said to have resulted from successful containment but which in fact saw clear adumbration before the height of the Cold War—might have

---

[68] These are primarily the Institute of World Economy and International Relations and the United States of America Institute. For evidence of the significance of the distinction between Varga's views and those more in the Stalinist mold for current foreign policy debates in the Soviet Union, see a vigorous defense of Varga and an attack, equally vigorous, on his dogmatic critics in "Tvorcheskoe nasledie E. S. Vargi," Mirovaia Ekonomika i mezhdunarodnye otnosheniia, No. 1 (January 1970), pp. 123–31; "Zhizennyi i tvorcheskii put' revolutionera-uchenogo," Mirovaia Ekonomika i Mezhdunarodnye Otnosheniia, no. 11 (November 1969), pp. 14–20; and Griffiths, "Images, Politics, Arms Control."

[69] Professor Spanier in his essay (Chapter 8 of this volume) criticizes me for ignoring systemic explanations. It is precisely because of the high probability of some kind of Soviet-U.S. conflict stemming from the nature of the postwar international system which prompted me to assert that the scope and intensity of the adversary relationship might have been more limited had the U.S. pursued different policies, not that there would not have been an adversary relationship. In no way do I focus, Spanier notwithstanding, "entirely upon American behavior." What I do assert (and what has been long denied) is that what the United States did after World War II did make a difference.

persisted beyond 1946–47, rather than be constricted by the xenophobic anti-intellectual climate of the *Zhdanovshchina*.

To be sure, even this scenario may be excessively optimistic. However, it at least suggests that American decision makers might have been better prepared to respond to changes in Soviet conduct following Stalin's death (which warranted encouragement) if their image of Soviet and Communist behavior had been one which assumed the existence of significantly divergent opinions among Communists in Moscow and elsewhere and one which assumed that external behavior affected the internal political dialogue within the Soviet Union and the world-Communist movement. A less-determinist and mechanistic image might, therefore, have prepared the U.S. to respond to Malenkov's doctrinal pronouncements in 1954 or to Khrushchev's moves in 1955. Instead, because American policy makers had so internalized the notion that Soviet behavioral changes were only tactical, it was not until after the 1962 Cuban missile crisis that there was general recognition of the limited adversary nature of Soviet-American relations and of the cybernetic and reactive dimensions[70] of the sources of Soviet conduct.

[70] For a view stressing the nonreactive, internal-system determined nature of Soviet foreign policy, see Uri Ra'anan, "The Changing American-Soviet Balance: Some Political Implications," prepared for the Subcommittee on National Security and International Operations of the Committee on Government and Operations, United States, 92nd Congress, 2nd Session.

7

CHOICES IN THE POSTWAR WORLD (2):
Containment and China

I

My purpose in this article is to make the case that if, in 1949, the United States had recognized the new Chinese Communist regime, exploited Mao's long-standing suspicions of Stalin, catered to China's national interest and expressions of desire for American support, the Sino-Soviet split would have erupted much earlier. Moreover, in such circumstances, the Chinese might not have intervened in the Korean War, Washington might not have felt compelled to fight in Vietnam against what it thought to be Chinese expansionism via its Hanoi proxy, and the entire course of the postwar world might have been different. Instead, shortsighted American policy in 1949, dictated by a combination of internal American politics and gross American ignorance about the relationships within the Communist world, forced Peking into Moscow's embrace.

The burden of my case rests on two contentions that I will try to demonstrate with documentary evidence. The first contention is that the relations between Mao and Stalin in the thirties and forties, indeed right up to Stalin's death in 1953, were relations of deep mutual mistrust and suspicion. Stalin believed that Mao was a potential Tito and consistently regarded him, as he regarded all "National Communists"

—Communists with independent bases of power—with enormous suspicion. He repeatedly—but unsuccessfully—sought to make a satellite of the Chinese Communist Party (CCP), to intervene in its internal affairs and to give it advice based on the needs and interests of the Soviet Union as Stalin perceived them. Mao emancipated himself and the CCP from Comintern control in the mid-1930s only after a long struggle, deliberately avoided several traps laid by Stalin to bring the CCP into greater dependence on Moscow, resented Stalin's lack of support to the CCP struggle against the Kuomintang in the Chinese Civil War, and concluded a one-sided alliance with Russia only after his bids for American support were rejected.

My second contention is that because of his suspicion of Stalin, Mao bid for American support as a counterweight to exclusive dependence on the Soviet Union right up to the middle of 1949, the year the Communists took power on the mainland. Barbara Tuchman has recorded the unsuccessful Chinese bids for American friendship in 1945 and 1946.[1] These bids came on the eve of U.S. intervention in the Chinese Civil War. A recent report by the Senate Committee on Foreign Relations, based on hitherto classified government documents, has now detailed Mao's bid for American recognition as late as the summer of 1949, after U.S. disengagement from the Chinese Civil War in 1948.[2] As soon as the Communists conquered the former Nationalist capital of Nanking in April, 1949, they initiated conversations with the American Ambassador Leighton Stuart, who remained behind. These conversations took place throughout May and June. On June 28, 1949, Mao personally invited Stuart to Peking in order to continue the discussions at the highest level, an initiative that the State Department recognized at the time to be of enormous significance. But President Truman vetoed Stuart's trip; four days earlier, he had received a letter from twenty-one senators warning against recognition of Communist China. It was this rebuff by the Americans, the second in four years, that resolved an ongoing debate within the Chinese Communist Party between an "internationalist" faction led by Liu Shao-ch'i that sought an exclusive alliance with the Soviet Union, and a Mao-Chou faction that sought to balance an alliance with Stalin against a new relationship with America.

When I first read an earlier draft of this paper at The American Political Science Association's Convention in September, 1972, I had to

[1] Barbara Tuchman, "If Mao Had Come to Washington: An Essay in Alternatives," *Foreign Affairs* (October, 1972): 44–64.

[2] Senate Committee on Foreign Relations Report, *The United States and Communist China in 1949 and 1950: The Question of Rapprochement and Recognition* (U.S. Government Printing Office, Washington, D.C., 1973).

make this case on the basis of then-fragmentary evidence.[3] Fortunately, in January, 1973, shortly after I presented my paper, the Senate Committee on Foreign Relations published a new study of Chinese-American relations in 1949, a study based upon classified proofs of the State Department's Foreign Relations series of 1949, classified transcripts of Foreign Relations committee hearings soon to be published, and interviews with former State Department officials.[4]

In what follows, I will first review the evidence of mutual mistrust between Mao and Stalin in the thirties and forties; then I will review the circumstances surrounding Mao's two requests for American support, first in 1944–46, then again in 1949. Finally, I will offer some concluding observations about the disturbingly high level of ignorance within the American government—both in 1949 and since—about the relationships within international communism.

If history is to be something other than a chronicle of events as they happened, the thoughtful historian must consider the likely consequences of paths that were not taken. Of course, there is no way of knowing with certainty the consequences of policies never adopted, but the imaginative reconstruction of such consequences is not only possible but necessary. Otherwise, history is reduced to a simplistic determinism in which whatever happened had to happen. History, after all, is made by men who make choices between alternative courses of action. Although these alternatives are often limited, the choice of one over another course of action is something for which politicians—and nations—should be held accountable, particularly when those choices have led to such disastrous results as were produced by American policy in Asia during the past two decades. This being the case, the charge of "revisionism" that John Spanier makes against me in this volume (Chapter 8) can only be welcomed. It is incumbent on the historian to be a "revisionist" in the sense that it is necessary to inquire whether different courses of action might have led to more positive results. In any case, the facts that follow should be sufficient to demonstrate that Spanier, like much of the U.S. government, misunderstood the relation-

---

[3] "Containment, China, and America," paper presented to the American Political Science Association Convention, Washington, D.C., September 5, 1972. At the time I wrote my APSA paper in September, 1972, the principal clue I had concerning the Chinese initiative in 1949 was contained in Seymour Topping, *Journey Between Two Chinas* (New York: Harper & Row, 1972). In that book, Topping described briefly a meeting between Huang Hua and Stuart. Tang Tsou also had a brief reference to it in *America's Failure in China* (Chicago: University of Chicago Press, 1963). I subsequently learned that Allen Whiting also referred to these developments in his testimony to the Senate Foreign Relations Committee in 1971. Evidently it was Whiting's testimony that provoked the Senate Foreign Relations Committee into releasing some of the relevant classified documents from 1949.

[4] Senate Committee Report, *The U.S. and Communist China in 1949 and 1950.*

ships within the international communist movement that obtained in
1949. To argue, as Spanier does, that "Mao's professed ideological commitments," his allegedly "unswerving loyalty to Moscow in the thirties
and forties," and his need for a foreign enemy all dictated a Cold War
with the United States, is simply to ignore those facts.

II

The crucial insight concerning Stalin's attitude towards foreign Communist leaders is not that Stalin was indifferent to the fate of communism outside the Soviet Union, but that he was prepared to sacrifice
foreign Communists to the interests of the USSR and his own power.
Indeed, he was prepared to allow the destruction of foreign Communists, if it was necessary, as it seemed to be in Greece in 1944–45, to
serve his "higher" interests. Moreover, Stalin had a paranoiac distrust
of any foreign Communist leader who pursued, or seemed to pursue,
independent policies that were not subordinated to Stalin's policies.
Stalin ruthlessly and systematically purged the Comintern in the late
twenties and early thirties of any leaders with a shred of independence.
He systematically infiltrated foreign Communist parties and secret police networks with men who were loyal to him personally. It was his
crude attempt to infiltrate the Yugoslav party, police, and army that
precipitated the break with Tito in 1948. If such attempts to infiltrate the
Chinese Communist Party failed, once Mao emancipated himself from
the Comintern in 1935, it was not for Stalin's lack of effort.

The relationship between Mao and Stalin in the two decades prior to
the establishment of the Sino-Soviet alliance in February, 1950, was one
of deep-seated mutual fears and suspicions. Stalin, for his part, long
suspected, not without reason, that Mao, who came to power after a
long struggle with the Comintern, was a potential "Tito." Mao, for his
part, must have deeply resented Stalin's persistent efforts to intervene
in the internal affairs of the CCP, to subjugate it to his own will and to
the needs of Stalin's policy, and to eradicate any traces of independence.

That Stalin regarded Mao as a "Tito" right up to the Chinese intervention in the Korean War is evident from the testimony of Mao himself. In a speech Mao made in September, 1962, to the 10th Plenum of
the Central Committee, he said that the "roots" of the conflict with the
Russians "rose a long time ago," because in 1945 "Stalin blocked the
Chinese revolution, saying that we must not fight a civil war but must
collaborate with Chiang Kai-shek." After the victory of the revolution,
which Mao carried out against Stalin's advice, continued Mao, Stalin
"again suspected that China would be like Yugoslavia and I would turn
into a 'Tito.' " Stalin, continued Mao, only "began to have confidence

in us" in the winter of 1950, after China intervened in the Korean War.[5]

The roots of mutual mistrust between Mao and Stalin far antedate 1945, however. From the time it was founded in 1921, until the mid-1930s, the Chinese Communist Party was a creature of the Comintern. It obeyed the dictates and served the interests of the Comintern, as these interests were perceived in Moscow. In the period between 1924 and 1927, those Comintern interests dictated a CCP alliance with the Kuomintang that led in 1927 to the virtual decimation of the CCP at the hands of Chiang Kai-shek. From mid-1928, until late 1930, the remnants of the CCP were placed by the Comintern in the hands of Li Li-san. Li took charge of the CCP immediately following the Sixth Congress of the Party which was held in Moscow in mid-1928. Li's urban-based revolutionary strategy proved by the end of 1930 to be a disaster and Li was recalled to Moscow where he spent the next fifteen years of his life.[6]

The failure of Li's urban-based revolutionary strategy led to Li's recall but not to the end of Comintern control over the CCP. In 1931, the Comintern designated the so-called "28 Bolsheviks," Chinese Communists trained in Moscow, to take over the party. From 1931 to late 1934, the beginning of the Long March, Mao had to fight a continuing, and losing, battle against the "28 Bolsheviks." As John Rue has written of this period of Mao's opposition, on the eve of the Long March:

> By the time the Red Armies set out on the Long March, Mao had every reason to feel a deep repugnance for Stalinist methods of controlling non-Soviet parties. In 1931, when Mao was at the height of his power . . . the 28 Bolsheviks had begun their struggle against his ideas on political and military strategy. By 1934, with the support of the Comintern, they had removed him and his most active supporters from all influential positions in the party, army, and government. They had rejected and condemned his agrarian and military policies and replaced them with policies modeled after the practice of the Soviet government and the CPSU. In implementing their "further bolshevization of the CCP" they had adopted the terroristic policies of the Soviet political police and anticipated in the small Soviet districts of South China the great purges in the Soviet Union.[7]

[5] For the translation of this important speech by Mao, see *Chinese Law and Government*, vol. 1, no. 4 (Winter, 1968–69):88–89. I am indebted to an unpublished paper by Stuart Schram for calling this speech to my attention. Schram's suggestive paper is titled "Some Reflections on Mao Tse-tung's Attitude Toward the Soviets, 1957–62."

[6] Li Li-san suddenly reappeared, along with Stalin's Red Army, in Manchuria in 1945, and evidently was designated by Stalin to take over the reins of the CCP.

[7] John Rue, *Mao Tse-tung in Opposition* (Stanford, Calif.: Stanford University Press, 1965), p. 265.

Stalin's efforts to "bolshevize" the CCP in the early 1930s were consistent with his efforts to make puppets of all foreign Communist parties represented in the Comintern. By the early 1930s, Stalin systematically purged all foreign Communist leaders with any trace of independent thought and ruthlessly transformed the Comintern from a potential revolutionary instrument into an instrument of his foreign policy.[8]

In these circumstances, it is scarcely surprising that once he reasserted control over the CCP in the midst of the Long March, at the Tsunyi Conference in January, 1935, Mao rejected Stalin's advice to settle his guerrilla army in Sinkiang, a frontier province bordering on Soviet Central Asia. In such a location, Mao's army would have been easy for Stalin to control from the Soviet Union. Instead, Mao chose a more exposed site in Yenan, a site that was better suited for the struggle with Japan but also was unsuited for easy communication with the Soviet Union. As Malcolm Mackintosh has written:

> The whole episode illustrated Stalin's preference for a communist base bordering on Soviet territory, and Mao's skill in avoiding what he probably regarded as a dangerous trap.[9]

The relations between the CCP and Moscow during the Yenan period are still obscure. Radio contact was established between Moscow and the Chinese Communists as early as 1936. But subsequent contact was maintained by Stalin through so-called Tass correspondents assigned to Yenan who were in fact agents of the Soviet secret police. According to one recent Soviet source, Mao surrounded these Stalinist agents with security personnel of his own, kept them isolated, and regarded them with extreme suspicion.[10]

Once the Japanese invaded China in 1937, Mao and Stalin, for reasons of their own, worked towards the establishment of a united front with Chiang Kai-shek's Nationalist army. Mao supported the Nationalist struggle against the Japanese in the double hope of preventing the Japanese conquest of China and increasing Communist strength in North China by appealing to broad Nationalist sentiments. Stalin, for his part, sought to check the threat of an expanding Japanese militarism. Con-

---

[8] Franz Brokenau, *World Communism* (Ann Arbor: University of Michigan Press, 1962).

[9] Malcom Mackintosh, "Sino-Soviet Relations in a U.S.-China Crisis," unpublished paper. For additional evidence that Stalin wanted the Long March to settle in Sinkiang, see Warren Kuo, *Analytical History of the Chinese Communist Party* (Taipei: Institute of International Relations, 1970), Book III, p. 200.

[10] O. Vladimirov and V. Riazantsev, *Stranitsii politichesko: biografii Mao Tsetunga* (Moscow), p. 53; cited by Steven I. Levine, "Soviet American Rivalry in Manchuria and the Cold War: A Framework of Analysis," paper prepared for the Columbia University Seminar on Modern East Asia, May 9, 1973. I am indebted to Mr. Levine for calling this source to my attention and for other insights into Sino-Soviet relations in this period.

trary to the notion (advanced by Spanier in Chapter 8 of this volume) that the CCP was at this time an unwilling tool of the Kremlin, Robert North has pointed out that "both the Chinese and Russian leaders had been considering the problem of opposing Japanese expansion more effectively and, independently, had reached several of the same conclusions concerning a broad united front."[11] Charles McLane, another student of the period, even suggests that the Chinese Communists adopted the notion of a united front with Chiang before the Russians.[12] In any case, he goes on, "We can, I think, assume only a parallel and not a closely coordinated working out of the united front policy in Moscow and in China."[13]

After Germany plunged the Soviet Union into a European war in 1941, Stalin left Mao to his own devices. When in August, 1945, Moscow returned to the Far East by joining the war against Japan and occupying Manchuria and part of Korea, there could have been little joy in Yenan. First of all, in August, 1945, Moscow signed a treaty with Chiang Kaishek which the CCP leadership can only have regarded as a betrayal. The Chinese Communist leadership tried to put the best possible face on the Soviet action but confessed to its own cadres that "Soviet policy cannot be understood."[14] The sense of betrayal must have been intensified when, as Mao indicated in the quotation cited earlier, Stalin advised him sometime in 1945 to stop fighting the Nationalists and to collaborate with them instead.

At the same time, Stalin evidently resumed his long-standing efforts to bring the CCP under his control. When Soviet troops appeared in Manchuria in late 1945 and early 1946, they brought with them Li Li-san, the CCP leader who had been disgraced in 1930 but who had spent the intervening fifteen years in Moscow. Li Li-san and Mao had been bitter enemies in the late twenties and it seems quite likely that Stalin had been grooming Li to take over the reins of the CCP at the end of the war.[15]

While it might be argued that prior to the outbreak of the Civil War, Stalin was merely skeptical of the CCP ability to win such a war, and was therefore advising caution on Mao out of good will, Stalin's policy during the entire course of the Civil War leads to a different conclusion

[11] Robert North, *Moscow and the Chinese Communists* (Stanford, Calif.: Stanford University Press, 1963), p. 177.

[12] Charles McLane, *Soviet Policy and the Chinese Communists* (New York: Columbia University Press, 1958), p. 78.

[13] Ibid.

[14] Warren I. Cohen, *America's Response to China* (New York: Wiley, 1971), p. 182, citing a mimeographed transcript of a CCP lecture to cadres on August 30, 1945.

[15] This is the argument of J. M. Mackintosh in *Strategy and Tactics of Soviet Foreign Policy* (New York: Oxford, 1962) p. 39; see also F. C. Jones, *Manchuria Since 1931* (London: Oxford, 1949) p. 235; also *New York Times*, Oct. 11, 1946, p. 10.

—namely, that he had little desire to see an independent Mao take power, or to see China run by a strong central government. As Garthoff has suggested, Stalin probably preferred a weak China run by the Nationalists in which the Russians could exercise leverage both through the Chinese Communists and through dissident warlords—what Levine aptly calls a "weak neighbor" policy.[16] This conclusion is suggested by a variety of Soviet actions during the Civil War. As late as 1948, the Russians offered to mediate a settlement. As late as January, 1949, Stalin was busy negotiating an abortive treaty with the Nationalist government, then headed by Acting President Li Tsung-jen. In April, 1949, when the Nationalist capital of Nanking fell to the Communists, the Soviet ambassador was the only foreign diplomat to follow the Nationalists in their retreat southward.

Stalin's policies in the borderlands between Russia and China during the Civil War point to the same conclusion. These policies were designed not to ease Mao's path to power but rather to increase Soviet influence and to exploit natural resources. In Sinkiang, for example, as late as 1949, "the Soviet ambassador in China was negotiating with the National Government over important economic and transportation concessions. . . . During the very months when the Chinese Communist armies were driving rapidly into the Northwest, Moscow appeared intent upon obtaining a special position there."[17]

A similar pattern was evident in Manchuria during the Civil War. Shortly after the Soviet Union occupied Manchuria in 1945, it began to strip Manchuria of its industrial and military assets. As Garthoff has pointed out: "The Soviet looting of Manchurian 'reparations' is inconsistent with the contention that the Russians handed Manchuria over to the Chinese Communists so that they could have a base to defeat the Nationalists. If that were the case, why destroy the major part of the great Mukden arsenals which could have given the Chinese Communists the wherewithal to fight?"[18]

Stalin's patently imperialistic designs on the borderlands had already been revealed at the Yalta Conference in 1945 and in the treaty Stalin negotiated with Chiang Kai-shek in the same year. At Yalta, and in the negotiations with the Nationalists, Stalin put in a claim to a sphere of influence in all the important borderlands: Manchuria, Mongolia, and Sinkiang. Indeed, the claims against the borderlands made by Stalin in 1945 were quite similar both to the Tsarist claims against a tottering

[16] Levine, "Soviet American Rivalry."

[17] Howard Boorman, "The Borderlands and the Sino-Soviet Alliance," in *Moscow-Peking Axis* (New York: Harper & Row, 1957) p. 178.

[18] Raymond Garthoff, *Sino-Soviet Military Relations* (New York: Praeger, 1966), p. 83.

Manchu Dynasty in 1902 and to the subsequent claims that Stalin would make on Mao in 1950.

Throughout the four years of Civil war between Mao and Chiang Kai-shek, Soviet military assistance to the Chinese Communists was minimal. After a careful review of the evidence, Garthoff concludes that "it is evident that the Russians permitted the Chinese Communists to seize only small amounts of tanks and aircraft in Manchuria. . . . The items the Communists seized from the Nationalists (including the U.S. material originally supplied to the Nationalist armies), and not Soviet-supplied weapons, provided the Chinese Communist forces with the implements for winning the Civil War."[19]

By the mid-1940s, Stalin's suspicions of Mao must have been even more greatly intensified by Mao's overt assertions of ideological independence. As early as 1942, Mao launched a "rectification" campaign within the CCP, one of whose purposes was to "remold" those comrades who looked upon Moscow as the only Mecca. In 1946, Liu Shao-ch'i told Anna Louise Strong, a prominent American fellow-traveller then visiting Yenan, that Mao had developed an Asian brand of Marxism and thus, by implication, was the leader of the Asian revolution. When Miss Strong arrived in Moscow in 1949, after touring Eastern Europe and spreading the word about Mao's original brand of communism, Stalin had her thrown into jail. At about the same time, Mikhail Borodin, a Comintern leader who had strongly sympathized with the Chinese Communists in the thirties, was also arrested by Stalin. These actions came at a time when Stalin was systematically purging all real or suspected "National Communists" in Eastern Europe, including Gomulka, Rajk, and Pauker.[20]

Stalin blatantly intervened in the internal affairs of the Eastern European Communist parties—intervention that led to the split with Tito, and it seems likely that he never gave up hope of replacing Mao at the head of the CCP, or at least of cultivating relations with the more "internationalist" leaders of the CCP. Once Mao's armies won the Civil War, the opportunity for infiltrating Stalin's secret police into the CCP were minimal. But there is some evidence to link Stalin to Kao Kang, a prominent CCP leader in Manchuria who was purged by Mao in 1954 after Stalin died. In 1956, Klaus Mehnert talked with Chinese who said that Kao had "cooperated more closely with Stalin than was permissible for a provincial governor." In the spring of 1956, Peking tended to support this speculation by officially charging that Kao Kang's group

[19] Ibid., p. 84.
[20] For the details of the Anna Louise Strong case, see Phillip Jaffe, "The Strange Case of Anna Louise Strong," *Survey* (October 1964):129–140.

had represented "reactionary forces" both "at home and abroad."[21] Mehnert considers it likely that Stalin, "when he saw his Manchurian venture collapsing after Mao's victory throughout China, had encouraged the formation of a government more or less independent of Peking in order to make it a satellite of Moscow—like Outer Mongolia."

After Mao took power in October, 1949, the longstanding mutual fears and suspicions that existed between Stalin and Mao did not disappear. As we have already noted, Mao said in 1962 that even after the CCP won power on the mainland, Stalin did not trust him. "After the victory of the revolution, he again suspected that China would be like Yugoslavia, and I would turn into a Tito." Moreover, continued Mao in the same speech, even when he went to Moscow to negotiate the Sino-Soviet Treaty of Alliance in January-February 1950, "this also involved a struggle. He (Stalin) did not want to sign it, but finally agreed after two months of negotiations."[22]

That Treaty has rightly been called the last of the unequal treaties. One of its provisions called for joint exploitation of uranium resources in Sinkiang, a provision which was revoked only in 1954, after Stalin's death, when Khrushchev and Bulganin flew to Peking to put the Sino-Soviet alliance on a new and more equal footing. Another provision of the Treaty gave Stalin naval bases at Port Arthur and Dairen on the Manchurian coast. In September, 1952, Stalin used the Korean war as a wedge to extend Soviet occupation of Port Arthur indefinitely. The Russians agreed to withdraw from Port Arthur, to turn over the Soviet installations there without compensation, and to abandon all their special rights in Manchuria only after Stalin's death. In sum, although Mao's intervention in the Korean War must have reassured Stalin about his loyalty, Mao must have strongly resented the "colonialist-like" demands that Stalin made upon China between 1950 and 1953. On this point we have the testimony of Khrushchev:

> Stalin jeopardized China's alliance with the Soviet Union and thus endangered the solidarity of the Soviet camp by demanding too much in return for aid. Stalin faced Mao Tse-tung . . . with a series of economic demands smacking of colonialism. He insisted that he, Stalin, must have the final word on the development of Communism, within China as he had in other countries of the Soviet bloc. Mao was extremely embittered by Stalin's insistence on jointly controlled companies and mining and industrial concessions. He refused to submit to Stalin's authority over Chinese affairs. Had it not been for the hardness of U.S. policy towards

[21] Klaus Mehnert, *Peking and Moscow* (New York: G. P. Putnam, 1963), p. 252.
[22] See note no. 5.

Communist China, the Peking government might well have decided to break openly with Moscow as Marshal Tito did in 1948.
The situation was said to have been eased by Mao's visit to Russia
in 1949–50. But tenseness in relations continued right up to the
time of Stalin's death in 1953.[23]

To sum up this portion of the argument, the evidence is overwhelming
that as of 1949–50, on the eve of the Korean War, relations between Mao
and Stalin were charged with mutual fear and suspicions. An alliance
between Peking and Moscow was probable once the Cold War began
both for ideological reasons and because the U.S., by its intervention
in the Chinese Civil War, had shown itself to be hostile to the CCP. But
the nature of the Sino-Soviet alliance was still very much in question.
Indeed, there exists compelling evidence which shows that Mao and
Chou En-lai both wanted an alliance with the Soviet Union to be
balanced with diplomatic and economic relations with the United
States.[24] It is to this evidence that we now turn.

III

In the period from 1944 to 1946, as World War II drew to a close
and on the eve of the civil war between the Communists and Nationalists, Mao made several efforts to obtain American support. The first such
effort came in 1944. Already after Japan attacked Pearl Harbor, according to one careful observer, the Chinese Communists had become "extremely friendly toward the United States, not only on the surface, but
even in their educational programs."[25] In 1944, July 4th was celebrated
in Yenan with tremendous enthusiasm and fulsome praise to Roosevelt,
whose policies were lauded as expressions of the great tradition of
freedom and democracy in the United States. On Roosevelt's re-election in 1944, Mao sent him a message of congratulations. In the summer
of 1944, the American Observer Group, or the Dixie Mission, arrived in
Yenan as a prelude to broader cooperation between Washington and
the Communists. All of these events must have given Stalin's intelli-
gence agents in Yenan much food for thought.

In January, 1945, Mao and Chou asked for a meeting with Roosevelt
to coordinate military strategy against Japan, but the request was refused. Roosevelt accepted the ill-reasoned advice of Ambassador Hurley
against the advice of the great majority of the China specialists in the

---

[23] Sydney Gruson, reporting Khrushchev's secret speech in the New York Times, February, 1956.

[24] See, for example, Lyman Van Slyke, ed., The Chinese Communist Movement (Stanford,
Calif.: Stanford University Press, 1968), p. 218ff.

[25] Cohen, America's Response to China, p. 174.

State Department. In August, 1945, around the time of the Japanese surrender, the CCP again sought American neutrality in their struggle with the Nationalists and once again were rebuffed. The Communists claimed for their forces the right to liberate territory held by the Japanese, and refused to go along with Chiang Kai-shek's orders to remain in place. But American forces and the American government began openly to side with the Nationalists. American forces liberated key points in North China holding them for the Nationalists; the Americans also began to provide transportation to facilitate the movement of Nationalist troops into areas that the Nationalists otherwise could not reach before the Communists.[26]

After Hurley resigned in late November, 1945, the Communists, sensing a softening of American policy, made still another overture to Washington. Chou told Marshall that the CCP "is prepared to cooperate with the United States in matters both of a local and national character. . . ." and hinted again that Mao would welcome an opportunity to visit the United States.[27] Again in 1945—and early 1946—CCP leaders made an extraordinary bid for better relations with the United States. In several conversations with American foreign service officers in Yenan, Mao indicated that postwar China would be dependent on U.S. aid for reconstruction and that the U.S. was the only country able to provide such assistance.[28] But clearly another reason was Mao's fear of, and mistrust of, Stalin.

Although the United States initially supported the Chinese Nationalists in the civil war on the mainland which began in 1946, by late 1948 it had begun to disengage from the war and to write off the Nationalists and their island refuge of Taiwan. As early as October, 1948, the State Department ruled out the use of American armed forces to defend Taiwan. And, in 1949, the Joint Chiefs of Staff reaffirmed their view that overt American military action to deny Taiwan to the Communists would not be justified.[29] In short, by early 1949 it was clear that the United States was not going to intervene with troops to prevent the collapse of the Nationalist armies on the mainland or to protect Taiwan against Communist invasion from the mainland. Moreover, State Department policy makers at the time, although not overly optimistic about the short-term prospects for improving relations with Communist China, did hope for "the early demise of the developing Sino-Soviet relationship" and did realize that "historically there had always been tension

[26] Ibid., p. 182.
[27] Ibid.
[28] John Paton Davies, Jr., *Dragon By the Tail* (New York: W. W. Norton, 1972), pp. 321, 404.
[29] Tang Tsou, *America's Failure in China* (Chicago: University of Chicago Press, 1963), p. 201.

between Russia and China," tension they mistakenly believed "stemmed from the vast border the two countries shared."[30] By and large, Secretary of State Acheson and his chief subordinates in the State Department were ignorant of the true nature of the relationship between Mao and Stalin in the thirties and forties, but they did correctly perceive the strength of Chinese nationalism, and they did appreciate the fact that Soviet territorial ambitions in the borderlands were bound to strengthen the forces leading to a rift, a rift they hoped to encourage.

> They . . . realized that China, regardless of her leadership's ideology, was in a xenophobic mood and that this xenophobia would be turned against any foreign intruder the Chinese felt threatened their sovereignty. While the Administration knew (sic) that these forces were working primarily against the West in 1949, it also thought that they could work against the Soviets. Operating on this assumption, the State Department formulated an American policy that would to the greatest extent possible allow those forces to operate unhindered against the Soviet Union.[31]

It is apparent, however, that while the State Department correctly perceived the potentiality over the long run for the development of a rift between Moscow and Peking, it greatly underestimated the already-existing potential of 1949. Thus, in March, 1949, two months before the Chinese began making overtures to the United States, Acheson predicted in an excutive session of the Senate Committee on Foreign Relations that there would be an "initial" period of close Sino-Soviet relations, and W. Walton Butterworth, then Director of the Office of Far Eastern Affairs, cautioned against any early hope for "Titoism"; only over "the long pull' would Chinese nationalism "exert an influence."[32] Acheson made the same point in his National Press Club speech in January, 1950, when he vividly described Russian imperialistic activity in China going back to Tsarist days and predicted that over the long run "we must not undertake to deflect from the Russians to ourselves the righteous anger, the wrath and hatred of the Chinese people which must develop. It would be folly to deflect it to ourselves."[33]

But while Acheson and his State Department advisors correctly perceived the importance of Chinese nationalism and of Soviet territorial ambitions, thus predicting a rift over the "long pull," they completely failed to take the measure of the long-standing ideologically-based

[30] Senate Committee Report, *The United States and Communist China in 1949 and 1950*, p. 3.
[31] Ibid., p. 3.
[32] Ibid.
[33] Ibid., p. 4.

tensions between Mao and Stalin that had their roots in Stalin's un-successful efforts to gain control over the CCP. That is why the State Department, as of early 1949, greatly underestimated the short-term prospects for a rift between Mao and Stalin. Then, as later, the role of ideology as a divisive element in the Sino-Soviet relationship was never comprehended.

It is in part for this reason that Acheson and the State Department did not look upon recognition of the new Communist regime in China as a burning issue. If the expectation was—as it was—that there was inevitably to be an initial period of close Sino-Soviet relations, there was clearly no urgency attached to dealing with, and recognizing, the new regime. Moreover, by mid-1949, sixteen Republican and five Dem-ocratic Senators had written a letter to President Truman warning against recognizing Communist China. These and other domestic po-litical pressures must have encouraged Acheson and his subordinates not to think in terms of moving too quickly on the recognition question.

On the Chinese side, however, there was a sense of urgency, one accelerated by a serious internal debate that raged through the spring and summer of 1949. On the one side, Mao and Chou En-lai, "while supporting friendship and general collaboration with Russia, want, nevertheless, to pursue a more independent line and particularly believe that Communist China should seek a working relationship with the United States and Britain in the interest of trade and other dealings of advantage to China."[34] Clearly another advantage to Mao and Chou of developing a new relationship with the United States was to make the new regime less dependent on Stalin.

Another more "pro-Soviet" group of leaders, more "internationalist" minded and led by Liu Shao-ch'i, were urging an exclusive relationship with Moscow. In the fall of 1948, Liu had been the author of a very important document on the importance of "internationalism," a docu-ment that appears to have set off subsequent debate.

The balance between the Maoists and the "internationalists" was still uncertain in the spring and summer of 1949. It was at this time that Mao tentatively began to explore with the American Ambassador in China, Leighton Stuart, the prospect for future relations. The recently released study of the Senate Foreign Relations Committee describes in consider-able detail the conversations that took place between Huang Hua—a man whose career has been closely tied to Chou En-lai—and Ambas-sador Stuart, between May 13 and June 28, 1949. It concludes:

[34] As reported by Tillman Durdin, *New York Times*, September 17 and 18, 1949, and cited in Senate Committee Report, *The United States and Communist China in 1949 and 1950*, p. 9, fn.

There were . . . in the spring of 1949 . . . indications suggesting that at least certain elements within the Chinese Communist Party were trying to develop closer relations with the West and avoid falling into the Soviet orbit. This group which had clearly been in the ascendancy in 1944 was on the decline in 1949 but was still active as the Huang-Stuart conversations and other evidence at the time suggests.[35]

Among the "other evidence" cited by the study indicating a clear Chinese desire to establish relations with the United States was Mao's important speech on June 15, 1949. In that speech, Mao said that:

The Chinese people wish to have friendly cooperation with people of all countries and to resume and expand international trade in order to develop production and promote economic prosperity.[36]

Both Edmund Stuart and Consul General Clubb in Peking "interpreted the speech in an optimistic light and saw in it reason to pursue Communist overtures."[37] Two weeks later, on June 28, Huang Hua reported to the American Ambassador that "he had received a message from Mao Tse-tung and Chou En-lai assuring me that they would welcome me to Peiping if I wished to visit Yenching University."[38] Stuart informed the State Department of this overture on June 30. It was interpreted by John Davies of the Policy Planning Staff as an "extremely significant" overture. But, on July 1, Secretary of State Acheson, citing a decision reached at the "highest level," instructed Stuart that "under no circumstances should he visit Peiping."[39] Four days before Huang's invitation, sixteen Republican and five Democratic Senators signed a letter to President Truman urging him not to recognize the Chinese Communists.

In sum, it is apparent that in the spring and summer of 1949, at least one group of Chinese Communist leaders, including Mao and Chou En-lai, were again probing the possibility of a relationship with the United States that would have made the new Chinese regime less dependent on the Russians. But the overtures made by Mao and Chou were rebuffed by President Truman out of fear of rising Congressional opposition, led by the Republicans, to abandonment of Chiang Kai-shek. Thus, for the second time in four years, an important overture to Washington from Mao and Chou En-lai was rebuffed. Mao, because Washington

[35] Senate Committee Report, United States and Communist China in 1949 and 1950, p. 9.
[36] Ibid.
[37] Ibid.
[38] Ibid., p. 10.
[39] Ibid., p. 10.

offered him no alternative, was forced reluctantly to go along with the "internationalist" faction led by Liu Shao-ch'i which was arguing for an exclusive alliance with the Soviet Union.

If this analysis is correct, it sheds new light on the relationship between Mao and Liu Shao-ch'i, the leader who was one of Mao's first victims during the purges carried out in the Cultural Revolution. Liu was singled out by Mao early in the Cultural Revolution as "China's Khrushchev," as the symbol of "modern revisionism," as the dogmatic follower of the Soviet model. It seems likely, then, that the crucial debate between the "internationalist" and "nationalist" factions in Peking in the spring and summer of 1949 was never fully resolved. Indeed, it must have been aggravated in the late fifties and early sixties when Mao became increasingly disillusioned with the Soviet alliance, began to view the Russians as an enemy even greater than the American "imperialists," and systematically excluded from positions of power all leaders with "pro-Soviet" inclinations.[40]

Of course, no one can know what might have been the outcome if Truman had allowed Ambassador Stuart to take up Mao's invitation to visit him in Peking in early July, 1949. Mao's "lean to one side" speech was made on June 30, 1949, a day before Truman vetoed Stuart's trip. Thus, it is clear that that speech was made before Mao knew whether Stuart would accept his invitation. Indeed, it seems likely that Mao made the speech to conciliate Stalin and his own "internationalist" faction at home while at the same time holding out a hand to the Americans. But the "lean to one side" speech itself could hardly have been very reassuring to Stalin. It was anything but a declaration of obeisance. Indeed, in the course of that lengthy speech, Mao never once mentioned Stalin's name by itself as a source of inspiration for the CCP, a rhetorical practice then common in Eastern Europe. Mao mentioned Stalin only in connection with Lenin, Marx, and Engels—an indication that he was accepting the Communist tradition but not Stalin's exclusive interpretation of it. In the same speech, moreover, Mao spelled out his conception of "People's Democracy," a concept that was different in important respects from the Stalinist version of how to consolidate state power and about which Mao and Stalin were to wage polemics for several years.

In sum, the "lean to one side" speech was probably an attempt by Mao to take out some insurance against the tremors that would certainly have been aroused in Moscow by the sudden appearance in Peking of the American Ambassador. But Mao probably sought to demonstrate to Washington that although Peking was going to "lean to one side,"

[40] This list includes Marshal Peng Te-Huai, Liu Shao-ch'i, Lin Piao, Lo Jui Ch'ing, Peng Chen, and others.

it did not want to lean exclusively to one side. The abrupt rejection by Truman of Mao's overture probably led Mao to conclude that the United States was going to be hostile in the postwar world. It must have greatly strengthened the hand of the "internationalist" faction within the CCP.

In Washington, the "lean to one side" speech was either willfully distorted or misunderstood. Within a few weeks of the speech, Acheson, on July 18, sent Phillip Jessup a top-secret memorandum setting down the policy of containing communism in Asia and instructing Jessup to draw up a program of action to achieve this purpose. Acheson told Jessup of his desire "to make absolutely certain that we are neglecting no opportunity that would be within our capabilities to achieve the purpose of halting the spread of totalitarian communism in Asia." Twelve days later, in his "Letter of Transmittal" to Truman, Acheson, introducing the China White Paper, wrote that the Chinese Communist leaders had "foresworn their Chinese heritage and have publicly announced their subservience to a foreign power, Russia. . . ." Neither in the White Paper nor elsewhere did Acheson reveal that the Chinese Communists were making overtures to the United States only weeks earlier.

IV

The crucial question remains: why did Truman and Acheson reject the overture made by Mao in the summer of 1949? More specifically, why is it that the American government was able to recognize, and deal with, "Titoism" in Yugoslavia but not in China? There are three not mutually incompatible explanations. The first is that the China question in 1949 had become a question not only, or even primarily, of foreign policy; it had become a question of domestic politics. An active "China lobby" had developed within Congress, led largely by conservative Republicans, but also including conservative Democrats. This pro-Chiang lobby which influenced U.S.-China policy against recognition of the Communists had no equivalent when it came to U.S. policy toward Yugoslavia. It is an intriguing question whether, if Dewey had won the election of 1948, he might have neutralized the "China lobby" and been in a better position than Truman to recognize the new Communist regime. Some twenty-four years later, Nixon could deal with Peking much more easily than any Democratic president.

A second reason why the United States was able to deal with Tito and not with Mao was undoubtedly the fact that Tito publicly broke with Stalin in 1948–49, whereas Mao did not.

A third factor—an inadequate American perception of Communist

China—requires more explanation. The crucial insight into Sino-Soviet relations in 1949 was not the "Sinological" insight of the China specialists inside or outside the U.S. government: namely, that Chinese Communists were more "nationalist" than communist and could *ultimately* be weaned away from Moscow. The crucial insight was that Mao and Stalin never trusted each other, that the Chinese Communist Party had developed independently of the Comintern and made its own revolution, and that *as of 1949*, relations between Mao and Stalin were sufficiently strained so that the United States could effectively compete with Moscow for influence in China. The China specialists within and outside government were insufficiently aware of the history of the communist movement to appreciate this crucial point. (Tang Tsou, in *America's Failure in China*, convincingly has made this case.) On the other hand, many of those who were familiar with the history of international communism too easily assumed that communism was more or less monolithic.

Of the influential men in government in 1949, the record suggests that only George Kennan had taken the real measure of the Chinese Communists. Writing in 1945, Kennan, then in Moscow, argued that relations between Moscow and Yenan were "subtle and obscure." But he concluded that Yenan might enjoy a "surprising degree of independence" because: (1) the Chinese Communist Party had little reason to be grateful to the USSR—it had survived and grown not because of, but in spite of, Moscow; (2) the CCP had developed its own brand of Marxism and indigenous traditions; (3) the CCP was no fugitive band of conspirators—for ten years it had had a regime, army and civil administration; and (4) the CCP had taken on nationalist coloration.[41] This was a subtle, brilliant, and truly prophetic analysis for any year, particularly for the year 1945.

On the other hand, it seems clear that Truman, Acheson, and Marshall all gravely underestimated the differences between Mao and Stalin and the historic differences between Chinese and Russian Communism. In September, 1949, when British Foreign Secretary Ernest Bevin warned Acheson that if the United States was too obdurate it "would drive China into the arms of Russia," Acheson replied "they were there already."[42] By the winter of 1950, when British Prime Minister Attlee observed to President Truman that opinions differed on the extent to which the Chinese Communists were satellites of the Russians, Truman responded:

[41] Cited by Dean Acheson, *Present At the Creation* (New York: W. W. Norton, 1969), p. 202.
[42] Ibid., p. 328.

I said that in my opinion the Chinese Communists were Russian satellites. The problem we were facing was part of a pattern. After Korea, it would be Indo-China, then Hong Kong, then Malaya.[43]

There is, perhaps, a deeper explanation of the failure of American policymakers in 1949 to take the measure of the Chinese Communists. For a variety of reasons having to do largely with America's particular historical experience, "only infrequently do Americans really enter the texture of a foreign society," and then often with a sense of impatience to change it. Behind this incapacity lies the absence of any clear-cut vision of politics, of power, or of history, other than a superficial Wilsonism with its "world of self-determined, self-governing nations with mild disputes and nondisruptive internal issues until the end of history, a history kept busy by discrete crises and gradual changes rather than by cataclysms and deep transmutations. . . ."[44] The United States has a set of abstract principles and disembodied "formulas" but no philosophy of history or "clear-cut vision of the main trends."[45] The absence of such a clear-cut vision of history, and of politics, inevitably makes our analyses of foreign nations and societies superficial. One great strength of our Communist adversaries during the Cold War has not been the skill of their diplomacy but the insights (even if occasionally misleading) into the dynamics of foreign societies provided by Marxism.

[43] Harry Truman, *Memoirs,* vol. 2 (New York: Doubleday, 1956) p. 399.
[44] Stanley Hoffman, *Gulliver's Troubles* (New York: McGraw Hill, 1968), p. 210.
[45] Ibid.

8

THE CHOICES WE DID NOT HAVE:
In Defense of Containment

PRIMITIVE AND SOPHISTICATED REVISIONISM

Dexter Perkins, the distinguished American historian, once defined revisionism as "an after-the-event interpretation of American partici-pation in war, with the accent on the errors and blunders that provoked the struggle and on the folly of the whole enterprise."[1] More specifi-cally, there are two types of revisionism: primitive and sophisticated. The former suggests that the responsibility for war, whether hot or cold, falls on the U.S.: that American vital interests were not threatened and therefore there was no cause for the nation's involvement, and that the reason it became involved was due to the manipulations of political leaders, propaganda, and the "merchants of death," the military-industrial-financial interests. It is this type of revisionism, which has followed every American war since the United States established its independence, that will concern us primarily.[2] For if the revisionists are

Copyright © 1974 by John Spanier.

[1] Dexter Perkins, *Foreign Policy and the American Spirit* (Ithaca, N.Y.: Cornell University Press, 1957), p. 107.

[2] As seen in Chapter 5 of this volume, Senator J. William Fulbright has come close to embracing this position; a critical assessment of his views is presented towards the end of this essay. For some of the principal books by revisionist writers, see Gar Alperovitz, *Atomic Diplomacy* (New York: Vintage Books, 1965), and *Cold War Essays* (New York: Anchor Books, 1970); D. F. Fleming, *The Cold War and Its Origins, 1917–1960*, 2 vols. (Garden City,

correct, with regard to World War II and its immediate aftermath, then containment would have been unnecessary. But we shall also examine a more sophisticated form of revisionism which has arisen during this period.[3] It too focuses on the errors of American policy, but it does not assert that but for our actions the postwar bipolar conflict could have been avoided;[4] it only suggests that the scope of this adversary relationship might have been more limited had we pursued different policies. It does not deny the reality of a postwar threat to American security interests and it rejects the belief that conflict and war are the products of wicked leaders or profit-hungry systems; by and large, it attributes American responsibility for the conflicts with Russia and China to the misperceptions of the Communist threats by American policy makers.

One reason for the recurrent appearance of revisionism, no doubt, is the widespread disenchantment which has tended to follow the high aspirations accompanying the wartime efforts. The nation went to war in 1941 in the struggle against Fascism. But Germany hardly had been defeated when the apparently even greater threat from Russia arose; Japan's surrender was quickly followed by the collapse of Nationalist China and the birth of the Chinese People's Republic which, together with Soviet Russia, condemned the U.S. as the bastion of world reaction and defined it as their principal enemy. The confrontation of a seemingly more menacing danger to American security than the one just defeated was eventually bound to raise questions: Why had we become involved in World War II?[5] How had our alliance with one of the Big Three (the USSR) during the war become transformed into an intense adversary relationship? Had this postwar conflict been inevitable or could we have conducted our policy differently and avoided this struggle? And could we not have prevented the collapse of another ally (Chiang Kai-Shek's China), or at least established better relations with the successor regime?

N.Y.: Doubleday and Co., 1961); Lloyd C. Gardner *Architects of Illusion,* (Chicago: Quadrangle Books, 1970); Gabriel Kolko, *The Politics of War* (New York: Random House, 1968), and (with Joyce Kolko) *The Limits of Power* (New York: Harper & Row, 1972); Walter LaFeber, *America, Russia, and the Cold War, 1945–1971,* second edition (New York: John Wiley & Sons, 1972); Carl Oglesby and Richard Shaull, *Containment and Change* (New York: The Macmillan Co., 1967); Thomas G. Paterson, "The Abortive American Loan to Russia and the Origins of the Cold War, 1943–1946," *Journal of American History* (June, 1969): 70–92; William A. Williams, *The Tragedy of American Diplomacy,* revised edition (New York: World Publishing Company, 1962).

[3] See Chapters 6 and 7, by Zimmerman and Zagoria in this book.

[4] For a discussion of various interpretations and dates of origins for the Cold War, see Paul Seabury, *The Rise and Decline of the Cold War* (New York: Basic Books, 1967), pp. 3–17.

[5] For example, Bruce M. Russett, *No Clear and Present Danger* (New York: Harper Torchbooks, 1972) for a tortured interpretation.

The timing for the appearance of revisionism about the origins of the Cold War, however, is in large measure due to the Vietnam War. For the war in that hapless country disenchanted many who had formerly supported containment. If Vietnam was the end product of our prior policy, did this not condemn the entire record of American foreign policy since World War II? If the reasons we had become involved in Vietnam no longer appeared as persuasive by the late 1960s as they had been earlier in that decade, were the officially given reasons—and the "orthodox" historical interpretations—for our involvement in the Cold War not perhaps equally specious? In any case, after twenty odd years of conflict, could anyone say that the U.S. was more secure and prosperous despite all of its toil? Would the country not have been better off had it never become involved in the Cold War which, in large—if not full—measure, it had precipitated?

AMERICAN PROVOCATIONS AND THE LEGITIMACY OF RUSSIAN INTERESTS

Primitive revisionism assigns responsibility for the Cold War to five American policies during World War II. The first one was the failure to open up the Second Front earlier than 1944. This aroused Stalin to suspect that the U.S. and Britain were waiting for Germany and Russia to exhaust one another and leave the two Western states to dictate the peace terms. Second, the American insistence upon national self-determination in Eastern Europe—which would presumably have resulted in the establishment of anti-Communist governments—constituted an attempt to drive Russia out of Eastern Europe and extend American influence to Russia's frontiers. Third, Truman's succession to the Presidency resulted in the launching of an intensive anti-Communist policy. Fourth, Hiroshima initiated an "atomic diplomacy" against Russia, which reinforced Russia's sense of insecurity stemming from three invasions in just over a century by technologically more advanced Western states. Fifth, generous economic loans to help rebuild a devastated Russia were withheld instead of being extended as a token of American friendship and benevolent intentions.

The blame for these policies is basically distributed among three causes: (1) certain policy makers, particularly President Truman and certain advisors such as Harriman and Forrestal, as well as such bureaucrats as Kennan; (2) specific policies which may not have been intended to antagonize Stalin, such as the postponement of the invasion of France, or others which were clearly provocative, such as the atomic diplomacy; (3) and the counter-revolutionary and imperialist nature of American foreign policy. Paradoxically, although only the latter interpretation is a determinist one, it simultaneously emphasizes that American policy reflected the capitalist economic system and class structure and yet blames the U.S. for acting as it did, even though presumably it could not have acted in any other way. Thus even the capitalist interpretation shares, at least in spirit, the belief that but for the provocative nature of U.S. behavior the bipolar clash after 1945 would not have occurred.

By contrast, Soviet Russia's purposes are perceived as strictly defensive, limited to the defense of Russia's borders, although this included some "defensive expansionism"[6] in Eastern Europe to establish a Russian security belt throughout the area. But Russia did not threaten any vital American interests. Indeed, Russian policy had no inner dynamics of its own, no independent purposes or goals. It was viewed as essentially reactive to prewar anti-Soviet Western acts: the Allied intervention in Russia at the end of World War I in order to overthrow the Soviet regime, and, after the failure of that attempt, the establishment by France of the *cordon sanitaire* in Eastern Europe to keep the Soviet virus from infecting Europe; the West's rejection of Soviet efforts in the mid- and late-1930s to build an alliance against Hitler; and, especially, the Munich agreement in 1938, which, by destroying Czechoslovakia, in effect opened Hitler's gateway to the East. In short, Western efforts to ostracize and ultimately destroy the Soviet Union, as well as attempts to turn the Hitlerian threat away from the West and toward Russia, were considered the primary reasons for the existence of Soviet hostility.

This attitude, interestingly enough, was shared by America's wartime leaders.[7] Consequently, it was thought, the West had only to demonstrate its good intentions and prove its friendliness. The question was not *whether* Soviet cooperation could be won for the postwar world, only *how* it could be gained. And if Western efforts did bear fruit and create good will, what conflicts of interest could not be settled peacefully in the future? The revisionist's argument, however, is that Western efforts produced not good will but additional misgivings and hostilities.

We need not detain ourselves long to deal with their charges. This has been done at some length elsewhere.[8] A brief look at just one of these charges—that the U.S. employed atomic diplomacy, not to compel Japan to surrender (because Japan was already defeated and on the verge of surrender) but to coerce Russia into a European settlement

[6] Louis J. Halle, *The Cold War as History* (New York: Harper and Row, 1967), pp. 10–19.

[7] William H. McNeill, *America, Britain and Russia* (New York: Oxford University Press, 1953); Herbert Feis, *Churchill, Roosevelt, Stalin* (Princeton, N.J.: Princeton University Press, 1957).

[8] See especially John Lewis Gaddis, *The United States and the Origins of the Cold War, 1941–1947* (New York: Columbia University Press, 1972).

favorable to this country[9]—reveals the shallow nature of most of them. The charge is fiction but not fact. The Joint Chiefs of Staff, especially General Marshall and General MacArthur in the Pacific, continued to press for an invasion of Japan for they felt that despite the bomb an invasion was necessary to force Japan to surrender; they also continued to insist on Russian participation against the Japanese forces in Manchuria. Not a single public statement of atomic threat against the Soviet Union or, for that matter, one by a diplomat talking to his Russian counterpart was recorded during this period (in contrast to repeated Soviet threats during the Suez War and the later Berlin crises, as well as talk of "massive retaliation" by John Foster Dulles during the 1950s). The post-Hiroshima period witnessed Soviet pressure on Iran and even greater pressure on Turkey, hardly signs of the constraint and timidity that the bomb is supposed to have inspired in the Kremlin, and the additional lack of American success in removing the allegedly frightened Soviets from Eastern Europe—had that been the U.S. aim—further emasculates the accusation of atomic diplomacy. Indeed, as Adam Ulam has noted, "what *is* astounding is that no attempt was made by the United States to exploit politically the monopoly of this weapon of unique destructiveness when it came to the peace settlement in Europe or Asia." In any event, despite the revisionist arguments to the contrary, "*Even Soviet sources* . . . do not accuse the United States of threatening the Soviet Union in 1945."[10]

A more pertinent reason for the failure of U.S. wartime policies, and one ignored by the revisionists in their attempt to discredit these policies, was the dynamics of Soviet behavior, which stemmed at least in part from the nature of the Soviet regime. Even in the immediate postwar period, however, Washington had not yet fundamentally rethought its wartime assumptions about Soviet policy.[11] Admittedly, the Truman Administration recognized that Big Three (U.S., U.K., and U.S.S.R.) cooperation had ended, and it realized that the time when the U.S. needed to demonstrate goodwill toward the Soviet Union in order to overcome the latter's suspicions had passed. No further concessions would be made to preserve the surface friendship with the Soviet Union. Paper agreements, written in such general terms that they actually hid divergent purposes, were no longer regarded as demonstrating such friendship. Something more than paper agreements was needed: Russian words would have to be matched by Russian deeds.

[9] Alperovitz, *Atomic Diplomacy*.

[10] Adam B. Ulam, *The Rivals* (New York: The Viking Press, 1971), p. 82 (Italics in Ulam).

[11] The process of reevaluation and the conflicting evaluations are analyzed in John W. Spanier, *American Foreign Policy Since World War II*, Fourth rev. ed., (New York: Praeger Publishers, 1971), pp. 31–38.

The American Secretary of State, James Byrnes, called this new line the "policy of patience with firmness." This phrase meant that the U.S. would take a firm position whenever the Soviet Union became intransigent, and that the U.S. would not compromise simply in order to reach a quick agreement. This change in official American attitude toward the Soviet Union was not, however, a fundamental one. A firm line was to be followed only on concrete issues. The assumption was that if the United States took a tougher bargaining position and no longer seemed in a hurry to resolve particular points of tension, the Soviet rulers would see the pointlessness of their obduracy and agree to fair compromise solutions of their differences with the United States and the West. In short, American firmness would make the Russians "reasonable." For they were regarded as "unreasonable" merely on particular issues; the Soviet Union was still considered to be a typical nation-state. That this "unreasonableness" might stem from the nature of Soviet regime had not yet been fully accepted at the highest levels of American policy-making. The recognition of its revolutionary character came with Kennan's famous telegram of February, 1946, and his later "X" article which suggested that Soviet policy did indeed possess a drive of its own.[12] The hostility of the leaders who came to power in 1917 stemmed from an ideology which was preconceived and deduced from first principles long before the Bolshevik Revolution and subsequent anti-Soviet Western actions.[13]

Surely, this analysis provided the administration with a more comprehensive and—if one may be forgiven for using a much-abused word —"realistic" basis for its policies than the modified version of the wartime attitude which continued to prevail during much of the eighteen months between Japan's surrender and the announcement of the Truman Doctrine, a period during which Churchill's Fulton address was critically received and public pressure for demobilization remained intense. To criticize Kennan's analysis as "mechanistic," as Zimmerman does,[14] is to forget that the policy makers needed *some* conceptual foundation upon which to base policy if they were to do more than flounder around with a series of ad hoc reactions to Soviet challenges in response to what was increasingly perceived in Washington to be a coherent and persistent Soviet policy aimed at dominating Europe.

[12] See Chapter 2 of this volume; also *Memoirs 1925–1950* (Boston: Little, Brown and Company, 1967), pp. 354–67. Walter Millis, *The Forrestal Diaries* (New York: Viking, 1952), pp. 135–40.

[13] Whether ideology or power impels Soviet foreign policy—which, as Gati indicates in Chapter 4, is somewhat confused in the "X" article—is very clear in Kennan's analysis, *Russia and the West Under Lenin and Stalin* (Boston: Little, Brown and Company, 1961), pp. 179–83.

[14] See Chapter 6 of this volume.

In addition, the mood of the country needed to be turned around. It would have been too much to expect that the American public would change suddenly from an attitude of friendliness toward the Soviet Union—inspired largely by the picture of Russian wartime bravery and endurance and by hopes for peaceful postwar cooperation—to a hostile mood shortly after the war. The American "reservoir of good will" for the Soviet Union could not be emptied that quickly. Moreover, the desire for peace was too strong. The United States wished to be left alone to preoccupy itself once more with domestic affairs. The end of the war signaled the end of "power politics" and the restoration of normal peacetime harmony among nations.

It was Soviet behavior which shifted American opinion against Russia, but it was Kennan's explanation—even if represented by the President (in the Truman Doctrine) in brighter and more contrasting colors—that helped the latter mobilize public support for containment.[15] If the tone of the Doctrine was more universalistic than Kennan had intended and if it divided the world too sharply into Free and Slave Worlds, it was not inconsistent with the cosmic goals which had guided America's crusades during World Wars I and II. Ever since Lincoln's phrase that a country half-slave, half-free could not survive, Americans have felt that this was equally true for the world. Once the nation became involved in wars overseas, Americans have thus embarked on crusades in the name of democracy and humanity. These global purposes, ironically, have been best articulated by the very liberal spokesmen who today are most critical of the universality of the Truman Doctrine.[16] During most of the Cold War, however, as Gati has noted,[17] American behavior was always more limitationist than the official rhetoric suggested.

STATE SYSTEM AND ORIGINS OF THE COLD WAR

A more substantial criticism of American policy is surely the failure to analyze American-Soviet behavior in systemic terms. A focus on the interactions of two great powers, as Zimmerman claims, would have stressed the significance that each respective policy held for the other and, in this context, it would have indicated the capacity of the Soviet Union's leaders to "learn," to adapt their behavior and change their

[15] See Chapter 1 of this volume.

[16] For various expressions of this crusading spirit during World War II, of the Pax Americana as the Pax Humana by various liberal spokesmen, see Seabury, Rise and Decline of Cold War, pp. 39–45.

[17] Gati, Chapter 4; see also his "Another Grand Debate? The Limitationist Critique of American Foreign Policy," World Politics (October 1968), pp. 133–51.

attitudes in response to the behavior of other states.[18] The implication of this conceptually sound point of view is that if American policy makers had acted on the basis of "third-level analysis,"[19] the United States might have acted so as to reduce rather than reinforce the Kremlin's "siege mentality," avoided the worst days of the Cold War, and helped produce in the 1940s the more limited adversary relationship that finally flowered during the 1960s and 1970s.

In relationship to the initiation of the Cold War, however, this criticism is unpersuasive. It occurs in the same type of vacuum that, as Zimmerman concludes, makes the essentialist and mechanistic explanations of Soviet foreign policy so unconvincing. It ignores that American wartime policy was based upon precisely such a "cybernetic approach." Since Western animosity during the interwar period was considered the primary cause for Soviet hostility, a wartime policy of conciliation and cooperation with Russia would have replaced distrust with trust and assured peaceful postwar relations. Furthermore, this criticism also ignores that Stalin was suspicious not just of capitalists. He was suspicious of his colleagues, of his Red Army soldiers who had seen war-wracked Eastern Europe and Germany and, as was soon to become evident, of Tito and Mao Tse-tung. It would have been a miracle if Stalin had not been suspicious of the U.S. and Britain, no matter how benevolent the intentions of their leaders! In any event, although Zimmerman talks in systemic terms, he, like the other critics, ends up by focusing essentially upon American behavior—its alleged misperceptions of the Kremlin and the international Communist movement—and faults it. Interestingly enough, not one word is said that perhaps the U.S. might have learned from its wartime experiences with Moscow and that American policy after 1946–47 might have had some justification because of the failure of Washington's "cybernetic" approach to Russia from 1941 to 1945. After all, if Stalin possessed a siege mentality which attributed hostile intentions to his adversaries, is it really surprising that his prophesies about capitalist behavior became self-fulfilling?

Nevertheless, Zimmerman, in theory at least, does emphasize the great utility of analyzing Soviet and American foreign policies in terms of their interactions with one another. Primitive revisionists, who compose the bulk of the revisionists, pay no attention to the state system at all. This is all the more surprising since Russia, as a long time player

[18] See Chapter 6 of this volume.

[19] J. David Singer, "The Level of Analysis Problem in International Relations," *World Politics* (October, 1961), pp. 80–82, and Kenneth N. Waltz, *Man, the State and War* (New York: Columbia University Press, 1959), p. 159.

of "power politics," was bound to feel fearful in terms of the state system's norms of behavior. If each state were the guardian of its own security in the essentially anarchical international system, each would regard other states as potential adversaries who might threaten its fundamental interests; and, moreover, since conflict was therefore an inherent feature of the system, the end of one war and defeat of one enemy would witness the appearance of another potential opponent. Thus Russia had to assure itself of a strong position for the struggle it could expect after Germany's collapse. Russia had, after all, capitulated to Germany during World War I; more than a century earlier, Napoleon had also invaded Russia and almost won. Stalin was well aware of the state system's rules of behavior and of Russia's historical experience. In 1931, even before the German threat had reappeared, he had urged full speed ahead on Soviet industrialization because "to slacken the pace would mean to lag behind; and those who lag behind are beaten. . . . We are fifty or a hundred years behind the advanced countries. We must make good this lag in ten years. Either we do it or they crush us."[20] Stalin had been right. Hitler almost crushed Soviet Russia, just as World War I had, in fact, helped bring down the Czarist system. And now, as this war was ending, Russia confronted yet another Western power whose population was almost as big as Russia's, whose industrial strength was far greater, and whose enormous military power had, in the closing days of the war, been augmented by the technological discovery of how to split the atom.

Thus, as World War II came to a close and in the months immediately afterward, Russia's actions were largely typical of a great power: the imposition of Russian control on Poland, Hungary, Bulgaria, and Rumania, turning them into satellites (Yugoslavia was already under Tito's control, and Czechoslovakia was living under the Red Army's shadow), and the attempts to dominate Iran—to effect a breakthrough to the Mediterranean by pressuring Turkey, demanding the administration of an Italian colony in North Africa and a share in the control of the Ruhr industry in West Germany while insisting on unilateral control of East Germany. In short, Soviet power had advanced behind the retreating German armies and ended up in the center of Europe.

These were the actions that led to the American containment policy. As weary and destroyed as Russia was by the war, it emerged as the major power on the Eurasian land mass as all the other former major powers in Europe collapsed. Germany was in ruins, France never recovered from its defeat and occupation, and Britain foundered soon

---

[20] Quoted by Isaac Deutscher, *Stalin* (New York: Oxford University Press, 1949), p. 328.

after victory. Nowhere in Europe was there any countervailing power. The only such power existed outside Europe.

The postwar falling-out among the Allies and their ensuing rivalry was almost a replay of the conflict that occurred after the disintegration of the coalition that had defeated Napoleon. At the end of that lengthy war, Czarist Russia, after an exhausting struggle, ended with soldiers in Paris and a close ally in Prussia. The Czar was particularly adamant about retaining control of Poland (its boundaries were quite different from those of contemporary Poland). All entreaties for him to withdraw his troops behind Russia's frontiers were in vain. It was only after Britain, Austria, and a defeated France signed a triple alliance, reputedly ready to go to war if the Czar remained stubborn, that a new balance satisfactory to all the great powers was worked out (including a part of Poland for the Czar) and ratified at the Congress of Vienna in 1815.

In simple terms, the post-1945 conflict substituted Soviet Russia for Czarist Russia and the United States for Britain. The differences in ideology between the two Russias, or the differences in political complexion and economic systems between the two English-speaking nations, were not, in the context of the balance-of-power analysis, the key factors in breaking up the respective wartime alliances against Napoleon and Hitler and aligning the principal powers on opposite sides. The key issue in each case was the postwar distribution of power. In terms of the state system's logic, even had Russia in 1945 been a capitalist state like the United States (or the latter a Communist state like Russia), the bipolar division of power after Germany's defeat would have brought on the Cold War. They became enemies because, as the only two powerful states left, each had the ability to inflict enormous damage on the other. As Paul Seabury has noted, bipolarity was "a contradiction in which two powers—America and Russia—were by historical circumstances thrown into a posture of confrontation which neither had actually 'willed,' yet one from which extrication was difficult."[21] Or, as Louis Halle has pointed out, the historical circumstances of 1945 "had an ineluctable quality that left the Russians little choice but to move as they did. Moving as they did, they compelled the United States and its allies to move in response. And so the Cold War was joined." As Halle suggests, "This is not fundamentally a case of the wicked against the virtuous. Fundamentally . . . we the observers may properly feel sorry for both parties, caught, as they are, in a situation of irreducible dilemma."[22]

21 Seabury, *Rise and Decline of Cold War*, p. 59.
22 Halle, *Cold War as History*, p. XIII.

No wonder primitive revisionists avoid a systemic analysis: They would be less able to freely assign blame, hold the U.S. almost exclusively responsible for the Cold War, and assert that the wartime period should have resulted in an era of good feelings. Implicitly, at least, the revisionists seem to assume that if states—like Stalin's Russia—were interested merely in the protection of their homelands, even if this entailed slight "defensive expansionism," and were—again like Stalin— allegedly willing to recognize other great powers' primacy in their respective spheres of influence, a natural harmony of interests and peace would emerge. In short, fundamentally, primitive revisionism assumes that international rivalry and war are abnormal and avoidable, that war is a "great aberration," that America can avoid involvement in war if *she* has but the will to do so; and if she does become involved it is due to wicked leaders, wicked policies, or a wicked system. These assumptions stand in clear contradiction to those inherent in the state system level of analysis, or indeed to the very nature of modern international relations.

One final note: The presumption of anti-Communism as a principal motive of postwar American foreign policy assumes that the Cold War was somehow not the typical power struggle inherent in an anarchic state system that leaves each state to be its protector and therefore compels it to concern itself with its power status relative to other potentially hostile states. The advocates of this view suggest that but for anti-Communist motivations, there would have been no struggle. Systemically, this suggestion is dubious; what is less dubious is that anti-Communism provided U.S. leaders with a powerful tool for mobilizing public and Congressional support for policies launched for strategic reasons.[23] Ideologically, it justified the use of "power politics" to a nation which has generally condemned the use of power internationally as evil, antithetical to the humane and democratic values for which it proudly proclaims it stands; it also made it easier to arouse a people who had historically been preoccupied domestically and regarded foreign policy as essentially burdensome, costly, and distracting and who were not at all eager for further external involvement after four years of total war.

COMMUNIST POLYCENTRISM AND MAO TSE-TITO

A more recent and sophisticated revisionist critique of American policy during the early Cold War period has centered on the diversity

[23] For Acheson, see Ronald J. Stupak, *The Shaping of Foreign Policy*, (Racine, Wis.: The Odyssey Press, 1969), pp. 47–64; and for Dulles, the persuasive book by Michael Guhin, *John Foster Dulles* (New York: Columbia University Press, 1972), especially pp. 129–58.

which first appeared within the Communist world movement at that time but is said to have gone unrecognized because of American policy makers' image of a monolithic Communist conspiracy controlled and directed from the Kremlin. Had this emerging polycentrism been recognized by Washington, it is contended, American policy presumably could have reinforced this trend, played off one Communist state against another, and avoided the worst days of the Cold War.[24]

Zagoria is more specific. He argues persuasively that if the U.S. had recognized the new Chinese Communist regime, exploited Mao's long-standing suspicions of Stalin, catered to China's national interest and expressions of desire for American support, the Sino-Soviet split would have erupted earlier. Perhaps, in these circumstances, the Chinese intervention in the Korean War might not have occurred, and Washington would not have felt compelled to fight in Vietnam to contain what it perceived to be Chinese expansion via its Hanoi proxy. Instead, U.S. policy forced Peking and Moscow to join hands.

It is probably true that the U.S. underestimated the differences within the Communist movement, but the question remains that had it been more aware of the diversity of views and pursued more differentiated policies toward the various Communist states, would the U.S. have avoided the colder days of the postwar conflicts with Russia and Communist China? Starobin, usually cited to demonstrate the emerging polycentrism after the war, specifically says no; it was precisely this incipient polycentrism which made the Cold War inevitable because for Stalin the conflict was the means of subordinating the international movement to Soviet control![25]

In any event, the indications about the Chinese Communists appeared more ambiguous in the late 1940s than they appear today with the benefit of hindsight. Among the factors supporting the theme of Chinese Communist independence are the following: Mao's claim to ideological pre-eminence, the Asian Marx and Lenin all in one; Mao's organization of the peasantry rather than the proletariat as the basis of his movement; statements by Mao and other Chinese leaders professing friendship for the U.S. and declarations that the U.S. more than any other country could help China in its efforts to modernize; and the reports from Foreign Service officers who felt not only that Mao would defeat Chiang but that the Chinese Communists could be weaned away from the Kremlin to lean in America's direction.

On the other hand, can Mao's professed ideological commitments be dismissed so lightly? Barbara Tuchman, for example, has said that "Be-

[24] See Chapters 6 and 7 by Zimmerman and Zagoria, respectively, in this volume.
[25] Joseph R. Starobin, "Origins of the Cold War," Foreign Affairs (July 1969), pp. 681–96.

fore everything else the Chinese Communists were pragmatists."[26] But does this imply that *all* options, including establishing better relations with the U.S., were open to Mao in 1949, that the ideology was meaningless and served merely to rationalize whatever courses the Chinese leader chose on the basis of some pragmatic criteria completely divorced from any ideological influences? If not, would it not be more persuasive to argue that to the extent ideology provided Mao and his colleagues with a particular perception of the world, defined certain social, economic, and political forces, and prescribed long-range goals, Communist China's hostility to the U.S. in the early days after the success of the revolution was a virtual certainty? Revolutionary leaders, after capturing state power, generally have been very militant. Their long, costly, and painful struggle, a struggle sustained by the myth of the revolution, finally has been rewarded. The vision of the secular New Jerusalem still is very much alive and compelling. It is only later that the responsibilities of power, growth of bureaucracy, and general aging process begin to diminish this vision.

Second, the public record of the Chinese Communist party was one of loyally following Moscow's policy shifts, whether this required a common front with Chiang against the Japanese invaders in the 1930s, blessing the Nazi-Soviet Nonaggression Pact and the Soviet-Japanese Neutrality Pact, or swallowing Stalin's 1945 Treaty of Friendship and Alliance with Chiang, pledging Soviet support for the Nationalist Government. To be sure, this does not necessarily indicate that Mao was Stalin's puppet. Some of Stalin's moves undoubtedly coincided with Mao's own interest—for instance, establishing a common front with Chiang against the Japanese invaders. Others, such as Stalin's treaty with Chiang, clearly did not. As Adam Ulam has noted with regard to the latter, "Had the Chinese Communists been anything but a disciplined party accustomed to accepting Moscow's words as final, they would have cried out in bitterness at this new betrayal."[27] They did not then; nor had they done so earlier. However critical the Chinese may have been, as good Communists, they supported Moscow's decisions. Thus, until almost the moment of final victory, when they ignored Stalin's advice to enter a coalition government with the Nationalists, Mao had given few signs of independence.

Contemporary critics, in brief, may be underestimating not only the degree of Moscow's control but, more importantly, the scope of *common interests* shared by Russia and the Chinese Communists *at that time*. Was

[26] Barbara W. Tuchman, "If Mao Had Come to Washington: An Essay in Alternatives," *Foreign Affairs* (October, 1972), p. 50. Also see John Gillings, "A Shameful Tale," *The New York Review of Books*, November 16, 1972, pp. 7–12 for a similar point of view but with a revisionist twist.

[27] Adam B. Ulam, *Expansion and Coexistence* (New York: Praeger Publishers, 1968), p. 476.

not Mao's final success assisted immeasurably by the Soviet provision of arms taken from the Japanese, by Soviet refusal to permit Nationalist troops to land in Manchuria, and also by the Red Army's delayed withdrawal from Manchuria until the Chinese Communist army had gained a sufficient grip on this key area where Chiang's army received its first major defeats, defeats from which it never recovered? Would Mao not also have known that he would still be dependent upon Stalin for economic aid, military assistance and protection and diplomatic support after he had established his government? Perhaps the U.S. could have supplied these elements, but quite apart from its willingness to do so, was Mao really ready to turn to the U.S? Given Mao's ideological commitments, his perception of the world divided into two camps, and his condemnation of those who expected to remain independent in the struggle between these two camps, perhaps it was first necessary for the Chinese leader to discover that ideological ties did not prevent his principal fraternal ally from becoming his principal enemy. The need thereafter not to confront the U.S. and USSR simultaneously and to use the former against the latter may have been as much a prerequisite for Mao to become less "ideological" and more "pragmatic" in foreign policy as the growth of Soviet power since the late 1960s seems to have been the prerequisite for Washington's "pragmatic" turn to Peking.

Lastly, even if the arguments about ideology and the public loyalty of Mao to Stalin should be found wanting by some critics, there is yet one other powerful consideration: the need for the new regime which had not yet consolidated or legitimated its power to have a foreign enemy. The belief in a hostile capitalist world was surely helpful for a new and still somewhat-insecure regime seeking a monopoly of political power and demanding sacrifices from its people for "building socialism." The U.S. obviously was a better candidate for this external enemy than was the Soviet Union. The fact that a number of Foreign Service Officers believed that Communist China would pursue a national and independent foreign policy and seek a closer American relationship was, among other factors, due to a denigration of the role of ideology (Vincent, for example, had read neither *The Communist Manifesto, State and Revolution,* nor any works by Mao!), a consequent belief that the Chinese Communists were a Chinese version of a European Democratic Socialist Party, and a confusion between popular support for Mao and the democratic character of Chinese Communism (ignoring the elitist and disciplined nature of the Party seeking to exploit popular dissatisfaction.)[28] Deeply and personally committed to the welfare of the Chinese people, completely alienated from the corrupt and inef-

[28] Tang Tsou, *America's Failure in China: 1941–50* (Chicago: The University of Chicago Press, 1963), pp. 202–36; Herbert Feis, *The China Tangle* (Princeton, N.J.: Princeton University Press, 1953), pp. 260–64.

ficient Nationalist government whose weaknesses they analyzed accurately, these diplomats wanted to believe the best of the Communists
—that they would provide the Chinese people with a government that
cared for them while maintaining the traditional friendly Sino-American
ties.

Interestingly enough, Zagoria was not always so convinced of the
relative lack of ideological influence on the Chinese Communist outlook and policies as he is now; nor was he once so certain that the
Sino-Soviet split could have been achieved earlier, that it would become
so deep that the chasm would be virtually unbridgeable, and that
Washington could—and should—have exploited this conflict among
the two large Communist parties for its own advantage all along, even
before the official establishment of the Chinese People's Republic.
Carefully separating himself from the school of thinkers who held that
a break between Russia and China was inevitable, Zagoria used to stress
that "while there are serious differences of interest and outlook between Russia and China, the overriding common aims of both, their
joint commitment to an international revolutionary process which they
believe is historically inevitable and which they believe it is their duty
to aid, their shared determination to establish Communism throughout
the world, sets limits on conflict between the two."[29] Emphasizing that
"one cannot stress too much that the partners to the Sino-Soviet alliance
are dedicated to a common purpose and bound together by a common
ideology,"[30] Zagoria specifically rejected the term "national interests"
in an analysis of the relationship between Moscow and Peking; he
preferred the term "revolutionary interests" because the former "fails to
take account of the urge to expedite the revolutionary process so central to both Russian and Chinese actions. While the pursuit of this goal
is influenced by national viewpoints, the goal of international revolution itself goes beyond such traditional goals of nation states as security and survival."[31] Sino-Soviet differences were primarily differences
of priority and timing, for the two powers "have much more in common
with each other than with the Western world. . . ."[32] Of course, this was
written in the early 1960s, and the fashionable intellectual currents
have changed since that time.

In view of the ambiguity of evidence about the Chinese Communists,
it is perhaps all the more surprising that American policy-makers *did*
attempt to exploit potential Chinese-Russian differences and were *not*

[29] Donald S. Zagoria, *The Sino-Soviet Conflict, 1956–1961* (Princeton, N.J.: Princeton University Press, 1962), p. 4.
    [30] Ibid., p. 8.
    [31] Ibid., p. 19.
    [32] Ibid., p. 22.

blind to possible polycentric tendencies within the Communist world. It was Secretary Acheson's belief that the two Communist regimes would eventually clash, notwithstanding common ideological worldviews. Acheson predicted that Russia's appetite for a sphere of influence in Manchuria and northern China would alienate Chinese nationalism. The implications of this point of view are clear: If the Chinese Communists were genuinely concerned with the preservation of China's national interest, they would resist Soviet penetration; Mao Tse-tung might, therefore, be a potential Tito. On the other hand, if Mao proved himself to be subservient to Russia, he would lose the support of the Chinese people. Since he would have shown that he served not the interests of China but those of another power, his regime would be identified with foreign rule. Given time, Acheson declared, the Chinese people would throw off this "foreign yoke."[33] Thus, whichever of these two developments occurred, the United States could only gain from the antithesis between Communism and Chinese nationalism.

This analysis of Sino-Soviet relations indicated that the United States must first disentangle itself from Chiang Kai-shek. Until this disassociation had been completed, the United States would remain identified with the government rejected by the Chinese people. This could only foster the growth of anti-American sentiment in China. It was precisely this that had to be avoided, for the attention of the Chinese people should not be diverted from the Soviet Union's actions. Under no circumstances, Acheson emphasized, must we "deflect from the Russians to ourselves the righteous anger, and the wrath, and the hatred of the Chinese people which must develop."[34] Only by disengaging ourselves from Chiang Kai-shek could the United States exploit the alleged clash of interests between China and Russia.

The first step taken by the Administration to implement this policy was the release of a White Paper which argued that the Nationalists had lost control of the mainland despite adequate American economic and military aid. The clear implication was that Chiang was no longer worthy of American support; hence, American recognition of Chiang's government as the official government of China should be withdrawn. Conversely, it was suggested that the Communists should be recognized as the official government of China, both as a matter of fact and as a gesture of friendship. A second act was an announcement that American forces would not be used to defend Formosa, and that the Administration would no longer provide the Nationalists with military aid or

[33] State Department, *United States Relations with China, 1944–1949* (Washington, D.C.: Government Printing Office, 1949), pp. xvi–xvii.

[34] Dean Acheson, "Crisis in Asia—An Examination of U.S. Policy," *State Department Bulletin,* January 23, 1950, pp. 113–14.

advice: "The United States Government will not pursue a course which will lead to involvement in the civil conflict in China."[35] This opened the way for the Chinese Communists to take Formosa—an event which was expected before the end of 1950. The Communist Government would then be the only claimant to represent China, and the United States could extend it recognition (the Republic no longer being in a position to demand support for a non-existent Nationalist regime). Chiang, through whom containment had been impossible because he had been not a container but a sieve, would have been eliminated; containment of Russia could then be implemented through "Mao Tse-tito."

Significantly, before events could show whether Mao would indeed follow such an independent course of policy, war had broken out in Korea, and American-Chinese relations had passed a point of no return for the next two decades. In that period—until in the late 1960s the threat of Russian power began to move the U.S. and China toward one another again—Washington's share of responsibility for the lamentable state of Sino-American relations cannot be denied. The virulent nature of American domestic politics, the viciousness of McCarthyism, the inflexibility of the Eisenhower era, the lack of courage of the Kennedy and Johnson administrations to make even the slightest moves toward a possible détente with Peking, played their role; if the new Chinese regime needed an "imperialist" enemy, the U.S. seemed willing to please. But this does not mean that the Chinese Communist regime can be absolved from responsibility for its poor relations with the U.S. For a new nation allegedly anxious for good relations with this country, the seizure of American consular personnel and property in violation of diplomatic practice was hardly calculated to bring about this objective; and the frequent anti-American campaigns did much to convince Washington of the correctness of its perception of Communist China's hostility. Peking was, after all, hardly blameless in alienating Washington and Moscow simultaneously; it takes effort to manage to make enemies of the two greatest powers on earth.

WHY DIDN'T STALIN HAVE THE FORESIGHT?

The criticisms of American foreign policy we have reviewed up to this point all share one characteristic: a double standard of judgment. While pointing to American misperceptions, overreactions, lack of foresight and wisdom, it makes no similar criticisms or demands of Stalin or Mao. After all, was the Soviet leader not perhaps guilty of the same type of mistakes attributed to Roosevelt and Truman? The

---

[35] Ibid., January 16, 1950, p. 79.

latter were expected to place themselves in Stalin's position in order to give them a better insight into Russia's needs and wants, and thus formulate American policies so that they would meet both Russian and American interests while simultaneously creating a more solid basis for postwar cooperation. Why could Stalin not have placed himself in the American President's place?

Of all the revisionist charges the delay of the Second Front as a major factor in arousing Stalin's suspicions has perhaps the most substance. When the front was postponed from 1942 to 1943 to 1944, Stalin, Russia's dictator, became very bitter. He brusquely rejected Allied explanations that sufficient invasion barges for such an enormous undertaking were not available; and he especially denounced Prime Minister Churchill for declaring that there would be no invasion until the Germans were so weakened that Allied forces would not have to suffer forbiddingly high losses. To Stalin, this was no explanation, for the Russians accepted huge losses of men as a matter of course. It was no wonder, then, that the Russians should dismiss these Allied explanations. But if Roosevelt was expected to overcome Stalin's apprehensions about the capitalist powers' intentions, is it too much to expect the Soviet leader to understand the American and British leaders' hesitations about the possible failure and enormous loss of life that might be suffered if the largest sea invasion ever attempted in history were launched prematurely?

Or, take the accusation that the United States sought to push the Soviets out of Eastern Europe. For Stalin, the area was obviously Russia's security belt. Roosevelt understood this and wanted Russia to have "friendly neighbors." He also understood that there was little that the U.S. could do to prevent the establishment of a dominant Soviet position, in any case; the Red army would decide the matter. (The alleged American purpose of rolling back Soviet power was no more true in 1944–45 than it was in 1953, 1956, or 1968 when the USSR could deter U.S. intervention and the latter had already long acquiesed in and accepted Soviet domination.)

The crux of the problem for the President was the way the U.S. legitimated its conduct of war in terms of democratic purposes. American power had to be "righteous" power. This meant painting those who fight on our side in democratic colors, punishing our enemies completely, and ensuring that our purposes—articulated during World War II in the Atlantic Charter and Four Freedoms—would not be sullied. Hence a Darlan deal created an outrage; Churchill's suppression of the Greek Communists and support for the "reactionary" monarchical government was widely denounced. Not surprisingly, if lapses of democratic principles were quickly condemned, Roosevelt was in a dilemma in Eastern Europe, for how could he concede the area to Stalin without violating the principle of national self-determination? In the specific case of Poland, such a lapse might endanger the Democratic Polish-American vote, the consensus the President needed for the conduct of the war, and Senate support for the United Nations, which for Roosevelt was the linchpin of future peace. "Any indications that the big powers were preparing to divide Europe up into spheres of influence might be as damaging to the United Nations as the Allies' World War I secret agreements had been to the League of Nations."[36]

What Roosevelt expected—as he would have with domestic adversaries[37]—was that "as one politician to one another," Stalin would understand his problem and thus "go easy" in exercising his control. The Yalta Declaration on Liberated Europe was Roosevelt's attempt to reconcile the unreconcilable: Stalin's domination of Eastern Europe with the American penchant to be fighting the good fight on behalf of the noble principles of the Atlantic Charter. But such hypocrisy—to expect free elections to be reconciled with Soviet domination—could hardly survive public scrutiny, particularly given Stalin's brutal methods of establishing Soviet domination. The irony of the whole situation was that Stalin could have had his security belt had he only shown more sensitivity towards Western public opinion. For in America and Britain, there existed a great amount of good will toward the Soviet Union at the end of the war. Had the Soviet Union left Poland, Hungary, Rumania, and Bulgaria internally autonomous while securing control of their foreign policies, as it did in postwar Czechoslovakia, it could have avoided arousing and alienating America and Britain. The Western states believed that coalition governments that included Communists could be friendly to the Russians *and* to the West. Eduard Beneš in Czechoslovakia seemed a symbol of this model for Eastern Europe—until the Russians later overthrew his coalition government.

Why did the Soviets behave in this manner? One major reason would seem to have been the ideologically induced expectation that the immediate postwar period would be one of social and political upheaval and, therefore, would be an opportune time for the extension of Soviet power. It was anticipated that the United States would suffer another depression once war production ceased and, as a result, it would withdraw once more into its traditional isolationist posture. During the war, Roosevelt had in fact told Stalin that American troops would be withdrawn from Europe within two years of Germany's surrender. At the

---

36 Gaddis, *U.S. and Origins of Cold War*, pp. 149–50. Chapter 5 presents an excellent analysis of FDR's dilemma on Eastern Europe and especially Poland.

37 Gaddis Smith, *American Diplomacy During the Second World War, 1941–1945* (New York: John Wiley and Sons, 1965), p. 9.

same time, Russia knew that the instability of Europe once Germany was defeated would not last forever, and that Western capitalism would eventually recover. Thus the opportunity brought on by the fluidity of the immediate postwar situation had to be seized.[38] Stalin was unable to overcome his own ideological background. If American policy makers are said to have wrongly identified Stalin with Hitler and mistaken Russia's limited and legitimate aims for world revolution, it was in good part Stalin's fault—at least if we used the revisionists' standard of judgment.

To admit Soviet or Chinese errors would, of course, nullify or emasculate the revisionist thesis that the U.S. is primarily to blame for the Cold War. Occasionally such an admission does surface, such as Zagoria's comment that "the Chinese Communists have to bear some portion of the blame for their unhappy relations with the United States during the past decades. More specifically, they could have adopted a more conciliatory approach to the United States in the crucial year of 1949 and strengthened those forces within the American government who were in fact arguing for their recognition."[39] But such brief comments, almost hidden in the midst of lengthy analyses largely blaming Washington, provide little balance.

POWER VERSUS MORALITY

The revisionist onslaught on the containment policy has recently been strengthened by some prominent liberal critics who now look back in despair and anguish, confessing to the error of their former ways, with regard both to Vietnam and to the earlier Cold War, which they once fervently supported. Their revulsion against containment-through-power and their repentance for having supported this policy in the past demonstrates that they share many of the revisionists' views about the conduct of international politics and that they, too, tend to look back at American foreign policy primarily—if not exclusively—through the prism of Vietnam.

We have already noted the American penchant for moralizing power, domestically and internationally, in terms of democratic purposes. The bipolar nature of the Cold War lent itself particularly well to this penchant, for the distribution of power made it easy to practice *Realpolitik* and disguise the struggle for power and security endemic in the state

[38] Paul E. Zinner, "The Ideological Bases of Soviet Foreign Policy," *World Politics* (July 1952): 497–98.

[39] Donald S. Zagoria, "Containment, China, and America," p. 3, paper presented at the National Convention of the American Political Science Association on September 5, 1972, in Washington, D.C. A revised version of this paper appears as Chapter 7 of this volume.

system as ideological politics, a struggle for the realization of democratic values. But Vietnam, not surprisingly, witnessed the reassertion of this deep-seated attitude toward the international exercise of power as immoral and corrupting. Once power politics no longer could be moralized in the context of the democracy-dictatorship dichotomy, the sense of guilt awakened by its employment returned.[40] Vietnam seemed to prove again that in the use of power the nation had forsaken its moral traditions and violated its own democratic and liberal professions. Not surprisingly, sensitive men deeply committed to humane values—and daily watching the employment of power in the form of violence in history's first televised war—repented their former support of containment as if in their former support they had acted as unknowing sinners. Thus Senator Fulbright, who had been a leading advocate of postwar foreign policy while it could be disguised as a moral conflict, now attacked America's global role as evidence of an "arrogance of power." He did not merely assert that the United States had overextended itself and that our commitments needed to be cut down to our capacities, nor did he say that Vietnam had been an unwise commitment and that the basic policy of containment had been a correct one. He stated something far more fundamental: that it is the exercise of power per se which had made the U.S. arrogant. Power itself is a corrupting factor; even if justified in moral terms, its use is immoral.[41]

Vietnam, in brief, and even the origins of the Cold War, were not perceived as the result of mistakes in judgment but products of sin! In this respect, Fulbright's criticism of American foreign policy was quite characteristic of many critics: when things seem to go wrong, ask not what errors might have occurred but seek out who is guilty. Whereas previous analyses and so-called orthodox interpretations held the Soviet Union to be largely responsible for the Cold War, the new critics select the United States as the sinner; the villain is no longer regarded as the Kremlin but the American Establishment (in the guise of the "national security managers" in the State and Defense Departments and C.I.A. and/or corporate capitalism, popularly known as the military-industrial complex). After all, the critics cannot do much to change the adversary's behavior; they can, however, by assuming that U.S. behavior is primarily responsible for the conflict, hope to change that behavior and expect to end the conflict.

If power is evil and its exercise is tantamount to abuse, abstention

[40] See Senator Fulbright's savage attack on power politics as "an endless, mindless, purposeless struggle for power" which is dangerously obsolete because of "its utter irrelevance to valid human needs" in J. William Fulbright, The Crippled Giant (New York: Vintage Books, 1972), pp. 7–9.

[41] J. William Fulbright, The Arrogance of Power (New York: Vintage Books, 1967), pp. 3–22.

from power politics and providing an example to the world of a truly just and democratic society is the obvious prescription and the moral thing to do. Or, as Fulbright has said in his own words, "the nation performs its essential function not in its capacity as a *power,* but in its capacity as a *society.*"[42] His principal foreign policy recommendation therefore is "to serve as an example of democracy to the world by the way we run our own society." Ronald Steel has said it even more eloquently:

> It is now time for us to turn away from global fantasies and begin our perfection of the human race within our own frontiers. There is a great deal to do at home within a society which a century after the liberation of the slaves still has not been able to grant the Negro full equality, a society which has been plagued with violence in the streets and guilt in the heart, which has achieved unprecedented material riches and yet is sick from a debilitating alienation, where the ideals of American democracy are mocked by the reality of racial prejudice, where individual decency is in constant conflict with social irresponsibility, where prosperity has assured neither justice nor tolerance, where private affluence dramatizes the shame of public squalor, where wealth has brought psychoanalysis, and where power has bred anxiety and fear. This is a society whose extraordinary achievements are now being overshadowed by the urgency of its unfulfilled promises and by dangerous strains in its social fabric.
>
> America's worth to the world will be measured not by the solutions she seeks to impose on others, but by the degree to which she achieves her own ideals at home. That is a fitting measure, and an arduous test, of America's greatness.[43]

In short, foreign policy is domestic policy.

One may, of course, ask whether social reform at home as a substitute for a strong defense is a feasible policy. This is not to say that enhancing national prosperity and increasing social justice is not important in its own right; it is only a question of whether or not one can be substituted for the other. The critics' response is that the struggle in the world has not been primarily military. They claim that it was not so at the end of World War II, when Russia was too weak to have been a military threat to Western Europe and was motivated mainly by "morbid fears" for her security; nor are the threats of Russia and China

---

[42] Fulbright, *The Arrogance of Power,* p. 256 (The italics are Fulbright's). In this connection, see also the Senator's distinction between the America of Lincoln and Adlai Stevenson —"generous and humane"—and the America of Teddy Roosevelt, of power and superpatriots (pp. 245–47).

[43] Ronald Steel, *Pax Americana* (New York: The Viking Press, 1967), pp. 353–54.

fundamentally military today. The conflict, they say, has been nothing more than an ideological struggle to see whether Russian Communism —and after 1949, Chinese Communism as well—or American-style democracy would win the "hearts and minds of the world's people." Accordingly, arms build-ups and tough anti-Communist policies are to be condemned as weapons which presumably cannot stop communism as an idea and social message. Instead, since communism is portrayed as a product of hunger, disease, and social injustice, only social action, vigorously pursued, could "win" such a struggle. Thus granting priority to domestic policy is—amazingly!—consistent with the needs of foreign policy. It follows that America can "come home," win the international ideological struggle, and be true to itself. Virtue, not power, becomes the key to foreign policy. *America's influence should come from its moral strength as a good and just society. Arms, alliances, and spheres of influence are not the answer; a redistribution of income, racial justice, environmental concern—all worthy ends in themselves—are advocated as the nation's most effective instruments of foreign policy.* The recommendation for a significant budgetary shift from the armed services to the social services follows logically.

Although this policy calls for a return of American policy to the traditional purpose of serving as a beacon of a morally superior society, which we considered ourselves to be at the time of our birth, Fulbright disclaims the isolationist label. Intellectually, a liberal critic like Fulbright —or his conservative colleague, Taft,[44] twenty years earlier—knows that the U.S. is involved in world affairs and cannot isolate herself politically and militarily as she did before World War II or, better yet, before World War I. But *emotionally,* the isolationist urge still holds an attraction. The gap between Fulbright's intellectual realization and *nostalgia* for a previous era is spanned by an internationalism which he defines as the "classical internationalism" of Woodrow Wilson and Franklin Roosevelt:

> We believe in international cooperation through international institutions. We would like to try to keep the peace through the United Nations, and we would like to try to assist the poor countries through institutions like the World Bank. We do not think the United Nations is a failure; we think it has never been tried.[45]

Thus, just as he juxtaposes domestic reform with power, so the Senator also juxtaposes the "practical idealism" of the U.N. Charter to the "old balance-of-power system," which he calls a "discredited failure"

---

[44] Robert A. Taft, *A Foreign Policy for Americans* (New York: Doubleday and Company, 1951).

[45] Fulbright in Chapter 5 of this volume, pp. 79–80.

for having twice this century erupted into world wars plus a cold war. Given the danger of not surviving another hot war, "it is myopic to dismiss the idea of an effective world peace-keeping organization as a visionary ideal—or as anything, indeed, but an immediate, practical necessity."[46] Sounding like Cordell Hull, the Senator castigates the Truman Administration for its "unrealistic 'realism' " and its "conversion from Wilson to Machiavelli," asserting that the U.N. has not worked because its members have not wanted it to work. To make it work, he says, they merely require the desire. They need only to stop using the international organization as an instrument of national policy, to subordinate short-term nationalistic advantages to the long-run advantages of humanity and all nations, and to treat the U.N. "as a potential world-security community."[47] And that is the heart of the matter for the Senator and many of the non-Marxist critics, as it was for President Roosevelt during World War II. The U.N. represents more than an organization of nations to abolish war; rather, it is the embodiment of a new spirit of internationalism which hopefully will erode nationalism and replace it with international harmony. In brief, devotion to the U.N. constitutes a rejection of the assertion of national egotism and an act of atonement for the sin of employing power politics—in this instance, for having ravaged Indochina and earlier having provoked Soviet Russia. In the final analysis, therefore, revisionism and criticism of Vietnam telescope and take us back to fundamentals: a re-examination of the philosophical assumptions and orientations underlying different ways of analyzing and understanding the relations of nations.

REVISIONISM REVISITED

The appeal of revisionism in a period of weariness and disillusionment—after two decades of extensive global involvement, unprecedented effort and sacrifice and weathering of constant crises, climaxed by a costly and divisive war—is understandable. The danger of revisionism, especially the more common primitive version, however, is that its themes may become part of the new conventional wisdom. To be more brutal about it: contemporary revisionism—most especially primitive revisionism—has pretensions of being the new Versailles guilt literature. An age that tends to debunk the 1930s and casts doubts upon the validity of the immediate post-1945 analogy of Stalin's Russia to Hitler's Germany has forgotten that the revisionism of the interwar years set the intellectual and moral tone which Hitler so successfully exploited from 1933–39: that Germany had actually not been primarily

[46] Ibid., p. 81.
[47] Ibid., p. 80.

responsible for World War I; that the Versailles peace treaty had been punitive and unfair; that Germany's claims against France and England were therefore legitimate grievances and Hitler the legitimate—although rather vulgar—spokesman for these grievances; that the Western democracies, having wronged Germany, had no moral right to oppose Germany's claims, which were advanced in the name of national self-determination. The result was Western guilt and paralysis; Germany was perceived not as an adversary but as a victim.

The new Versailles literature too points its fingers at the U.S., not the Soviet Union or Communist China, as the party primarily, if not exclusively, responsible for the Cold War. If only American leaders had not misperceived the Soviet Union as a threat, had been willing to recognize her limited and legitimate ambitions in Eastern Europe, had not tried to push her out of this area—with or without nuclear threats —there would have been no Cold War. Perhaps instead of writing his "X" article, George Kennan could have written then what he has more recently written of the present post-Cold War era: that the U.S. had little more to fear from Russia now than it did in 1910.[48] And if the U.S. had only been willing to give the Chinese Communists the even break that the latter were purportedly willing to give us, the Sino-American conflict need not have erupted either; or, according to the more sophisticated revisionists, Washington could have used the Chinese Communists against Russia, if a limited conflict with that country was not avoidable. *Thus have Russia and Communist China become transformed into the victims of American policy and the Cold War turned into a fairy tale.*

At the heart of this revisionist tale, then, lies a curiously inverted logic: American policies are presented as essentially provocative—whether or not they were intended to be—while the behavior of America's adversaries is seen as an expression of their legitimate national interests. *We* are the guilty party; the obvious prescription is the abdication of America's role in the world as "global policeman." "Come home, America," is surely advisable if America is such a blunderer or aggressor. In short, behind most revisionists stands the ghost of isolationism—old or new.[49] But while revisionism, as an after-the-events interpretation, finds it easy to stress the hostile intentions and blunders that purportedly provoked the conflict, is its claim to trace accurately the consequences of alternative policies which never occurred intellectually warranted? Its assertion that the world—and certainly the U.S. —would have been better off and happier had this country acted in

[48] See Kennan, Chapter 3 of this volume.

[49] For an interestingly argued case for the validity of a new isolationist stance for the U.S., see Robert W. Tucker, *A New Isolationism* (New York: Universe Books, 1972).

other ways can hardly be done with any mathematical precision; history cannot, like a clock, be set back and replayed with policies quite different to those actually pursued, thus producing different outcomes. This kind of historical recreation rests upon assumptions which, by the very nature of this kind of logic, cannot be proven. Written at a time when earlier passions are forgotten, when it is all too easy to argue that a little more wisdom and tolerance and restraint could have avoided conflict—at least total conflict—this recreation simply brushes aside the assumptions underlying yesterday's policies as if they had little or no basis in reality, as if they all were products of the imagination of either hostile or well-intentioned leaders who misunderstood and misperceived the world around them. It is over this issue, as well as the future role of the U.S. in the world, that the revisionists and their critics long will continue their debate.

PART THREE

THE DYNAMICS OF THE COLD WAR ERA

9

THE COMPETITIVE RELATIONSHIP

The dates May 22, 1947, and May 22, 1972, span exactly twenty-five years. On May 22, 1947, President Truman signed a Congressional bill committing the United States to support Greece and Turkey against Soviet designs, and the U.S. thereby assumed overtly the direct leadership of the West in containing Soviet influence. The Truman doctrine committed the U.S., in President Truman's own words, "to support free peoples who are resisting attempted subjugation by armed minorities or by outside pressures." Twenty-five years later to the day another U.S. President landed in Moscow, declaring to the Soviet leaders that "we meet at a moment when we can make peaceful cooperation a reality." The agreement signed at the conclusion of President Nixon's visit to Moscow did, indeed, reflect the appearance of a more mixed U.S.-Soviet relationship in which new cooperative links began somewhat to offset the competitive character of the relationship between the two powers.

Viewing the last twenty-five years of the Cold War as a political process, this study seeks to evaluate the conduct of the two competitors

Copyright © 1974 by Zbigniew Brzezinski. A condensed version of this study appeared under the title, "How the Cold War Was Played," in *Foreign Affairs*, October, 1972. The author wishes to acknowledge the support provided by the Research Institute on Communist Affairs of Columbia University and his obligation to Miss Toby Trister, his assistant, for her help in research and for the preparation of the appendix.

and to draw some implications from the preceding for the future of U.S.-Soviet relations. Its purpose is thus neither to seek the causes of the Cold War, nor to assign moral or historical responsibility for it.[1]

To accomplish the above, two steps must be taken. The first is to identify the principal phases of the Cold War, viewing it as a process of conflict-competition. The purpose of the periodization is to delineate phases of time in which the competitive process was dominated by a discernible pattern of relations; in its simplest form, this involves identifying phases in which one or the other side seemed to hold the political initiative, either on the basis of a relatively crystallized strategy and/or through more assertive behavior. In the study which follows, six phases are identified (see Appendix B). Given the particular focus of the study, they rather differ from those found in the available histories of the Cold War.[2]

Secondly, it is necessary to focus on several dynamic components at work in the competitive process, the interaction of which shaped the relative performance of the two powers. To reduce this task to manageable proportions, reference will be made within the several phases of the competition to the relative international standing of the two rivals, to their relative economic power, to their relative military power, and to the relative clarity and purposefulness of national policy, including the degree of domestic support for that policy. Obviously, not only for reasons of space but also because of the very nature of the topics, some of the assessments made will be quite arbitrary.[3]

---

[1] See Appendix A for a critical review of texts relevant to the origins of the Cold War.

[2] In fact, most studies of the Cold War are structured around key seminal events with reference to particular confrontations. See, for example, Herbert Feis, *From Trust to Terror: The Onset of the Cold War, 1945–1960* (New York: W. W. Norton, 1970), which concerns specific conflicts and clashes between the two powers essentially chronologically and geographically defined. Adam Ulam in *Expansion and Coexistence* (New York: Praeger, 1968) talks primarily about very broad patterns in the relationship, such as "the end of an era," "changing directions—1950–1956," and so forth. In his book dealing specifically with American-Soviet competition, *The Rivals* (New York: Viking Press, 1971), Ulam talks about three broad phases: "The Era of American Omnipotence," "New Worlds Emerging," and "Lost Opportunities." Andre Fontaine in *History of the Cold War* (New York: Pantheon Books, 1968) speaks broadly of "The Duel" during the years 1945–1950, within which he examines specific confrontations, and then of "From the Korean War to the Present," which is strictly chronological. I have not come across in the literature any periodization based on predominant patterns in the competitive relationship, as is attempted in what follows.

[3] Of the above four components, two can be treated with a certain degree of precision. Even though data on economic and military power of the two major powers is not precise, there is sufficient information to permit broad, but reasonably accurate, comparisons at the various stages of the Cold War. The issue is more complex with regard to international standing and national policy. International standing cannot be defined precisely, but as used here it is meant to capsulate the overall degree of influence that either power could exercise on the international community and extract from that community needed political support. U.N. votes at critical juncture points may be one useful measure, but it will also be occasionally necessary to make some impressionistic judgments concerning the overall

Finally, it must be acknowledged that this study sees the Cold War as more the product of lengthy and probably ineluctable historical forces and less as the result of human error and evil, though doubtless at any given juncture both error and evil were present and contributed to the shaping of the process. Nonetheless, two great powers, differentiated by divergent centuries-long experience and separated by sharply differing ideological perspectives, yet thrust into political proximity as a consequence of the shattering of the earlier international system, could hardly avoid being plunged into a competitive relationship. In brief, this is less a matter of Stalin or of Dulles and more of de Tocqueville.

PHASE I: SHAPING OF THE CONFRONTATION, 1945–47

This phase was essentially a preliminary one. Neither the U.S. nor the USSR were directly pitted against each other at this time. The U.S. was still inclined, at least on European matters, to defer to the British, although pursuing a unilateral policy in the Far East; the Soviet Union saw as its principal interlocutor the Anglo-Saxons rather than the USA, pure and simple. Within both societies, active debates concerning the likely nature of postwar developments were yielding conflicting estimates and advice: in the U.S. the issue came out into the open with the Truman-Wallace split; in the Soviet Union there were overtones of it in Zhdanov's more militant posture, while the Varga debate (about the postwar prospects of capitalism)—though more muted than the corresponding discussions in the U.S.—indicated analytical disagreements concerning the future of the capitalist system.

The key signals for the respective sides, helping each to reinforce its maturing interpretation of the other as implacably hostile, were provided by two significant speeches: Stalin's "electoral speech" of February, 1946, and Churchill's address at Fulton, Missouri, in March of the same year. Each side could easily find in the respective address a conceptual confirmation for a pattern of behavior increasingly viewed as inimical to the other. To the Americans, Stalin's address, resurrecting the notion of international class warfare, fitted the arbitrary behavior of the Soviet Union in Eastern Europe, and seemed ominously portentous to the unsettled conditions of Greece and Western Europe. To the Soviets, Churchill's speech, calling in effect for an Anglo-Amer-

---

political climate towards the two major powers. National policy, finally, can be judged by the extent that it appeared to be reasonably coherent or fragmented, confident or cautious, purposeful or drifting, expansive or defensive, and—quite important—commanding or lacking domestic popular support.

ican alliance, revived old notions of capitalist encirclement and seemed to fit established presumptions concerning capitalist hostility.

Neither side was operating yet on the basis of clear-cut policies, backed by firm domestic support. Internal U.S. divisions continued into the Presidential campaign of 1948, and it was only in 1947–48 that a more crystallized American view emerged, backed by bipartisan support. George Kennan's famous article in *Foreign Affairs* (July 1947) —reprinted as Chapter 2 of this volume—represented in that respect a historic watershed. On the Soviet side, while the assumption of Western hostility was deeply ingrained in the official ideology, widespread popular disaffection, economic dislocations, and the gradual re-imposition of Stalinist controls after relative wartime relaxation, all reflected a very basic domestic weakness of the system as a whole, sharpening for Stalin the dilemmas of moderation or militancy (with the latter apparently advocated not only by Zhdanov but in very early postwar phases also by Tito and his associates in Yugoslavia and Bulgaria).

The international context in which the emerging hostility was crystallizing was clearly to U.S. advantage. While the Soviet Union emerged from the war with vastly enhanced prestige, with much accumulated good will even within the United States, and with highly subservient and influential Communist parties playing key roles in such countries as France and Italy, the Soviet position in the world was still very inferior to that of the United States. The Western hemisphere was firmly in the American grip; Africa and the Middle East were politically controlled by America's allies (with American economic assets expanding particularly rapidly in the Middle East); the Southern Asia arc was still part of the British Empire, while Iran already in 1946 was seeking U.S. political assistance against the Soviet Union; Nationalist China was striving to consolidate its authority, and Japan was subject to an exclusive U.S. occupation.

In terms of international influence, the U.S. could count on the overwhelming support of members of the newly constituted U.N. Perhaps the first critical issue confronting the international community— one that represented an important test case—involved the resolution introduced by the United States on the threat to the political independence and territorial integrity of Greece. Voted on October 21, 1947, the U.S. was backed by forty members; eleven abstained; and six voted against. Of the six negative votes, three were cast by the Soviet Union (including the Ukraine and Byelorussia); and it was supported by the Communist governments of Poland, Czechoslovakia, and Yugoslavia. More interesting were the neutrals who abstained: several Arab countries, India and Afghanistan, three Scandinavian countries (two of which, Norway and Denmark, were subsequently to become members of NATO), and Guatemala. The vote was thus symbolic of U.S. global pre-eminence, but it also pointed broadly to areas where in the years ahead U.S. influence was to recede.

Economically and militarily, the relationship also favored the United States, though the military aspect was clouded by some uncertainties. The U.S. emerged from the war with its gross national product (GNP) actually increased, and in the years 1945–47 it ranged somewhere around $300 billion (in 1966 dollars).[4] The Soviet Union, on the other hand, had suffered grievously during the war and by 1947 its GNP was probably less than one-third that of the United States (roughly equal to that of contemporary India or China). Economic conditions in the Soviet Union verged on poverty, with starvation even occurring in some places.[5] While the United States was in a position to extend economic assistance to its allies, the Soviet Union was taking recourse to an extensive program of stripping, dismantling and seizing the industrial assets of the Central European and Manchurian areas under its control.

The military picture was not as clear cut. Neither side could afford to maintain the enormous forces that were at their disposal at the conclusion of the war. American armed forces, which at their peak numbered some 12.3 million men, were rapidly demobilized, because of domestic political pressures and economic need. By 1947 American ground forces had shrunk to about only 670,000 men, organized into thirteen not fully staffed divisions. At their peak, Soviet armed forces numbered about 11.3 million men. Contrary to postwar myths, the Soviet Union did not refrain from large-scale demobilization. A demobilization of the Soviet army was an economic necessity, given wartime devastation and enormous manpower losses. Accordingly, a significant reduction did take place, and by 1947 the Soviet Union had only approximately 2.8 million men under arms.[6]

For political reasons, the Soviet government chose to keep its demobilization a secret; in fact, Soviet political interests were served by the widely accepted postwar view that Stalin kept his armed forces essentially undiminished. As a result, contemporary Western estimates of Soviet military strength were considerably higher than reality, and

[4] U.S. Congress, Joint Economic Committee, *Soviet Economic Performance, 1966–1967* (Washington, D.C., 1968), pp. 11, 16.

[5] "By now, as I had predicted, famine was under way. Soon I was receiving reports about deaths from starvation. Then cannibalism started. . . . I found a scene of horror. . . . The woman had the corpse of her own child on the table and was cutting it up. She was chattering away as she worked, 'We've already eaten Manechka. Now we'll salt down Vanechka. This will keep us for some time.' Can you imagine? This woman had gone crazy with hunger and butchered her own children!" *Khrushchev Remembers,* translated and edited by Strobe Talbott (Boston: Little, Brown and Company, 1970), pp. 234–35.

[6] Nikita Khrushchev, *Pravda,* January 15, 1960.

the Soviet Union did nothing to disabuse the West of this fact.[7] The element of uncertainty in the military relationship was introduced by the U.S. monopoly over atomic bombs. Presumably because of this fact, it suited the Soviet Union not to disabuse the West of the otherwise politically costly notion that it was only the U.S. (and the U.K.) that disarmed following the war. Western overestimates of Soviet strength (abetted by deliberate Soviet discounting of the strategic importance of atomic weapons) provided an important counter to the American atomic monopoly, perhaps inhibiting the American side from exploiting it politically. Moreover, in the immediate postwar era there was considerable uncertainty both as to the actual destructiveness of the new atomic weapons and the American capacity to deliver these weapons on Soviet targets.[8] Because of lags in production and the termination of some atomic facilities, the United States' atomic stockpile by 1947 was well under 100 bombs, with a cumulative damage-inflicting capacity roughly equal to that imposed on Nazi Germany during World War II,[9] and thus not on a scale sufficient to guarantee the effective destruction of the Soviet Union.

Both sides were thus in an ambiguous position. Unsettled political and social conditions in the West, as well as the Soviet advantage on the ground favored the Soviet Union in the event of hostilities in Europe. American nuclear monopoly as well as the vastly superior American economy—not to speak of the general exhaustion of the Soviet society—boded ill for the Soviet Union in the event of any protracted conflict. The standoff that followed, in a variety of limited confrontations, was logical, especially in view of the absence of directly conflicting political goals. The West, vastly overestimating Soviet strength, did not contest Soviet primacy in Central Europe, fearing, instead, a Soviet push Westward. The Soviet Union, preoccupied with consolidating its wartime gains and concerned lest the West exploit its weaknesses, only half-heartedly probed the newly established perimeters.[10]

[7] For example, the New York Times of May 12, 1947, in a comprehensive "World Military Survey" estimated the Soviet ground forces as ranging from 3.5 million men to 4.1 million men, organized in 200 or more divisions and backed by an additional one million men in its air forces and navy, for a total of over 5 million men under arms (or roughly double the actuality). Moreover, data released by Stalin concerning Soviet wartime arms production (30,000 tanks per annum, 40,000 planes per annum, and 120,000 artillery pieces per annum) was an impressive reminder of the capacity of the dislocated Soviet economy to sustain a very major war effort (Joseph Stalin, speech of February 9, 1946).

[8] In 1946, only one bomber group in the Strategic Air Command was equipped and trained to carry nuclear weapons. George H. Quester, Nuclear Diplomacy (New York: Dunella Publishing Co., 1970), p. 34.

[9] Ibid., p. 5.

[10] At the Potsdam Conference, the Soviet Union did indicate an interest in obtaining additional control over areas in the Mediterranean. During this phase, the Soviet Union succeeded in retaining all of its wartime conquests, with the exception of a pullback from northern Iran, and additionally it gained parts of Germany occupied during the war by American forces but earlier assigned to the Soviet zone of occupation.

PHASE II: SOVIET PROBES, 1948–52

The confrontation between the United States and the Soviet Union crystallized during the second phase. Not only did more direct conflicts actually develop, but both sides came to be guided by increasingly antithetical political concepts. Within both societies there emerged a form of political consensus: in the United States the crushing defeat of Wallace and the appearance of bipartisan support for an actively anti-Soviet policy signalled the end of postwar uncertainty; in the Soviet Union (as well as in Eastern Europe) the imposition of Stalinist terror created an atmosphere of a beleaguered camp ("imperialist encirclement"), dominated by implacable ideological hostility towards its rivals.

The Cold War now became primarily an American-Soviet affair. By 1947, the United States had assumed responsibility for British undertakings in Greece and Turkey and, more generally, it took the lead in fashioning the strategy of the West.[11] American goals were expressed succinctly in the concept of "containment." Essentially, the strategy rested on two premises: Soviet expansion must be halted, both by military and political means, and this in turn will create the preconditions for an eventual mellowing or even breaking up of the Soviet system.[12] The Soviet position was not spelled out publicly with the same degree of precision, but Soviet actions indicated an accelerated effort to subordinate Eastern Europe to full Soviet control, while Soviet probes in Berlin and Korea appeared to have been aimed both at the consolidation of existing Communist power and, had an American response been lacking, also the expansion of the Soviet sphere.

During this phase, the United States continued to enjoy decisive advantages in economic power and international influence, though its relative military position in some respects actually worsened. In spite of a brief bout with recessional tendencies, the U.S. economy grew during this phase to over $400 billion (in 1966 dollars), and the U.S. was able to undertake a massive program of injecting its capital into Western Europe, thus reinforcing a vital political link. Data on the Soviet GNP can be estimated only in very broad terms: Soviet postwar recovery was pressed energetically and the Soviet economy passed its prewar levels, with the GNP crossing the $150 billion mark (in 1966 dollars) by the time of Stalin's death.[13]

[11] See George F. Kennan, *Memoirs, 1925–1950* (Boston: Little, Brown and Company, 1967), and Dean Acheson, *Present at the Creation: My Years in the State Department* (New York: W. W. Norton, 1969).

[12] For a revealing review and discussion, see Charles Gati, "What Containment Meant," *Foreign Policy* no. 7 (Summer 1972) and, in the same issue, "Interview with George F. Kennan" (both are reprinted in this volume as Chapters 4 and 3, respectively).

[13] Joint Economic Committee, *Soviet Economic Performance*, pp. 11, 16. See also *Economic*

The international climate was similarly skewed to U.S. advantage. The coup in Czechoslovakia, the Berlin blockade, the defection of Yugoslavia (with its overtones of Soviet bullying), the purge trials in Eastern Europe, and eventually the invasion of South Korea all created a distinctly anti-Soviet mood. Reflecting this international climate, the American-sponsored plan for the international control of atomic energy (the Baruch Plan) was approved in June, 1948, by the U.N. Security Council, though vetoed by the USSR, with Syria, Argentina, and Colombia joining the U.S. and its West European allies. More significant still was the General Assembly vote of November, 1950, on the "Uniting for Peace" resolution, precipitated by the Korean conflict. Approved by 52 votes to 5, with two abstentions (India and Argentina), the vote found the Soviet Union completely isolated. However, probably a more accurate measure of international attitudes was provided by the February, 1951, vote condemning the Chinese intervention in the Korean War. The pro-U.S. vote was 47 to 7 with ten abstentions. India and Burma joined the Soviet Union in opposition to the resolution, while Egypt, Indonesia, Pakistan, Saudi Arabia, Sweden, Syria, Yemen, Yugoslavia, Algeria, and Afghanistan abstained. The southern arc of the Eurasian continent was thus beginning to divorce itself from a clear-cut identification with the United States.

Heightened international tensions, especially after the outbreak of Korean hostilities, prompted both powers to step up their military preparedness. Paradoxically, the tendency in the West at the time—in contrast to the earlier phase—was somewhat to underestimate Soviet strength. Soviet ground forces were built up rapidly in order to offset any Western atomic threat.[14] Soviet defense spending—despite a decline to under $30 billion in 1948 from its wartime high of about $50 billion[15]—was still more than twice that of the United States, and Soviet armed forces grew in manpower to almost 5 million men by the time of Stalin's death, a figure approximately one million above prevailing Western estimates,[16] and considerably in excess of the U.S. 1.6 million men under arms. American defense spending did not rise until the Korean War (having dropped precipitously from over $70 billion in 1945 to

Performance and the Military Burden in the Soviet Union, also by the U.S. Congress, Joint Economic Committee (Washington, D.C., 1970), p. 14.

[14] Khrushchev explicitly conceded this years later when he stated that Soviet armed forces were increased during this phase because of fears of Western "blackmail with the atomic bomb at a time when we did not yet have it." (Speech of January 15, 1960.)

[15] Quester, p. 293.

[16] Khrushchev indicated in January, 1960, that Soviet armed forces numbered 5.7 million men in 1955 but there were no major increases in military manpower between 1953 and 1955. See also Joint Economic Committee, Economic Performance and the Military Burden in the Soviet Union, p. 191.

under $12 billion by 1950), but then it did so rapidly, exceeding by 1952 in total dollar value Soviet military allocations. Nonetheless, in terms of mobilized manpower, the Soviet advantage during this phase ranged from 3 to 1 (in 1949) to 2 to 1 (after the U.S. build-up from 1950 on).

More important in the shifting military relationship was the development by the Soviet Union of the atomic bomb. That development came earlier than American planners had expected and by 1951 the Soviet Union already possessed a modest stockpile of atomic bombs, estimated to number about sixty.[17] Although the Soviet stockpile was considerably smaller than the American (only about one-tenth of the estimated U.S. total in 1951)[18] and the Soviet delivery system depended on several hundred TU-4's (essentially copies of the U.S. B-29's and hence not suited for effective attack on the U.S.), and while the U.S. delivery capability was becoming increasingly sophisticated and longer-range, the existence of Soviet A-weapons did have an important psychological and political effect. It increased Western anxiety, for it seemed to offset Soviet vulnerability to an American atomic attack, as well as military occupation. Increasingly binding U.S. political and military commitments to Europe were hence designed to cancel any advantage the Soviet Union could derive from this new situation and thus to preserve inherent asymmetry in the American-Soviet relationship.

In evaluating this phase, it is difficult to avoid the conclusion that it saw the fulfillment of basic American political goals as broadly defined in the concept of containment, as well as some political-security developments which could hardly have been desired by Stalin and his associates: the creation of NATO, the beginning both of the economic recovery and even rearmament of Western Europe (including subsequently of West Germany and of Japan), as well as the direct political and military involvement of the United States in several countries along the periphery of the Soviet Union. The factor of military power was used by both sides only defensively. The U.S. made oblique atomic gestures during the Berlin crisis (by posting a squadron of bombers capable of carrying nuclear bombs in the U.K.), while Soviet military prowess may be assumed to have contributed to Western passivity during the Czechoslovak coup of 1948 and it certainly shielded the consolidation of Soviet domination of Eastern Europe.[19] On the other hand,

---

[17] Quester, p. 77.

[18] Ibid., p. 6.

[19] However, during this period there were indirect American actions designed, at the minimum, to maximize Soviet difficulties in Eastern Europe and, at the maximum, to weaken Soviet control. In the former category should be placed the various covert American mea-

even great Soviet military superiority on the ground could not be translated into an effective political asset in dealing with Tito's Yugoslavia, the only notable case of defection from Soviet control.

The historical significance of the Korean War, in addition to its crucial impact on U.S. rearmament, poses an especially tantalizing question: to what extent was it merely a Soviet miscalculation, based on the assumption of U.S. disengagement from the mainland of Asia and perhaps also stimulated by Stalin's desire (reflecting long-standing Russian interests) to transform a united Korea into a Soviet dependency (instead of a Chinese or even eventually a Japanese one), and to what extent was it a calculated move deliberately designed to stimulate American-Chinese hostility? Stalin's suspicions of China are well documented, while the predominant U.S. inclination prior to the Korean War was to seek some sort of an accommodation with the new government on the Chinese mainland. With the bitter Titoist experience still on Stalin's mind, and with many analogies in the Stalin-Mao relationship to the Stalin-Tito relationship, the Soviet leadership must have given some thought to the future of Soviet-Chinese and Chinese-American relations. In any case, even if Soviet concern was not the direct cause of the outbreak of the Korean War, the subsequent opportunity to stimulate a head-on clash between America and China must have been welcomed by Stalin, and deservedly so. The ensuing twenty years of American-Chinese hostility were certainly a net gain for the Soviet Union.

On balance, this phase of the Cold War can be said to have involved clashes reflecting a more assertive Soviet pattern of behavior, with the U.S. essentially responding to perceived threats. The consequence of the clashes were three major developments, all to U.S. advantage, in spite of relative U.S. military weakness: the launching of Western economic recovery and the shaping of a new political coalition; the initiation of a rapid U.S. military build-up designed to erase the Soviet advantage on the ground; the rebuff of the Soviet Union in two, and possibly even three, crisis areas: Berlin, Korea, and maybe Yugoslavia. Soviet military power was effective only in shielding the Soviet political predominance in Eastern Europe and that area was not even actively contested by the West.

---

sures, including some risky deep-penetration U.S. flights and air drops to aid the Ukrainian insurgent army and some Polish resistance activities; in the latter, there was the combined air-sea operation undertaken in the late 1940s, designed to start a guerrilla movement against the pro-Soviet Albanian regime, geographically isolated by Tito's defection. From the Soviet standpoint, these actions were doubtless viewed as at least potentially dangerous American probes, even though their scale was quite inconsequential.

PHASE III: THE RHETORIC OF ASSERTIVENESS AND THE POLICY OF STATUS QUO, 1953–57

The coincidence of apparent external successes with domestic political change in the United States (not only in leadership but, even more notably, in ideological climate) led to the next phase in the rivalry, a phase seemingly dominated by greater U.S. assertiveness.

The new American policy, articulated by the winning Republican side during the presidential election of 1952, seemed to signal a basic departure from the U.S. strategy of containment: the adoption instead of an offensive "policy of liberation" designed to roll back the Soviet Union from its newly acquired East European satellites. Implicitly committing the United States to back East European efforts to attain political independence, the policy postulated a direct challenge to the Soviet Union in the area of its greatest political sensitivity.[20]

Soviet leaders had cause to view this change in American tone with some anxiety. Their insecurity was doubtless heightened by a series of internal crises, the cumulative effect of which was to sharpen the contrast between the self-confident and, on the whole, self-satisfied America of the early Eisenhower years and the troubled Russia torn by post-Stalin dissensions. A grave and enduring political crisis ensued in the wake of Stalin's death, with internecine conflicts consuming the energies of the top Soviet leaders throughout this phase. Its eruption precipitated a marked decline in the effectiveness of Soviet control over Eastern Europe—the area at which the new U.S. policy ostensibly pointed—and it sparked a series of violent uprisings. Finally, Soviet uncertainty about the future of Sino-Soviet relations caused Soviet leaders to redress the more overtly irritating aspects of the relationship established between Stalin and Mao in 1949, but without quieting en-

---

[20] In an address to the American Political Science Association, reported by the *New York Times* on August 28, 1952, Mr. John Foster Dulles outlined "the liberation plan of Eisenhower" in the following terms:

(1) The President of the United States would declare that this country would never make any deals with the Soviet Union, to recognize its conquests, and to let it keep its captive peoples;

(2) Voice of America and other agencies will begin to stir up resistance behind the Iron Curtain, letting the Poles, Czechs, and others know that they have the moral backing of the U.S. government;

(3) Resistance movements which spring up among patriots will be supplied and integrated via air drops and other communications from private organizations such as the Committee for a Free Europe.

That the Soviets had every reason to take the above seriously is suggested by the following comments of a thoughtful American observer, C. L. Sulzberger: "What the Eisenhower Republicans would like to make very plain is that any such revolt of free peoples in the future would be supported by this country and Soviet intervention would be warned off by a clear threat that it would be met with American reprisals" (*New York Times*, May 16, 1952).

tirely Soviet anxieties about the future.[21] To be sure, Soviet concern lest America exploit actively their time of troubles may have been somewhat diminished by American passivity toward the June, 1953, collapse of the newly established East German regime and the subsequent intervention by the Soviet army to restore its authority. That crisis, however, was of very short duration and it could not be taken as a firm token of future U.S. conduct.

More significant from the Soviet point of view was the fact that during this phase the U.S. was beginning to acquire a strategic capability for inflicting significant damage on the Soviet Union which, coupled with the generally more crusading mood of Washington, seemed to lend credibility to the offensive character of the U.S. policy. U.S. military spending, though it declined somewhat from the Korean War peak of $61 billion, stabilized around the mid-$30 billion mark during the first Eisenhower administration, while manpower under arms ranged from 3.5 million to 2.8 million men. In effective manpower, the Soviet Union still retained a considerable edge (almost 2:1), since by 1955 its armed forces numbered some 5.7 million men, with Soviet defense spending for this period estimated as roughly equivalent to $30 billion per annum. The big margin, strategically and politically, was in respective nuclear vulnerability. The U.S. proclaimed itself committed to the doctrine of massive retaliation, and the modernization and expansion of the Strategic Air Command (SAC) did create during this phase, probably for the first time, a situation of high Soviet vulnerability to a large-scale U.S. atomic attack. By 1955, the U.S. nuclear weapons bomber fleet capable of undertaking two-way attack missions on the Soviet Union had grown to about 400 aircraft, and the total number of U.S. bombers capable of executing an atomic attack on the Soviet Union was in the vicinity of 1350; the corresponding Soviet figures were only about 40 and 350, respectively.[22]

This one-sided ratio must have caused Soviet leaders the greatest concern, especially when coupled with the changed U.S. rhetoric—and hence, perhaps, intentions. The U.S. now seemed to have both the capacity to inflict very heavy damage on the Soviet Union and to significantly impede any Soviet effort to seize Western Europe. Perhaps to deter the United States, though conceding the Soviet Union's own vulnerability, the then-Soviet Prime Minister Malenkov broke ideological precedent by suggesting in March, 1954, that a nuclear war would be "unbearable" for both sides (and not just spell the end of cap-

---

[21] Years later, Khrushchev acknowledged that "I remember that when I came back from China in 1954 I told my comrades, 'Conflict with China is inevitable'" (Khrushchev Remembers, p. 466).

[22] Quester, pp. 126–38, 295.

italism, as ideological propriety heretofore indicated). In fact, however, the Soviet Union at this stage did not have the capacity for making a nuclear war "unbearable" for the United States.

Moreover, Soviet atomic insecurity was heightened still further by the continuing economic gap and by persisting international isolation. The economic asymmetry remained roughly what it had been at the time of Stalin's death: if anything, the gap widened slightly in absolute figures, with the U.S. GNP reaching in 1955 the figure of $508 billion (in 1966 dollars), and the Soviet Union increasing its GNP to about $185 billion.[23] Relatively, the Soviet Union had moved up somewhat, with its GNP about 36 percent that of the United States. Nonetheless, the death of Stalin and the subsequent temptation on the part of competing Soviet leaders to cater more to domestic aspirations prompted a debate on whether or not to enhance the Soviet standard of living, necessarily at the expense of defense budgeting. The conflict between Malenkov and Khrushchev touched on that very issue, and it certainly must have made the Soviet leaders acutely aware of their economic constraints.[24]

However, the U.S. side during this phase also began to be increasingly apprehensive about its security. Even the very limited Soviet striking power created, for the first time, some domestic U.S. vulnerability to a Soviet nuclear attack, and this sense of vulnerability was heightened by two other developments, one of public and one of private concern. The first was the unexpectedly rapid Soviet acquisition of an H-bomb, with the Soviet Union testing an operational weapon before the United States did; and the second was the conclusion by a special RAND study that even with an inferior striking power the Soviet Union might be able to launch a devastatingly effective first strike against U.S. SAC bases. The American side, accordingly, did not view the emerging power relationship with equanimity, even though the overall relationship was clearly skewed in U.S. favor.

On the international plane, despite stepped up Soviet activity, the overall picture remained basically unchanged from the days of the early fifties. Thus on the critical Hungarian issue of 1956, the Soviet Union could muster only eight votes (including three of its own) against the pro-U.S. total of 55, with 13 abstentions (again the Arab states, in-

[23] Joint Economic Committee, *Soviet Economic Performance, 1966–1967*, pp. 11, 16. See also *Economic Performance and the Military Burden in the Soviet Union*, also by the Joint Economic Committee, p. 14.

[24] In his memoirs Khrushchev indirectly reveals the Soviet sense of inadequacy, as well as high prestige sensitivity, when he oberves that on the arrival in Geneva for the Four Power talks, "Unfortunately, our own delegation found itself at a disadvantage from the very moment that we landed at the Geneva airport. The leaders of the other three delegations arrived in four-engine planes, and we arrived in modest two-engine Ilyushin (Il-15). Their planes were certainly more impressive than ours, and the comparison was somewhat embarrassing" (*Khrushchev Remembers*, p. 395).

cluding Egypt, plus Yugoslavia, Afghanistan, Cambodia, Finland, India, and Indonesia). On the less-polarized China issue, the U.S. held a similarly large margin until 1956, when the admission of new states began to reduce the U.S. edge.[25]

The combination of domestic and international strains led the Soviet side to initiate a series of steps pointing towards a détente in East-West relations. Even before Stalin's death, the Soviet side hinted that it might be willing to explore the possibility of a reunited but neutralized Germany, and some of the post-Stalin successors appeared to have been inclined to pursue this path. More significant was the Soviet readiness to conclude a peace treaty with Austria, resulting in the withdrawal of Soviet forces from that country. An accommodation with Yugoslavia terminated that particular crisis, while "the spirit of Geneva" —following the 1955 summit meeting—prompted publicly announced troop cuts[26] by both the Soviet and the American sides. The Soviet side was perhaps even surprised by the relative American readiness to accommodate, for the apparent willingness of the U.S. Republican Administration to stabilize the arms race did not appear to be entirely consistent with its more politically offensive rhetoric.

For the Soviet side, the critical turning point, prompting the termination of this particular phase in the Cold War and initiating a new one, probably came with the October-November crisis of 1956. The almost total U.S. passivity toward enormous Soviet indecision during what seemed for a while like the imminent collapse of Soviet rule throughout Eastern Europe, as well as toward the skillful Soviet exploitation of the unprecedented allied differences over the Suez affair, apparently convinced the Soviet leaders that American assertiveness was in fact only a domestically expedient myth.[27] Malenkov's views on mutual non-survivability had already been dropped by the new Khrushchev leadership and a novel tone of Soviet assertiveness increasingly began to be heard.

[25] Thus in 1955, out of 60 member states, 42 supported the U.S. position on the China issue, 12 were against, and 6 abstained. Two years later, in 1957, out of 82 member states, 48 supported the U.S., 27 were against, and 7 abstained.

[26] U.S. troops were cut from 3.5 million to 2.9 million, and on the Soviet side some Soviet forces were withdrawn from Eastern Europe (30,000 from East Germany and later some 60,000 from Hungary and Rumania). The Soviet Union also gave up its naval and military base at Porkkala in Finland.

[27] Khrushchev describes thus his assessment of the Suez affair: "Our use of our international influence to hold England, France and Israel's aggression against Egypt in 1956 was a historic turning point. Before that time, the Soviet Union—and Imperial Russia before it —had always treated the Near East as belonging to England and France. King Farouk had once asked Stalin to give him arms so that he could force Great Britain to evacuate its troops from Egypt, but Stalin refused. . . . When we first began to take an active interest in the affairs of Egypt, our attitude was cautious and our optimism was guarded" (Khrushchev Remembers, p. 431).

This phase of the Cold War, therefore, was essentially one of missed U.S. opportunities. It was the American side which failed to capitalize on the political and military momentum generated by the repulsion of Stalin's probes—either by exploiting to its own advantage the surfacing Soviet weaknesses or by taking advantage of the Soviet interest in a détente to engage the Soviet Union in a more binding arrangement. The doctrine of massive retaliation, accompanied by cuts in U.S. ground forces, left too narrow a margin between the extreme alternatives of war or peace for the U.S. policy makers to exploit the U.S. strategic preponderance. Subsequent U.S. passivity in late 1956 in turn appears to have provided the Soviet leaders with a new key interpretive signal, and the post-1953 Soviet anxiety about U.S. capabilities and intentions now gave way to a radically different Soviet reading of the rivalry. If from 1953–56 the Soviet Union can be said to have exaggerated its own strength in order to deter the United States from acting assertively, from 1957 on the Soviet leaders were inclined to exaggerate their own strength in order to exploit it on behalf of a more assertive Soviet behavior.

PHASE IV: PREMATURE SOVIET GLOBALISM, 1958–63

"The East Wind Prevails Over the West Wind": These words uttered in the Kremlin by Mao Tse-tung in late 1957 set the tone for the next phase of the Cold War. The Chinese leader succinctly summarized the emerging mood in Moscow, even though soon thereafter the Soviet and the Chinese leaders were to disagree about the more immediate policy implications of the allegedly new international balance of power.

Nonetheless, the combined effects of sudden Soviet space successes, of seeming American immobilism, of growing American anxiety about its (and its allies') vulnerability to Soviet strategic missiles, and of increasing Soviet diplomatic successes in breaking out from the U.S.-imposed geopolitical containment of the Soviet Union, was to infuse the Soviet leadership—and Khrushchev particularly—with an ebullient optimism. This was the era of increasingly frequent Soviet missile threats, as well as of economic forecasts pointing to Soviet supremacy over the United States within a decade.

The Soviet concept of détente changed accordingly. If in the earlier 1950s it was primarily designed to shore up a threatened status quo, in the late 1950s it was meant to help effect a change in it. Soviet leaders thus sought to combine summit diplomacy from a position of apparent strength with a recourse to open threats in order to compel the removal of the United States from Berlin, still the most sensitive spot in the East-West relationship. Khrushchev sought to accomplish this

goal without a head-on confrontation: hence détente diplomacy continued even as threats mounted, in the hope that political and psychological pressures would yield the desired results.

Soviet international activity acquired for the first time a distinctly
global range. Soviet involvement in the Middle East was widened and
politically deepened, Soviet ties with North Africa expanded, the Soviet
Union became deeply involved in the Congo crisis and developed
close political and even some ideological links with the new African
governments of Mali and Guinea, the Soviet Union provided extensive
support to President Sukarno of Indonesia, and—most symbolic of its
new policy—the Soviet Union began to aid, though at first rather
cautiously, the new Castro government in Cuba.

If Mao Tse-tung's remarks can be said to have set the tone for the
next phase, perhaps the key signal—in any case, so interpreted by the
other side—was provided by Khrushchev's so-called "national liberation struggle" speech of early 1961. Delivered almost literally on the
eve of inauguration of the new U.S. president—and read avidly by him
—his speech represented for the U.S. what almost a decade earlier
Dulles' concept of the "policy of liberation" probably meant to the
Soviet leaders: an ominous warning of an activist policy based on force,
even if not exercised through the application of direct force.

What Khrushchev appeared to be saying was that the balance of
power had tipped; that ideologically decisive change could now be
effected by "national liberation struggles," carried on under the pro-
tective umbrella of Soviet power; that Communist gains could be se-
curely protected; and that the West would have to yield even in Berlin,
where Soviet tactical advantages could be asserted under the protection of the newly acquired Soviet strategic capabilities.[28] In effect,
Khrushchev's policy seemed emulative of Dulles': "massive retaliation"
would deter U.S. counteractions, enabling the desired changes to
be effected at a lower threshold of risk.

This more assertive policy was pursued in an international atmosphere which, for the first time since World War II, was turning distinctly less favorable to the United States. By 1960, the U.S. was finding
itself in a minority on the China question (those abstaining as well
as opposed to the U.S. position were now more numerous, with 48

[28] This is not the place to explore the differences between the Soviet and the Chinese
strategies of the time. In their essence, both were offensive, but the Chinese were initially
willing to urge a more direct confrontation, backed by an overt willingness to go to a
nuclear war, in the belief that the West would back down. The Soviet passivity in the face
of the American nuclear threat during the Quemoy-Matsu crisis of 1958—directed, to be
sure, at China and not at the Soviet Union—led to a series of increasingly bitter disputes,
with the Chinese eventually shifting to an even purer, "do-it-yourself" revolutionary strategy, formulated by Lin Piao, a strategy no longer dependent on Soviet nuclear backing.

states backing the U.S., 36 opposed to the U.S. position, and 20 abstaining), and on the defensive on such issues as Cuba or the Congo. The question of Cuba became for the United States (especially after the debacle of the Bay of Pigs) what Hungary earlier had been for the Soviet Union: a source of embarrassment and strain, even in relations with friends. In the April, 1961, showdown, a resolution implicitly accusing the United States of aggression was defeated only because it had failed to acquire the two-thirds majority; it had obtained the support of 41 states, with 35 against and 20 abstentions. Those voting in favor included, in addition to Communist states, several Latin American states, as well as such states as Ireland and Ethiopia, which hitherto had supported the U.S. on most issues. The voting on the Congo question oscillated, depending on the specific issue, but the Soviet Union did find itself, on occasions, in the majority, with the United States abstaining.[29] The Soviet isolation of the fifties clearly was a thing of the past.

All of this contributed to an atmosphere which seemed to pit an energetic and assertive Soviet Union against a fumbling and defensive United States. Even the change in the U.S. presidency did not alter this relationship. Though John F. Kennedy assumed the presidency after waging a campaign in which American weakness (particularly the so-called missile gap) was one of his principal charges, events shortly after the inauguration seemed to bear out the self-confident mood of Soviet leaders. U.S. ineptitude during the aborted invasion of Cuba was followed shortly thereafter by U.S. passivity when the Soviet Union took unilateral action to effectively partition Berlin.

Yet the underlying reality of the relationship was more complex than its appearance, and that underlying reality was to surface before long. Politically, the change in the United States leadership did bring to the top a new and younger elite, which gained increasing self-confidence and which proceeded rapidly to build up U.S. military power. Within the Soviet Union, on the other hand, Khrushchev's personal position remained far from consolidated, with internal political struggles surfacing again, with unprecedented public displays of continued disagreement within the leadership manifesting themselves at the 22nd Party Congress. Moreover, the increasingly bitter struggle with China further complicated Soviet decision making, both forcing the Soviet Union to compete with China's militancy and somewhat reducing the Soviet Union's own room for maneuver.

Soviet economic bombast also did not measure up to reality. The

[29] For example, the vote of April 15, 1961, directed essentially against Belgium, a NATO ally of the U.S.: There were 61 states (including the Soviet Union) voting in favor of the resolution, against 5, with 33 abstaining (including the United States).

Soviet rate of growth began to wobble in the early 1960s, in contrast to the rapid rates of the 1950s, which Khrushchev apparently had simply projected into the future when announcing that the Soviet Union would surpass the United States by 1970. Moreover, the American economy, after the slowdown of the second half of the 1950s, began to accelerate, so much so that not only the absolute but even the relative gap between the two economies widened between 1961 and 1965. In 1958, the U.S. GNP stood at $519 billion (in 1966 dollars); the Soviet at $229 billion; with the difference being $290 billion and the Soviet GNP amounting to 44 percent of the U.S. In 1961, the respective figures were $575 billion versus $272 billion, with the difference being $303 billion, and the Soviet GNP amounting to 47 percent of the U.S. In 1965, the respective figures were $711 billion versus $330 billion, the difference being $381 billion and the relative Soviet standing 46 percent.[30] The dramatic economic reforms initiated by Khrushchev in 1957 clearly were not paying off.

Most significant of all, however, were developments in the military field. This phase marked the beginning of a new strategic competition with power measured increasingly by the number of missiles capable of inflicting strategic damage on the respective homelands of the two rivals. On the Soviet side, the number of men under arms actually decreased during these years. By 1960, the level had dropped to some 3.6 million men, and Khrushchev proposed to cut it further down to 2.4 million.[31] (The increased tensions in Berlin, however, prompted a freeze at around 3 million men.) At the same time, Soviet military expenditures continued to rise, approximately to $40 billion per annum, with the priorities put on modernization of equipment, and particularly on expansion of Soviet MRBM and ICBM strength.

The atmosphere created by Soviet boasting was very conducive to highly exaggerated U.S. estimates of Soviet power. In 1960, Soviet ICBM strength was semi-officially estimated as already around 100 missiles, and was projected to reach the impressive figure of 500 missiles by 1961.[32] In fact, however, during the Cuban missile crisis of October, 1962, the Soviet Union had only about 70 liquid-fueled ICBMs (of somewhat dubious reliability) capable of being targeted on the United States, and it did not reach the 500 mark until 1966–67. The new Kennedy administration, responding to what appeared to be both aggressive Soviet intentions as well as capabilities, sharply increased U.S.

[30] Joint Economic Committee, *Soviet Economic Performance, 1966–1967*, pp. 11, 16. See also *Economic Performance and the Military Burden in the Soviet Union*, also by the Joint Economic Committee, p. 14.

[31] Nikita Khrushchev's speech of January 15, 1960.

[32] See Thomas W. Wolfe, *Soviet Power and Europe, 1945–1970* (Baltimore: Johns Hopkins Press, 1970), p. 86, for citations.

defense spending, passing the $50 billion mark in 1962. Both U.S. strategic and conventional forces were reinforced. The former were designed to deny the Soviet Union the advantage of strategic threat; the latter were designed to meet head-on the new threat of insurgency and to enable the United States to wage the so-called two and one-half wars, both in Asia and Europe simultaneously. Moreover, according to then-Secretary of Defense McNamara, counterinsurgency forces were increased roughly by a factor of ten. Indeed, the missile gap—to the extent that it ever existed—was closed by late 1961, and the United States was in fact widening its strategic edge.[33] At the time of the Cuban missile crisis, the U.S. was in a position to deliver several times as devastating an attack on the Soviet Union as the Soviet Union could on the United States, even though by then American civilian losses might have been on the prohibitive scale of some 30 or so million fatalities.

From the Soviet point of view, however, the politically decisive factor was the realization by the Soviet decision makers of the fact that their society was several times more vulnerable than the American. This imposed a constraint on the Soviet use of strategic pressure even on behalf of moves in areas where the Soviet Union enjoyed a tactical advantage, as for example in Berlin. Furthermore, the rapid increase in NATO's nuclear firing power (by some 60 percent in 1961–63, as a consequence of deployment—according to Secretary McNamara—of "thousands of U.S. warheads") meant that a European conflict would quickly become a strategic one.

It was this asymmetry of power that led the Soviet Union to introduce MRBMs covertly into Cuba. Mikoyan confirmed this to a closed meeting of Communist ambassadors, held in Washington after the Cuban missile crisis (as recounted later by the Hungarian ambassador present).[34] By early 1962, the top Soviet leaders knew that in fact they did not have the strategic advantage they had claimed, and that American leaders *knew* this as well. What is even more important, the Soviet leaders probably knew what American leaders at the time could not yet know: that during the next several years the strategic gap would widen further in U.S. favor.

Thus, the Cuban confrontation in all likelihood was a last desperate gamble to achieve a payoff for an assertive Soviet strategy undertaken back in 1958. But that strategy rested on an insufficient base of power; it did not enjoy a sufficiently dynamic economic foundation nor the

[33] In 1961 the U.S. possessed 63 ICBMs and 96 Polaris missiles; by 1963, the figure had grown to 424 ICBMs and 224 Polaris missiles, giving it a total considerably above the 70 or so ICBMs the Soviet Union could muster during the Cuban missile crisis.

[34] For a full account of Mikoyan's visit to Washington shortly after the Cuban missile crisis, and the explanation of Soviet motives as provided by Mikoyan, see Janos Radvanyi, *Hungary and the Superpowers* (Stanford, Calif.: Hoover Institution Press, 1972), Chapter 15.

backing of an adequately developed military technology; and it over-estimated the revolutionary potential for radical change world-wide. As events during the next phase were to demonstrate, global conditions were not yet ripe for a Soviet policy that was meant to be both global and revolutionary. The casualty of this policy was the East-West dé-tente, which seemed within grasp in 1958 or 1960; the consequence of this policy was the massive U.S. strategic buildup of the early 1960s and a new phase in the Cold War, a phase dominated by increased U.S. assertiveness.

PHASE V: THE CRESTING OF AMERICAN GLOBALISM, 1963–68

The ideology for American globalism was provided by John Kennedy's inaugural address; American preponderance was dramatized by the Soviet backdown during the Cuban confrontation; the globalist policy came into its own during Lyndon Johnson's presidency, which coincided with the high water mark of the progressive post–World War II expansion of U.S. worldwide presence.[35]

The new phase did not involve a return to the dichotomic hostility of the 1950s. Indeed, American global assertiveness was initially accompanied by a stepped-up search for accommodation with the Soviet Union. The test ban agreement of 1963 and the establishment of the Washington-Moscow "hot line" represented major breakthroughs, signalling the growing recognition on the part of both powers of their stake in somehow stabilizing the arms race. This led by the end of the decade to the more formal U.S.-Soviet Strategic Arms Limitation Talks, creating in effect a standing U.S.-Soviet commission on strategic and political questions.

On the political plane, the new phase saw also a more active U.S. interest in developing closer ties with Eastern Europe. President Kennedy stressed during his electoral campaign the desirability of economic and cultural peaceful engagement with Eastern Europe, and President Johnson carried this approach even further, altering in October, 1966, the postwar U.S. priorities in Europe: heretofore German

[35] At its high point, the United States had over 1.2 million men under arms deployed abroad, based on 365 major U.S. military installations scattered throughout the globe, in addition to some 1600 minor facilities. U.S. defense commitments and assurances to foreign states included four major multi-lateral treaties, five bilateral defense treaties, five Congressional resolutions, nine executive agreements pertaining to defense arrangements with foreign states, as well as 34 additional executive declarations and communiques issued jointly with foreign governments, allowing for varying degrees of American commitment. Between 1950 and 1970, U.S. military aid to foreign states, in addition to the foregoing more direct American involvement, amounted to $53.8 billion.

reunification had been held to be the pre-condition for a European settlement; henceforth, East-West reconciliation was seen as laying the basis for a European settlement, eventually pointing to some resolution of the German question. Moreover, East-West reconciliation, it was expected, would help to increase East European independence from Soviet control.

The Soviet backdown in Cuba was widely regarded as signalling a protracted setback to Soviet global ambitions. American predominance was taken for granted, and American strategic superiority was blissfully portrayed as unchallengeable. Secretary McNamara went so far as to assert in 1965 that "Soviets have decided that they have lost the quantitative race, and they are not seeking to engage us in that contest. It means there is no indication that the Soviets are seeking to develop a strategic nuclear force as large as ours."[36]

If confident self-assertiveness was characteristic of the American mood during the initial years of this phase, anxiety and ambiguity appear to have dominated the Soviet outlook. At first, the change from Khrushchev to Brezhnev-Kosygin coincided with a distinct sense of letdown. The heroic competition with America—economic, political, and even spatial—had clearly ended in a defeat, symbolized towards the end of the decade by the American landing on the moon.[37] The Soviet leaders were evidently jolted by the directness of the 1962 American threat of a strategic attack on the USSR, and the Cuban debacle doubtless contributed to Khrushchev's fall from power in 1964. In addition, there is circumstantial evidence indicating that the post-Khrushchev Soviet leaders concluded that world affairs more generally were in a "reactionary" or "counter-revolutionary" phase, with the United States instigating the various international setbacks for "progressive" forces, deprived of Soviet nuclear protection. That appears to have been the meaning attached by Soviet leaders to the fall of Goulart in Brazil, March, 1964; Ben Bella in Algeria, June, 1965; Papandreou in Greece, July, 1965; Nkrumah in Ghana, February, 1966; and Sukarno in Indonesia, March, 1966—all statesmen whom Khrushchev

---

36 *Congressional Record*, vol. III, part 6, 89th Congress, 1st session, April 7, 1965, page 7271.

37 There is abundant evidence based on statements by Soviet spacemen and scientists, to the effect that the Soviet side had expected even as late as 1966 to beat the United States to the moon: Cosmonaut Komarov: "I can state positively that the Soviet Union will not be beaten by the United States in a race for a human being to go to the moon" (July 11, 1966). By 1968 there was less certainty. Cosmonaut Titov: "It is not very important to mankind who will reach the moon first" (December 20, 1968). See U.S. Senate, Committee on Aeronautical and Space Sciences, *Soviet Space Programs*, (Washington, D.C., December 1971), pp. 359–76.

had actively cultivated.[38] In the words of the official organ of the Italian Communist Party:

> For the policy of the *status quo* and the attempts to divide the world into zones of influence between the two super-powers, U.S. imperialism is gradually substituting a revised and corrected re-edition of the old policy of *roll back,* giving birth, within the framework of nuclear coexistence with the USSR (caused by reasons of *force majeure*), to a series of local interventions (economical, political, military) designed to modify the world equilibrium by means of setting up reactionary regimes, or by support given to them, and liquidation of the progressive forces and movements in individual countries.[39]

Soviet confidence was even further damaged by the widening rift with China, by the surfacing of liberal sentiments in Czechoslovakia, and by Israel's shattering defeat of Nasser's army, equipped and trained by the Soviet Union (including the embarrassing capture by the Israelis of some Soviet military advisors). The international gains of the preceding years appeared everywhere to be in jeopardy, with the prematurely assertive Soviet globalism prompting not only the massive U.S. military buildup but the global political American counteroffensive.

How to respond to American overtures, given this overall context, must have perplexed the Soviet leaders. On the one hand, there was something to be gained—if nothing else, at least time—by responding positively. Yet a positive response, given the overall context, could be a sign of weakness, and might be especially damaging to the Soviet position in Eastern Europe, still far from secure. This persisting insecurity prompted rather paranoiac Soviet reactions to American efforts to normalize relations with Eastern Europe; the effort was widely interpreted in the Soviet press and official statements as fundamentally counter-revolutionary.[40]

The Soviet response was, accordingly, cautious. In effect, for a while the new Soviet team did not have a foreign policy beyond that of re-

[38] Although Che Guevara's Bolivian adventure was not supported by the Soviet Union, his death in 1967 at the hands of U.S.-trained Bolivian rangers certainly fitted the pattern outlined above.

[39] *Rinascita,* August 4, 1967. Statements very much to this effect were presented by Brezhnev at the Soviet 50th anniversary celebration in Moscow and by Suslov to the International Communist meeting in Budapest, March, 1968. Tito, after a visit to Moscow in 1967, also reported this Soviet conclusion. In keeping with this assessment, Soviet commentators subsequently have referred to American foreign policy in the sixties as having been particularly "adventurist" in character. See, for example, A. A. Gromyko, "Present Trends in U.S. Foreign Policy," *SShA,* no. 3, (March, 1972).

[40] A good example of this paranoia is provided by G. A. Arbatov, "American Foreign Policy on the Threshold of the 1970's," *Orbis* (Spring 1971), p. 140.

trenchment and very ad hoc responses to new situations, such as that which arose in the Middle East in the wake of the Arab defeat and even more painfully in Czechoslovakia (where Soviet intervention was precipitated by fears that the entire Soviet structure in Eastern Europe might collapse). The drift contributed to a rather widespread sense of malaise, and perhaps even emboldened the Chinese to step up both their anti-Soviet polemics and border tensions.

However, as in the Soviet case during the preceding phase, American global assertiveness obscured a reality which was becoming steadily less favorable to the American side. The mounting U.S. engagement in the war in Vietnam, transforming what initially appeared to be a relatively limited shoring-up operation into a more massive and costly intervention, significantly reduced American freedom of action, prompted severe strains in the U.S. economy and society, absorbed much of the U.S. defense budget, and weakened the U.S. international position. As a result, the U.S. neither translated into deeds the vision held up in President Johnson's 1966 speech of East-West reconciliation in Europe, nor made the slightest move to complicate the Soviet decision to forcibly occupy in August, 1968, the increasingly liberal Czechoslovakia. Similarly, diplomatic passivity marked the U.S. posture in the Middle East—in part, because of the political need to reinforce waning domestic support for the Vietnamese war—with the result that before long the Soviet Union was able to reestablish and even widen its badly shaken position in the Mediterranean area.

In the meantime, Soviet diplomacy with regards to the Vietnamese war became increasingly skillful. Its essence can be described with the words: "opportunity-exploitation" and "risk-reduction." The war had the effect of increasing disproportionately the American stake in Soviet good will[41] and at the same time it significantly decreased American international standing. The world-wide good will generated in the early sixties by President Kennedy's image and by widespread admiration for his conduct of the Cuban missile crisis, gradually gave way to increasingly critical assessments of the U.S. role in Vietnam and—though briefly—also in the Dominican Republic. The U.S. position in the U.N. became progressively weaker. While still able to block the entry of Communist China, the combined votes of those opposing the United States and abstaining was now consistently larger than the pro-U.S. vote. Moreover, several key U.S. allies—most notably France—were openly critical of U.S. policies in Asia, and increasingly inclined to engage in bilateral negotiations with China or Russia. France also detached herself from the military structure of NATO, though this step

---

[41] In 1968 there were even rather advanced preparations for a visit to Moscow by President Johnson. The visit was aborted by the Soviet invasion of Czechoslovakia.

was matched by the quiet weakening of links between the Warsaw Pact and Rumania.

On the economic plane, the situation was more mixed. The American economy continued to grow steadily, but the Soviet economy regained much of its forward momentum and resumed its upward climb relative to the United States. By 1967, the U.S. GNP stood at $762 billion; the Soviet at $372 billion, or 49 percent of the U.S. total,[42] although the Soviet economy continued to be plagued by operational inefficiency and lack of adequate technological innovation. However, inflationary trends were beginning to beset the United States, with the war in Vietnam making it increasingly difficult for the United States to pursue its domestic programs of social renewal.

The biggest change, however, was to come in the military relationship. On the surface, U.S. supremacy seemed secure. In 1965, Defense Secretary McNamara estimated that in terms of delivery systems, "we have a superiority of approximately 3 or 4 to 1. . . . In qualitative terms, it's impossible to come up with a precise evaluation but it far exceeds 3 or 4 to 1. . . . The programs we have under way are more than adequate to assure our superiority in the years ahead."[43] By 1968, the steady buildup in U.S. ground forces also gave the United States for the first time in the history of the rivalry a lead in the number of men under arms (3.5 million versus 3.47 million). However, this particular increase was due primarily to the Vietnamese war, as was also the case with the continuing increase in U.S. military expenditures from $52 billion in 1965 to over $80 billion in 1968.[44]

In reality, despite Secretary McNamara's extraordinary optimism, the military balance was quietly shifting away from U.S. supremacy. It gradually became clear that some time earlier in the decade—presumably sometime before the Cuban crisis, though the outcome of the crisis obviously reinforced the decision—the Soviet leadership decided to respond to the American missile buildup with one of its own, thereby eventually making good on Khrushchev's premature claims. Soviet defense spending moved steadily upward, crossing the $50 billion mark in 1967 and reaching $55 billion in 1968,[45] thereby effectively matching and even surpassing U.S. defense spending outside of the Vietnamese war effort. By 1968, the Soviet Union (with some 900 operational

[42] Joint Economic Committee, *Soviet Economic Performance, 1966–1967*, pp. 11, 16. See also *Economic Performance and the Military Burden in the Soviet Union*, also by the Joint Economic Committee, p. 14.

[43] *Congressional Record*, April 7, 1965, p. 7271.

[44] United States Arms Control and Disarmament Agency, *World Military Expenditures, 1970* (Washington, D.C., 1970), p. 18.

[45] Ibid.

ICBMs and the U.S. leveling off at 1054),[46] was well on the way to erasing the margins of superiority authoritatively claimed by Secretary McNamara three years earlier.

Though by 1968 the United States still enjoyed a marked strategic edge,[47] the overriding reality of the military relationship was that now both sides had the capacity for destroying each other as viable societies, with neither possessing a decisive clear-cut first strike capability. Although this changed relationship imposed on both sides an increased obligation to consider closely the likely consequences of any unilateral application of force internationally, it meant a greater change for America, which until then had been relatively invulnerable.

Most important of all, however, was the conjunction between this change and the collapse within the United States of the postwar consensus concerning foreign affairs. Like the Soviet Union after the death of Stalin, by the latter part of the sixties the U.S. found itself in the midst of a deep political crisis, involving major convulsions within the ruling elite and a general crisis of social values. With the Vietnamese war precipitating a divisive national debate about foreign policy aims, the U.S. global engagement became increasingly devoid of positive domestic support. As a result, the initiative gradually passed to the Soviet side.

PHASE VI: SOVIET GLOBALISM AND THE SHAPING OF A MIXED RELATIONSHIP, 1969–

Just as Khrushchev's fall from power ushered in a period in the relationship dominated by American assertiveness, Johnson's fall from power in 1968 ushered in a new phase, dominated by rising Soviet self-confidence and expanding global involvement. Soviet analysts began to evaluate the world again in terms of the general crisis of capitalism, and Soviet leaders—though much more cautious in their pronouncements than was Khrushchev—were apparently concluding that the world was again shifting from a quiescent state into a dynamic condition, more favorable to "revolutionary" than "reactionary" trends.[48]

---

[46] USSR vs. USA: The ABM and the Changing Strategic and Military Balance, study by special American Security Council Committee (Washington, D.C., 1969), p. 36.

[47] Especially in strategic bombers—over 600 to less than 200 for the Soviets—and submarine-launched missiles targetable on respective homelands—656 to 45. Ibid., pp. 41 and 46.

[48] Brezhnev, in his report to the 24th Congress, March 30, 1971, asserted that "the crisis of capitalism continues to deepen." Similarly, a comprehensive review of "Current Problems of World Politics," by M. Kobrin in Mirovaia Ekonomika i Mezhdunarodnyie Otnosheniia (October, 1971) concludes that recent events "confirm the correctness of the conclusions of

This new phase also saw the emergence of a Soviet policy that was no longer primarily regional nor handicapped—as had been the case particularly under Khrushchev—by vast disproportion between ends and means. Exploiting both the domestic American malaise and the Vietnamese conflict, the Soviet leaders proceeded to fashion their own equivalent of the earlier Kennedy-Johnson combination of American globalism and bridge-building. The wider scope of the new Soviet strategy involved a rather different kind of policy from that pursued earlier by Khrushchev: his was not only globally premature but globally undifferentiated, spreading thinly still-thin Soviet resources, relying heavily on economic aid and ideology. His successors, putting more reliance on diplomacy and military presence, exploiting nationalism even while reducing Soviet economic aid significantly (and concentrating it on a few key targets), not only have been pursuing a more selective strategy, but have appeared to focus it on the vast Eurasian continent: isolating China in the East and flirting with Japan; consolidating the Soviet position in South Asia, while tying the U.S. down to the war in Vietnam; expanding their presence in the Mediterranean and in the Middle East; and seeking to draw Western Europe into closer economic and political ties—hopefully pointing to the "Finlandization" of Western Europe. The overall object appeared to be the attainment of a preponderant position on this vast continent. Continentalism rather than, as in the past, either regionalism (focused on Europe almost entirely) or premature globalism (undifferentiated in form) was the central character of the new Soviet policy.

This strategy coincided with the American re-examination of its foreign policy. The redefinition of American policy by 1972 was clearly leading the United States into increased reliance on a triangular pattern of politics, exploiting the Sino-Soviet cleavage to offset the Soviet Union and to gain increased leverage in bilateral American-Soviet relations. In response, the Soviet Union, obviously concerned about the new Washington-Peking relationship, sought to balance the negative consequences of any American-Chinese accommodation through its own initiatives vis-à-vis Washington. These initiatives were designed to convince the American side of the greater desirability of an American-Soviet accommodation. Beyond that, the Soviet Union still appeared to be counting on the possibility of a more pro-Soviet leadership in China after Mao, and in the meantime Soviet military pressure on

the 24th Congress concerning the continued deepening of the general crisis of capitalism." The above quotations are by no means atypical; many more could be cited and they reflect, obviously, a general evaluation.

China did result in the cooling down of Chinese border pressures.[49] Nonetheless, China came to represent a growing source of Soviet security concerns, necessitating major redeployment of forces and reallocation of resources.

The military dimensions of the American-Soviet relationship during this phase have been dominated by a new element of uncertainty. The pace of Soviet strategic and tactical buildup, as well as intensive development of home civil defense, appeared to indicate a desire to acquire a war-fighting capability in the context of parity[50]—which, if attained, could give the Soviet Union a significant edge in any protracted crisis bargaining. Soviet defense spending continued to rise (crossing the $55 billion mark by the late sixties), while American defense expenditures outside of the Vietnamese war remained unchanged. With the American strategic forces on a plateau since 1967, the Soviet Union was able by 1970 to match roughly the United States in the strategic sector,[51] while some of its programs could even be interpreted as seeking to obtain by the mid-seventies a decisive first-strike capability. Moreover, the Soviet Union made major strides toward the acquisition of effective naval power and long-range air- and sea-lift capabilities, and began to develop the argument that these forces would be able in the future to induce a U.S. recognition of "the inevitability and irreversibility of the social changes dictated by the will of the peoples."[52]

The result was that both powers were now checking each other, and—more dangerous—their power frequently overlapped (as in the

---

[49] There are strong grounds for concluding that the sudden September, 1969, Kosygin-Chou meeting in Peking was designed to deliver a Soviet ultimatum to China. It is a typical Soviet practice to have grave warnings delivered by the more moderate Soviet leaders in order to give these warnings greater credibility. There are also grounds for believing that the Soviet Union was involved in the abortive Lin Piao coup of August, 1971.

[50] For example, see David Holloway, *Technology, Management and the Soviet Military Establishment* (Adelphi Papers, IISS, 1971), pp. 7–8.

[51] With the U.S. strategic forces plateauing from 1967 on, by 1971 the strategic balance was as follows:

	U.S.	Soviet Union
ICBMs	1054	1550
Submarine missiles	655	580
Bombers	531	140

With many of the U.S. missiles equipped with MIRVs, the U.S. still commanded a major edge in the number of targeted warheads: 5,700 to 2,500. See *The Military Balance, 1971–72* IISS (London, 1972), and "Arms Control Implications of Current Defense Budgets," hearings, Committee on Foreign Relations, U.S. Senate, June–July, 1971 (Washington, 1971), especially p. 59.

[52] See A. Trofimenko, "Political Realism and the 'Realistic Deterrence' Strategy," *SShA*, no. 11 (November 1971).

Mediterranean). This prompted heightened pressures on them to develop more stable rules of behavior (such as the 1972 agreement on avoidance of naval incidents), but it also increased the probabilities of friction. The improved Soviet military posture was purchased at a high economic price, especially given the continuing disparity between the two economies. With a GNP in the early 1970s of about $500 billion (or under one-half that of the U.S.), the Soviet Union was attempting to match—perhaps even exceed—the U.S. military effort, with the costs and complexity of that effort growing at an almost exponential rate. Increased Soviet interest in somewhat moderating the military competition was doubtless thus stimulated in part by economic pressures, even if some sectors of the Soviet leadership (especially the military) may have continued to press in favor of a military posture that at a minimum assured the Soviet Union a reliable war-fighting capability[53] and at the maximum eventually a decisive first-strike capability.

Nonetheless, this most recent phase in the American-Soviet relationship also saw increased Soviet optimism concerning longer-range economic prospects. Premier Kosygin even revived—though in a moderated form—the earlier Soviet prognosis of an eventual victory over the United States in economic competition.[54] U.S. economic difficulties and tensions with its European and Japanese allies reinforced the Soviet expectations, even though the Soviet economy continued to suffer from inadequate scientific-technological innovation for which it sought remedies in periodic domestic economic reorganizations and in increased technological importation from the more advanced West.

What made for even greater uncertainty about the eventual outcome of this particular phase was the increasing importance of domestic political changes within both systems. The new bi-polar checking relationship, even though it heightened the risks of a crisis and posed an especially dangerous possibility of inadequate U.S. social staying power in the event of a prolonged and acute crisis, also meant that both sides were being pushed by the very nature of the checking relationship into a new competition, in which the domestic performance of the two systems was becoming an increasingly vital aspect of the competition. Their respective ability to cope with the rising social demands for the implementation of the concepts of liberty and

[53] The rather extensive Soviet civil defense programs (as well as the Soviet discussions of them) appear to be designed to that end. For a fuller discussion, see the research paper by Toby Trister, "Civil Defense and the Soviet Vision of Future War," January, 1972.

[54] "The total volume of the USSR's industrial and agricultural output in 1975 will exceed the present level of industrial and agricultural production in the USA. This, comrades, is an important landmark in the economic competition between the USSR and the capitalist countries" (Statement by Prime Minister Kosygin, *Pravda*, November 25, 1971).

equality (the former more in the Soviet Union; the latter more in the United States) was becoming an important ingredient in a competition that was now less a purely traditional one and more and more part of a global political process, increasingly inimical to sharp demarcating lines between the foreign and the domestic.

In this regard, both sides were plagued by major intangibles. Change in America—overtly turbulent—made for uncertainty about the character of America's involvement in world affairs and that in turn nurtured some of the Soviet optimism about the historical significance of this particular phase in the rivalry. Soviet—particularly Great Russian—nationalism was obviously attracted by the prospect of the Soviet Union emerging as the number-one world power, and this feeling, even more than ideology, provided the social propellant for sustained competition with the United States. Yet change in the Soviet Union, less visible and more repressed, was also taking place, and its eventual surfacing could have enormous implications. Increased social demands for a higher standard of living, intellectual dissent, generational unease, rising tensions between Great Russian nationalism and the more aroused nationalisms of the non-Russian nations, coupled with the conservative reaction of the ruling party elite, all cumulatively increased the importance of domestic considerations in Soviet foreign policy decision making.

The combined effect of increasing external complexity (symbolized by Vietnam for the United States and by China for the Soviet Union) and of rising domestic demands (in the U.S. for a re-examination of U.S. international commitments and in the Soviet Union for a higher standard of living) was to pressure both powers into limited but expanding accommodations. The number of bilateral U.S.-Soviet agreements continued to expand,[55] and the process culminated in May, 1972, with the Moscow summit. That meeting was held within days of an act of U.S. military compulsion directed largely against the Soviet Union: the mining of North Vietnamese ports. The Soviet failure to respond indicated the high Soviet political stake in the agreements, even though these agreements involved calculated gambles on both sides. In their essence, the Moscow agreements represented a clear short-term political gain for the Soviet side, and a short-term strategic gain for the American side; in the longer run, they could turn out to be

---

[55] These included a treaty barring the emplacement of nuclear weapons and other weapons of mass destruction on the seabed and ocean floors; a convention providing for the banning of the development and production of bacteriological weapons and toxins as well as for their destruction; improvements in the communications link between the Soviet Union and the United States, including the use of artificial earth satellites; bilateral talks on the avoidance of naval incidents; and so forth.

politically more beneficial to the American side, provided the longer run does not see the strategic relationship skewed to a considerable Soviet advantage.

On the political plane, the agreements involved an American acknowledgment of U.S.-Soviet parity as well as the legitimization of postwar Soviet gains in Eastern Europe (symbolized also by the related visit by Nixon to Warsaw, the first Presidential visit to a capital of an East European state not defying Moscow). In the longer run, the process of accommodation could dilute Soviet ideological militancy, provided that in the meantime the relationship of strategic parity is not upset. In that strategic relationship the agreements had the effect of halting the quantitative momentum of the Soviet deployment while leaving open the competition in its qualitative aspects, where the U.S. remains clearly superior; in the longer run, however, the existing Soviet quantitative advantage could become quite significant once the qualitative U.S. lead is erased.

This is why there is a sensitive interdependence between the political and the strategic aspects of the Moscow agreements, and the character of the next phase in the competitive relationship will be very much affected by the degree to which the U.S. Congress recognizes the interdependence. There is little reason to doubt that the Soviet leadership is sensitive to it.

CONCLUSION

Several additional observations emerge from our analysis of the different phases of the Cold War:

Cyclical pattern. The American-Soviet relationship appears to have been punctuated by alternating offensive and defensive phases, with neither side demonstrating the will nor the capacity for sustained political momentum. After the initial skirmishing had gradually given way to a sharper rivalry, the Soviet Union adopted a more offensive policy during 1948–52; the United States then gained the initiative and appeared to be on the political offensive during 1953–57; the Soviet Union in turn became more assertive and maintained an offensive posture during 1958–63; that policy collapsed in 1963 and during 1963–68 the United States pursued an activist global policy. However, by the late sixties the Soviet Union regained its momentum (while the U.S. was experiencing "an agonizing reappraisal" of its foreign policy), initiating the present phase in the relationship.

As the Soviet side gained in strength and self-confidence, its policies —both strategic and political—tended to emulate the American. In many respects, Soviet policy during the premature fourth phase was imitative of American policy during the third phase: American reliance on "massive retaliation" and "the policy of liberation" was later matched by Soviet nuclear threats and promises of support for "national liberation struggles." Similarly, the present phase of the relationship has seen strong reverse overtones of the political and strategic postures adopted by the United States during the fifth phase.

Relative performance.   In a narrow sense, the Soviet performance in the rivalry may be said to have been superior to the American—because, at least, the relative Soviet position improved considerably. From a general position of inferiority (in the context of reciprocal hostility) the Soviet Union has moved to a level approaching a global condominium with the United States (in the context of a more mixed cooperative-competitive relationship). Probably there still are some Soviet leaders arguing on behalf of preponderance as the Soviet goal for the next stage, and this is what makes the present phase so very critical. However, such a judgment must be qualified by the consideration that both sides succeeded in their basic defensive aims, even though in the last several years the Soviet Union has pierced southward (into the Middle East and Asia), through the weakest parts of the perimeters drawn by the U.S. policy of containment.

Given the nature of the Soviet system, Soviet leaders have been in a better position than the American policy makers to exploit politically whatever assets they had at their disposal. In that sense, Soviet policy has tended to be somewhat freer from objective restraints than the American side. The Soviet Union thus adopted offensive postures when an opportunity seemed to beckon, even if at a relative disadvantage in two or even three of the four comparable elements noted during each phase: relative international influence, respective military and economic power, domestic cohesion on behalf of national policy. In contrast, the United States tended to become more assertive only when all or most of these factors were favorable.[56] Moreover, even then

---

[56] Tables amplifying the dynamics of the competitive relationship are appended to this paper. In summary form, the relationship can be stated as follows:

Phase I   1945–47.   Preliminary Skirmishing
1	international standing	U.S. advantage
2	military power	probably a Soviet advantage
3	economic power	overwhelming U.S. advantage
4	domestic policy base	uncertainty in both

Phase II   1948–52.   Soviet Union Assertive
1	international standing	U.S. advantage
2	military power	marginal Soviet advantage?
3	economic power	decisive U.S. advantage
4	domestic policy base	U.S. advantage

the American stance tended to be more conservative, with its policies less consequential than the Soviet Union's and designed more to preserve America's relatively advantageous international position than to effect a decisive change in the American-Soviet relationship.

On the whole, throughout the relationship, both sides have been essentially prudent and restrained. Each has avoided pushing the other beyond the point of no return. In this regard, note must be taken of the extraordinarily salutary effect of nuclear weapons; in a more traditional setting, without the restraining effect of nuclear weapons, it is likely, given mutual hostility and occasionally very sharp provocations, that a major American-Soviet war would have occurred.

Missed opportunities. It is only natural that in a highly complex relationship between two remote powers, divided not only by distance but by ideology and culture, there should occur a number of instances in which one side has misinterpreted the intentions of the other, or miscalculated the anticipated reactions (or non-reactions) of the other, or simply interpreted as key signals actions or statements which perhaps were not meant to be key signals. Attention has already been drawn to the role played by several key "signals," irrespective of the subjective intention of the "signallers."

In addition, one may speculate about major opportunities which each side failed to exploit in order to alter fundamentally the relationship. Two such missed opportunities stand out. The first, America's, involved the years 1953–57 when the Soviet world was in the deepest disarray. A more active policy, combining a willingness to contrive a new European relationship (including perhaps a neutralized Germany) with a credible inclination to exploit Soviet difficulties in Eastern Europe, might have diluted the partition of Europe and maybe even

---

Phase III   1953–57.   United States Assertive
  1 international standing   U.S. advantage
  2 military power   U.S. advantage
  3 economic power   U.S. advantage
  4 domestic policy base   U.S. advantage
Phase IV   1958–63.   Soviet Union Assertive
  1 international standing   declining U.S. advantage
  2 military power   uncertain U.S. advantage
  3 economic power   U.S. advantage
  4 domestic policy base   probable U.S. advantage
Phase V   1963–68.   United States Assertive
  1 international standing   marginal U.S. advantage
  2 military power   clear U.S. advantage
  3 economic power   U.S. advantage
  4 domestic policy base   declining U.S. advantage
Phase VI   1969–.   Soviet Union Assertive
  1 international standing   roughly equal
  2 military power   marginal U.S. advantage?
  3 economic power   U.S. advantage
  4 domestic policy base   Soviet advantage

transformed the rivalry into a less-hostile relationship. Instead, the U.S. policy was one of rhetorical assertiveness, pointing towards the "liberation" of Eastern Europe, but in fact preoccupied with building up NATO, including in it a rearmed West Germany. Both the Cold War and the division of Europe were thereby perpetuated.

The other key opportunity missed appears to have come not long afterwards. Precisely because by 1958 the United States had given overt indications of a willingness to settle for the status quo, there seems to have existed an "objective" opportunity for a real détente. Instead, the Soviet leaders, who themselves had earlier fostered the détente (largely —it appears—for tactical reasons: to deflect U.S. hostility at a time of considerable U.S. preponderance), now decided to exploit what they construed to be an American psychological and political weakness to achieve a major breakthrough. The initiation of the Berlin crisis produced several years of acute tensions, launching in turn the massive U.S. strategic build-up of the Kennedy years, escalating the arms race, setting in motion the U.S. counteroffensive, and postponing by almost fifteen years any abatement in U.S.-Soviet hostility.

The role of military power. Because the two powers avoided a direct war, it is extremely difficult to assess the actual importance of absolute and relative military power to the unfolding pattern of the competition. To the extent that judgment may be hazarded, it does appear that one of the key reasons why so far every offensive phase has failed to attain its apparent objectives has been that the offensive side either lacked, or considered itself lacking, the needed margin of superiority in order to extract a decisive political advantage. The value of military power has thus been primarily defensive, but defensively it may well have been the critical factor.

However, it is noteworthy that in the two phases in which the U.S. has appeared to be the more assertive partner in the relationship, it was the United States which enjoyed an unambiguous military advantage. Thus it might be said that the United States has been more inclined to rely on military superiority as the basis for political assertiveness, even though it abstained from direct military probes of the opposite camp. On the other hand, the Soviet Union, even though militarily weaker, has been more inclined in its offensive phases to probe militarily or to use military pressure for political objectives, provided the overall context seemed to create favorable political circumstances and the basis for political confidence.

Until now, the stability of the relationship has not been tested by an assertive Soviet policy conducted in the context of clear Soviet military superiority.

The unclear but present danger. The acceptance of numerical parity in the American-Soviet military relationship raises two uncertainties about the future. The first pertains to the relative ability of the two political systems to engage effectively in protracted crisis bargaining, a bargaining which in the setting of relative parity would test to a far greater extent than ever before the psychological and political staying power of the two systems. A major crisis between the two powers would be likely to have especially unsettling consequences in the United States which heretofore based its deterrence of the Soviet Union on a significant margin of superiority. Since what the Russians could undertake prudently has depended in the past on what they thought they could do safely, the erosion of American superiority and the coincident overlapping of power could have the effect of widening the margins of Soviet initiatives.[57]

It is noteworthy that the Soviet Union has appeared lately to be somewhat less anxious than in the past to terminate rapidly third-party conflicts lest they escalate into a big-power confrontation. Soviet dilatory tactics during the India-Pakistan war of 1971 stood in contrast with the Soviet behavior during the earlier warfare of 1965, not to speak of Soviet eagerness to dampen the Middle Eastern war of 1967. Accordingly, we simply do not know to what extent Soviet prudence in the past was primarily a function of Soviet weakness rather than constituting an enduring aspect of Soviet behavior.

The second uncertainty arises out of the Moscow SALT of May 1972. The agreements permit qualitative improvements in the context of quantitative parity. These improvements—much more difficult to verify than quantitative expansion—could eventually threaten the parity arrangement. Indeed, because improvements in quality are more difficult to verify, anxieties may rise again unless additional agreements, providing for more verification and additional limitations (especially on testing), are not forthcoming within the next several years.

The next several years in the American-Soviet relationship are likely, therefore, to be very critical. They will determine whether the competitive relationship can be both stabilized and balanced by more cooperative elements, as indicated by the several U.S.-Soviet agreements announced in late May, 1972, or whether the competition again will assume an essentially hostile character. In the latter case, the outcome of a crisis between the two powers would depend very much not only on the relative power position of the two sides but also on the

---

[57] See Z. Brzezinski, "USA/USSR: The Power Relationship," in *International Negotiation,* Subcommittee on National Security and International Operations, Committee on Government Operations, U.S. Senate, Washington, D.C., 1971, pp. 8–12.

ability of the respective political systems to maintain domestic support for crisis-bargaining in the context of enormous psychological stress, with these two factors clearly interacting.[58]

The present character of the relationship. During phases two and three, the relationship between the two rivals operated in the context of bi-polar politics conducted on the basis of unified blocs. Phases three, four, and five saw the gradual emergence of polycentric politics, conducted in the context of bi-polar but still rather asymmetric power. Perhaps the best way to conceptualize the present phase of the relationship is to say that it involves a bi-polar checking power relationship, operating in the context of a multiple state interplay, with the Washington-Peking-Moscow triangle providing the critical political interplay. The relationship involves some overlapping power, with its potential for dangerous frictions, while the multiple state interplay (replacing the earlier bloc confrontations) makes for a more extensive but less intensive rivalry, balanced by increasing cooperation in certain specialized areas. Moreover, the Moscow agreements of 1972, while not terminating the rivalry, do involve a significant codification of "the rules of the game" under which the rivalry is to be conducted, and thus signify a change towards a more mixed relationship.

In that relationship the Soviet Union now possesses strategic power of a global character, but it still lacks the other attributes of a truly global power. Its policy and thrust are now of a continental character, and preponderance over the Eurasian continent appears to be currently its central objective. On the American side, the earlier policy of containment based largely on American efforts is being recast into a more complicated structure in which other states—notably China, Japan, and, hopefully, a more united Europe—are to help in offsetting the Soviet Union.

It hence appears unlikely that the earlier *Pax Americana* will give way in the foreseeable future to a new *Pax Sovietica*. Aside from the fact that the Soviet Union is economically far from being a global power, even its military might still lacks the truly global character of American military resources and deployment at the high point of American globalism. Moreover, nuclear proliferation, the appearance of the new American-Chinese-Soviet triangular relationship, as well as the enormous varieties of revolutionary change in the less developed nations, simply preclude the kind of world preponderance that the United States

[58] One can only speculate how American public opinion would have behaved, had the Soviet Union, instead of quietly complying, chosen to respond assertively to the U.S. act of compulsion inherent in the mining of North Vietnamese ports on the very eve of the Moscow summit.

at one time enjoyed. More important still, *Pax Americana,* to the extent that it ever existed, was in large measure the product of the genuine desire of many nations to commit the United States after World War II to global involvement. In fact, and contrary to the recent wave of conspiratorial, Manichean, or simply economically determinist historical "revisionism" of the Cold War, *Pax Americana* was as much the product of non-Americans urging the United States on as it was of American design.

In addition, United States society enjoyed—and still enjoys—enormous world-wide attraction. In the past, its seeming wealth and apparent freedom provided the source of its appeal. Today, its appeal appears to be its social and technological innovation; indeed, even its cultural turbulence is appealing to many. In contrast, both in the past and even more so today, Soviet society appears to most to be both backward and dull. Even revolutionary-minded elements consider the Soviet system to be a bureaucratic monstrosity. This absence of positive social appeal is a major Soviet weakness.

The wider picture.   The American-Soviet competition in the years ahead will be influenced to a degree greater than heretofore by domestic factors, as well as by changes in the global context. For much of the Cold War, both powers were able to superimpose the primacy of their competitive relationship over domestic aspirations, while the existence of hostile blocs and the enormous disproportion between American and Soviet power on the one hand, and the rest of the world on the other, reduced the significance of outside factors.

In the context of the bi-polar checking relationship and of the emerging multiple-state interplay, both America and Russia are becoming more susceptible to influences of internal and international origin. Both societies are facing increasingly articulate social demands, and in both societies a new planetary consciousness is emerging, focusing on the common stakes of all of mankind. Moreover, in both societies there is mounting awareness of the overwhelming complexity of social change in the developing parts of the world and a growing concern over the ability of existing international arrangements to cope with these problems effectively. Neither the American nor the Soviet leaderships can fully control domestic change or superimpose their will on international developments, though for the time being, the Soviet leadership is in a better position to manipulate and contain its domestic pressures for change. It is doubtful, however, that this relative advantage will be retained indefinitely.[59]

[59] See Z. Brzezinski, *Between Two Ages* (New York: Viking Press, 1970), Part III.

In addition, the Soviet Union confronts the unique challenge posed by China. China challenges both Soviet revolutionary purity and territorial integrity. The very scale of that challenge defies rational calculation and compensates for the obvious relative industrial and strategic weakness of the Chinese threat. It has already induced major Soviet strategic investments and troop redeployments, and there is little likelihood that in the years ahead China will cease to be a source of very major Soviet concern.

The combination of global and domestic complexity—assuming that in the meantime the bi-polar checking relationship is not suddenly skewed militarily in favor of one party—may over time induce progressively a more cooperative American-Soviet relationship, particularly in regard to a whole host of new problems confronting mankind. The agreements of 1972 already suggest that the Cold War is gradually being transformed from an implicitly apocalyptic conflict to an explicitly relativistic competition, in which both sides are bound by a common stake not only in avoiding a major war but in partially regularizing their rivalry. The competition is increasingly accepted as a continuing process which is partly inherent in the nature of things but which is also partly subject to increasing control and regularization.

This changing character of the competition—from a direct and antagonistic rivalry into a more mixed relationship, more responsive to international and internal influences—is more in keeping with the pluralist view of the world, with its emphasis on diversity, than with the monochromatic Soviet conception of the world. In the longer run, the combined effect of international pluralism as an enduring reality and of domestic pressures may therefore have a deeper effect on the nature of the Soviet system than of the American, provided that in the meantime the American system proves responsive to the need *both* for internal innovation and external staying power.

APPENDIX A: BIBLIOGRAPHICAL NOTE

The origins of the Cold War have been traced by some scholars to earlier wartime disagreements among erstwhile allies; other scholars have pointed to postwar conflicts of interest in central Europe; still others have argued that the Cold War really began in 1917, with the surfacing of ideological hostility as a major factor in international politics. Judgments have similarly differed concerning responsibility for its appearance. Some have seen it largely as the inevitable clash of interests among major powers, involving in large measure a pattern of action-reaction in stimulating the conflict, with the ideological factor acting as an added stimulus; others have pointed to Stalin's aggressiveness, especially in Central Europe, as the principal cause; others have argued that the major burden and responsibility for initiating the chain reaction rests on the United States, with some simply blaming American imperialism for imposing a hostile relationship on the peace-loving Stalinist Soviet Union.

Broadly speaking, Louis J. Halle, *The Cold War as History* (New York: Harper & Row, 1967); Walter LaFeber, *America, Russia, and the Cold War, 1945–1966* (New York: Wiley & Sons, 1967); Walter Lippmann, *The Cold War, A Study in U.S. Foreign Policy* (New York: Harper, 1947); John Lukacs, *A History of the Cold War* (New York: Doubleday, 1962); and Marshall Shulman, *Beyond the Cold War* (New Haven, Conn.: Yale University Press, 1966) fall into the first category of inevitable clashes of interest, as do also in part Martin F. Herz, *Beginnings of the Cold War* (Bloomington, Ind.: Indiana University Press, 1966) and Adam Ulam, "Rereading the Cold War," *Interplay* (March 1969), although the latter two stress more Soviet responsibility for the initiation of American-Soviet rivalry. Even greater emphasis on Soviet responsibility is put by Thomas A. Bailey, *America Faces Russia* (Ithaca, N.Y.: Cornell University Press, 1950); Desmond Donnelly, *Struggle for the World* (London: St. Martin's Press, 1965); Herbert Feis, *From Trust to Terror: The Onset of the Cold War, 1945–1950* (New York: W. W. Norton, 1970), and *Between War and Peace* (Princeton: Princeton University Press, 1960); and Andre Fontaine, *History of the Cold War*, 2 vols. (New York: Pantheon Books, 1968), with Bailey, Donnelly, and Fontaine stressing Soviet ideological hostility as an important factor in initiating the Cold War.

American responsibility, defined largely in big-power terms, is stressed by Isaac Deutscher ("Myths of the Cold War," in David Horowitz, *Containment and Revolution* (Boston: Beacon Press, 1967), Carl Marzani, *We Can Be Friends: Origins of the Cold War* (New York: Topical Books, 1952), and Frederick L. Schuman, *The Cold War: Retrospect* and *Prospect* (Baton Rouge: Louisiana State Press, 1962). American culpability, defined largely in ideological categories (imperialism, economic greed) is emphasized by Gar Alperovitz, *Atomic Diplomacy: Hiroshima and Potsdam* (New York: Simon & Schuster, 1965), and *Cold War Essays* (New York: Anchor Books, 1970); Denna F. Fleming, *The Cold War and Its Origins, 1917–1960* (New York: Doubleday, 1961); David Horowitz, *The Free World Colossus: A Critique of American Foreign Policy in the Cold War* (New York: Hill & Wang, 1965); Gabriel Kolko, *The Politics of War: The World and U.S. Foreign Policy, 1943–45* (New York: Random House, 1968); Christopher Lasch, in *Cold War Essays* by Gar Alperovitz (New York: Anchor Books, 1970); Ronald Steel, *Pax Americana* (New York: Viking Press, 1967); and William A. Williams, *The Tragedy of American Diplomacy* (New York: World Publishing Co., 1962).

APPENDIX B

THE DYNAMICS OF THE SOVIET-AMERICAN RELATIONSHIP

	Phase I (1945–47) Preliminary Skirmishing	Phase II (1948–52) Soviet Union Assertive	Phase III (1953–57) United States Assertive
International Standing	*U.S. Advantage* Truman Doctrine Economic recovery of Europe through the Marshall Plan Third World areas of Latin America, Asia, and Africa subject to U.S. or allied predominance Strong United Nations support for U.S. policies Unilateral Soviet actions in Eastern Europe	*U.S. Advantage* Hostile world reaction to coup in Czechoslovakia and subordination of Eastern Europe to Soviet control Unsuccessful Soviet probes in Berlin, Korea Defection of Yugoslavia United Nations support for U.S. policies continued Creation of NATO and beginning of rearmament of Western Europe	*U.S. Advantage* Dulles' "policy of liberation" for Eastern Europe Weakened Soviet control over Eastern Europe, as evidenced by 1953 East German revolt and 1956 Polish, Hungarian uprisings
Military Power	*Probably a Soviet Advantage* Men under arms: 　　　U.S.　　Soviet Union 1945　12.3 million　11.3 million 1947　670,000　2.8 million Soviet strength in European theater significantly superior to that of the West U.S. retains atomic bomb monopoly, but delivery systems remain weak	*Marginal Soviet Advantage?* Men under arms: 　　U.S.　　Soviet Union 　　1.6–2 million　5 million Defense Spending: 1950　$12 billion 1952　$30 billion　$30 billion Soviet development of atomic weapons, although stockpiles remain small relative to U.S. and delivery systems inferior	*U.S. Advantage* Men under arms: 　　U.S.　　Soviet Union 　2.8–3.5 million　5.7 million Defense Spending:　$30 billion　$30 billion Nuclear Bomber Fleets: two-way attack 　bombers:　400　40 total nuclear bombers:　1350　350

	Overwhelming U.S. Advantage	Decisive U.S. Advantage	U.S. Advantage
Economic Power	GNP* (app.) U.S. $300 billion Soviet Union $100 billion Severe economic dislocations persist in Soviet economy	GNP 1952: U.S. $400 billion Soviet Union $150 billion Large-scale U.S. economic aid to Western Europe continues	GNP 1955: U.S. $508 billion Soviet Union $185 billion
Domestic Policy Base	*Uncertainty in Both* Truman–Wallace Split Varga debates in Soviet Union over prospects of capitalism Widespread popular disaffection in the U.S.S.R.	*U.S. Advantage* Bipartisan support for U.S. foreign policy based on containment of Soviet Union Western economic recovery coupled with rapid U.S. military buildup Stalinist repression in the Soviet Union and Eastern Europe	*U.S. Advantage* Strident United States foreign policy pronouncements Political uncertainty in Soviet Union after death of Stalin and struggle for leadership between Khrushchev and Malenkov Soviet internal debates over economic priorities
Major Areas of Competition	Iran Turkey Greece Eastern Europe	Korea Berlin Czechoslovakia Yugoslavia	East Germany Poland Hungary Suez

* All GNP statistics are based on 1966 dollars.

Table continued on pp. 198–99.

	Phase IV (1958–63) **Soviet Union Assertive**	**Phase V (1963–68)** **United States Assertive**	**Phase VI (1969–)** **Soviet Union Assertive**
International Standing	*Declining U.S. Advantage* Soviet Union increases support of Third World national liberation movements and begins to pursue an active foreign policy, including nuclear threats United Nations support for U.S. position less sure on critical issues such as the Congo and representation of China	*Marginal U.S. Advantage* End of active Soviet foreign policy towards the Third World and major Soviet setbacks in Ghana, Indonesia, Algeria Establishment of the hot line and ratification of Test Ban Treaty U.S. involvement in Viet Nam escalates rapidly U.S. policy of "building bridges" to Eastern Europe not followed through and Soviet decision to invade Czechoslovakia remains unchallenged	*Roughly Equal* Expanding Soviet global involvement, especially on Eurasian continent Soviet friendship treaties with Egypt and India Legitimization of Soviet postwar gains in Eastern Europe in Bonn and Warsaw treaties Increase in Soviet-U.S. bilateral talks and agreements, such as SALT, and the 1972 Moscow summit pacts Admission of People's Republic of China to the United Nations, and U.S.-Chinese political contacts

Military Power	*Uncertain U.S. Advantage*
	
	Men under arms:
	        U.S. Soviet Union
	(app.) 2.5 million 3 million
	Defense spending:
	1961 $50 billion $40 billion
	Exaggerated U.S. estimates of Soviet power led to large increases in U.S. strategic and conventional forces under Kennedy, promoting a 3:1 U.S. strategic advantage by 1962.
		Clear U.S. Advantage
		
		Men under arms:
		     U.S. Soviet Union
		1968 3.5 million 3.47 million
		Defense spending:
		1968 $80 billion $55 billion
		ICBMs: 1054 900
		Neither U.S. nor Soviet Union has a clear-cut first-strike capability
		U.S. superiority remains unquestioned, but Soviet strategic capabilities expand rapidly
			Marginal U.S. Advantage?
			
			Soviet naval expansion and military buildup in the Mediterranean and Indian Oceans
			
			Strategic parity between U.S. and Soviet Union
			
			        U.S. Soviet Union
			ICBMs:
			1971 1054 1550
			Submarine
			missiles: 655 580
			Considerable U.S. advantage (of at least 2:1) in deliverable warheads

	U.S. Advantage		U.S. Advantage		U.S. Advantage	
Economic Power	GNP: 1961	U.S. $575 billion Soviet Union $272 billion	GNP: 1967	U.S. $762 billion Soviet Union $372 billion	GNP: 1970 approx.	U.S. $1,000 billion Soviet Union $500 billion
Domestic Policy Base	*Probable U.S. Advantage* Soviet space successes Improved Soviet strategic capabilities give rise to U.S. fears Khrushchev predicts Soviet economy will overtake U.S. in ten years		*Declining U.S. Advantage* Strains in U.S. society and economy due to Viet Nam war effort intensify Collapse of post-war foreign policy consensus in U.S.		*Soviet Advantage* Domestic upheaval over Viet Nam war continues Support for reduced military posture foreign policy commitments gains strength within U.S. Soviet propaganda on overtaking the U.S. economy is revived	
Major Areas of Competition	Congo Ghana Cuba Berlin Indonesia		Middle East (Jordan, Arab- Israeli War) Czechoslovakia Viet Nam Soviet setbacks in Brazil and Indonesia		India-Pakistan Viet Nam Middle East	

MARSHALL D. SHULMAN

10

BEYOND CONTAINMENT

I

We have been accustomed, during most of the past 25 years, to think of our security in terms of the containment of Soviet expansionism, relying largely upon a comfortable superiority in military power. A number of developments now call into question the adequacy of this conception and of our understanding of the nature of effective power in the modern world.

Among these developments have been changes in the military balance. Our strategic superiority over the Soviet Union was first constrained by the emergence of a condition of mutual deterrence, and more recently by the growth of Soviet strategic forces to a level of approximate parity. Coincidentally, there has been a substantial increase in Soviet conventional military capabilities with a global reach.

What effects this change in the military balance may be expected to have upon political developments is made more difficult to calculate by the evident paradox of our unprecedentedly large military power and our declining political influence in the world, a paradox which points up the limitations of arms as a source of effective power.

Original title: "What Does Security Mean Today?" Reprinted by permission of author and publisher from *Foreign Affairs* (July 1971). Copyright © 1971 by Council on Foreign Relations, Inc.

Since the end of World War II, events have pushed us toward a less Soviet-centric view of our security problems. Against a background of rapid and uncharted political changes in the world, the Soviet problem is perceived less in terms of expansion through the territorial control of contiguous areas than as a competition for political influence on a global basis. One effect of qualitative changes in weapons technology has been to make the strategic competition into a closed game, somewhat apart from the competition for political influence. Concurrently, the accelerated pace of technological change has altered the geography of politics, bringing distant areas within reach; it has given greater significance to forms of power based on new industrial technology; and it has resulted in profound upheavals in the domestic social orders of nations.

The persistent strength of nationalism as the most potent single force in international politics has fragmented the two-color maps of the world of a quarter-century ago; new nations and new political forces have with stubborn autonomy resisted the illusions of omnipotence of the two giant powers. Clearly, power in terms of capacity to exert one's will over other people is more variegated and limited than it appeared to be immediately following World War II.

The pace of change in the world has made it difficult to define the nature of the international system in which we find ourselves, and still more difficult to describe the kind of international order toward which we would like to move, in which we could improve our security and protect the values we hold important. Without such an effort, however, our actions lack direction.

The present climate of opinion, veering toward a withdrawal from international involvement and not yet prepared to sort out the lessons of the Vietnam experience, is not an auspicious one in which to reflect upon changes in the nature of power and the meaning of security. But if we are not to surrender to the drift of events, we must resist the vice of wide amplitudes of mood changes around stereotyped images to which democratic societies are prone. We need to rethink fundamental aspects of our foreign policy, bringing to bear more differentiated analyses of present problems and a sense of future direction.

II

In retrospect, it is now clear that the Soviet Union entered upon a new phase in its foreign policy in the mid-1960s. During the preceding decade Khrushchev had moved out from the Soviet periphery to a first pass at Africa and southern Asia. Accepting the concepts of nuclear deterrence and "peaceful coexistence," he began the modernization of strategic capabilities while greatly reducing Soviet conventional forces. In the competition with America, he put his reliance upon the anticipated economic superiority of the Soviet Union and the myth of a "shift in the balance of power" based upon the symbolic impact of the first Sputnik.

But the shortcomings of the Soviet economy made hollow his boasts of outstripping the United States, and the net effect of his efforts to gain political advantage from Sputnik was to stimulate higher American defense budgets, with the result that the Soviet strategic inferiority was in fact further deepened. The Congo crisis of 1960, in which the Soviet Union was unable to reach and support its chosen allies; the Cuban missile crisis, and the American naval blockade which capped it; and the powerful arsenal of U.S. conventional weapons brought to bear upon Vietnam after 1964—these were among the painful lessons experienced by the Russians during this period.

The result was a determination by the Soviet leadership which followed Khrushchev to acquire more rapidly the sinews of actual rather than symbolic military power, at whatever cost to the economy. Within a few years, there began to appear the various attributes of a diversified military capability. Rates of deployment of nuclear missiles rose steeply, and for all practical purposes the strategic inferiority under which the Soviet Union had labored was overcome, although qualitative improvements on the American side meanwhile made parity a dynamic condition rather than a plateau. Soviet conventional forces were now restored and modernized to play a wider and more flexible role. During this period, accelerated support for the navy achieved the historical transformation of the Soviet Union from a continental to a maritime power, capable of deploying its fleet in all the world's oceans. Concurrent improvements in mobile forces, including the Soviet "naval infantry," in firepower and in air and sea logistic capabilities, have given the Soviet Union the means of reaching distant local conflicts—whether to check anticipated American interventions or to bring military pressure to bear upon politically unstable trouble spots remains to be seen.

Economic and military aid programs, highly focused on a limited number of countries (about 70 percent of the economic assistance goes to Afghanistan, India, and the U.A.R., and the latter two are the main recipients of military assistance), continue to be of significant scale. In Eastern Europe there has been a reorganization of the Warsaw Pact forces to improve mobility and firepower, together with a continued effort to integrate the economies of the East European states, manifesting a primary Soviet concern with consolidating its control over the area.

That the central concept of this acquisition of power is to increase Soviet political influence on a global basis relative to that of the United States is underlined by the directions of an intensified and more sharply focused diplomatic effort since the mid-1960s. The most striking diplomatic moves have been the enlargement and greater flexibility of bilateral dealings with Western Europe, and with the Federal Republic of Germany in particular. The purpose is multiple—to encourage neutralist trends in Europe (which is to say, to reduce American influence in Europe); to gain juridical recognition for the German Democratic Republic and the Soviet position in Eastern Europe ("the acceptance of the realities of World War II settlements"); to inhibit Western European integration and the dominance of the Federal Republic in that grouping; and to increase trade and technological borrowing from the Western industrialized states. The proposal for a European Security Conference has been a feature of this diplomatic campaign, directed alternately at containing the Federal Republic and at isolating the United States from Western Europe as circumstances have required.

The most specific objective of near-term Soviet diplomacy has been to achieve a decisive influence in the Arab Middle East, both for its oil and other resources and as a gateway to the Indian Ocean and Africa. As an adjunct to this, the Soviet naval presence in the Mediterranean serves to neutralize the U.S. presence there and to symbolize Soviet power and interest.

The level of diplomatic effort in Africa and Latin America suggests longer-term aspirations, depending upon local opportunities. In Asia the Soviets have a dual objective: to contain the expansion of Chinese influence and to replace the British and American presence which they anticipate will be withdrawn from the area. Pragmatically, the Soviet Union has eschewed revolutionary movements (except in Vietnam) and cultivated its relations with established governments in order to influence their orientation in world politics. While courting Japanese businessmen, for both economic and political reasons, the U.S.S.R. has hammered away at Japanese security agreements with America and the growth of Japanese defense capabilities. On the subcontinent, Russia has become the principal external influence. It is a major arms supplier to India, and has begun to develop military sales to Pakistan and Ceylon. It has been negotiating shipping and air access to Singapore and has become the largest buyer of Malaysian rubber. It is becoming a naval presence in the Indian Ocean, growing by unobtrusive steps.

Paralleling the European Security Conference proposal, the Soviet Union has put forward a plan for a new collective security system in Asia, with itself as guarantor. So far, the proposal has not been enthusiastically received, although a few countries, notably Malaysia, have indicated interest in the plan as a hedge against the day when U.K. and U.S. withdrawal from the area might leave the way open to greater Chinese pressures.

It may be noted that these efforts are not inconsistent with long-term evolutionary trends toward traditional power politics and a diminished emphasis upon revolutionary transformations, at least in the near term. What have been added are a stronger military base and a global presence, orchestrated into a total effort to gain access and influence around the world. While the United States tends to think of its military, economic and diplomatic instrumentalities separately and to permit them a certain life of their own, the more fundamentally political outlook of the Soviet Union serves to harness them to specific political objectives. These different approaches may also to some extent reflect differences in governmental structure, with the more fully coordinated and centrally controlled Soviet apparatus better adapted to focus military, economic and diplomatic means toward political ends.

In the past, there has been a tendency to attribute a high degree of planning to Soviet policy, but more sophisticated and realistic recent studies suggest that Russian behavior in the world may be better understood as the result of three factors: a rather general long-term design, an interplay of bureaucratic pressures and interests, and a response to external opportunities. Although the design continues to be expressed in categorical ideological language, it reflects a general aspiration rather than a detailed prescription—perhaps with about the force of Avis' expressed determination to become "No. 1." The role of competing interests and bureaucracies in determining Soviet foreign policy is difficult to document, but there can be little doubt that it is an important factor, varying according to the particular issues involved, and that it has to be taken into account in understanding the mechanism by which Soviet behavior interacts with roughly similar mechanisms on the American side.

Finally, it is abundantly clear that a major factor in the emergence of a new phase of Soviet policy in the mid-1960s was a response to the perceived decline in U.S. prestige and influence around the world as a result of Vietnam. The first effects of the involvement of the United States in Vietnam in early 1965 were to raise apprehensions about U.S. bellicosity and its build-up of conventional capabilities. The second wave of effects stemmed from the indirect consequences of our involvement: the domestic disturbances, the tide of anti-militarism and anti-involvement in world affairs, the decline of confidence among our allies in the judgment of the American leadership. From Moscow, it became plausible to anticipate a reduction in the political influence of its major rival on every continent, and this anticipation encouraged a more active effort to increase Soviet political influence wherever opportunity presented itself.

For the most part, the effort to build the sinews of power was carried forward at moderate levels of tension, applying a lesson learned from the postwar period, i.e. that higher tensions simply mobilized and united the Western alliance. The détente policy has been on a country-by-country basis. It has proved most difficult to apply in the case of the United States, where the appeal for "normalization" of relations is undermined by the "anti-imperialist" campaign directed against the American presence around the world, and also by the insistence of the Soviet leaders on continuing the "ideological struggle" in harsh and uncompromising terms. Also, having smarted for so long under what they felt as the "arrogance" of American strategic superiority, the Soviet leadership is in a chesty mood, prepared to enjoy the advantages of a rising power position.

What are the prospects for the success of the Soviets in increasing their political influence in the world? One problem in answering is that the mixture of strengths and weaknesses in the Soviet position makes it difficult to characterize the fundamental power relationship between East and West. On the strategic military dimension, the condition called "parity" in fact reflects an asymmetrical balance, with some advantages on each side. The political effect of such a balance may depend largely upon subjective factors: the will and confidence of the respective leaderships, the mythology of power among the people. On conventional military capabilities outside Europe, the balance requires a region-by-region breakdown: compared to American, Soviet power is weaker but growing in the Mediterranean, stronger in the Indian Ocean and on the subcontinent, but relatively weaker in the Pacific and in Southeast Asia. The most serious Soviet deficiencies appear in the economic realm: institutional limitations, particularly in advanced technology. There are also serious economic limitations on the Western side: inflation, unemployment and growing competitive conflicts, but the strength of Western technological growth is increasingly recognized as a factor of effective power.

In political power, the comparison is between relative weaknesses —what someone has characterized as "competitive decadence." The internal strains in Western societies are painfully evident. Over the long run, creative processes may be at work, but at present the West European nations, struggling with domestic upheavals, do not find in the American experience any inspiration or source of confidence. For its part, the Soviet Union faces the prospect of continuing turbulence in Eastern Europe, a running conflict with China and its fragmenting consequences in the international communist movement, systemic rigidities at home, and not much luster in the Soviet model to attract emulation from abroad. This brief balance sheet illustrates the difficulty of weighing the effectiveness of various forms of power, in terms of political influence.

A further difficulty arises in assessing the prospects of the Soviet drive from the demonstrated resistance of smaller states to the subjugation of their will to the great powers. The transformation of military or even economic power into political advantage and influence has proved more difficult than the Soviet leadership had hoped when it first began to reach toward the underdeveloped nations in 1955.

"All trees do not grow to the sky." It would be an error to assume that the Soviet Union will automatically translate power into ever-spreading access and influence; recent Soviet gains have owed more to Western ineptitude than to Soviet effectiveness.

III

To the extent that the Soviet Union does succeed in expanding its role in the world, how much should this be a source of concern to us? In the past, we have been prone to assume that every gain for the Soviet Union, or for "world communism," was a loss for us, if not a threat. But have we not reached a point where we need to redefine our conception of the nature of the international system, and of our vital interests within that system?

It is evident that Russia is entering upon a phase of national growth like that which many other nations experienced in the nineteenth and early twentieth centuries, and is now pressing outward for a role commensurate with its status as one of the two superpowers in the world. But there are two levels of Soviet conduct: one represents an effort to bring about a change in power relations within the present international system in fairly traditional power-politics style; the other—if one takes seriously the residual ideological commitment of the Soviet Union—is to work toward a change in the nature of the international system itself, the rules and practices that govern international relations and the internal structure of societies. The former is an anachronism in a day when imperialism—in the sense of a dominion over other people—is increasingly difficult to maintain. The latter is of diminishing relevance in a world in which revolutionary change is everywhere in process, but for which the storehouse of Soviet Marxism has little to offer as a guide to the future.

In the international system as it is, and as it is becoming, change itself must be the fundamental starting point for any effort to codify relations among nations. No longer is it possible for nations to define their interests or seek their security in terms of hegemonial control over territory. The alternative to international anarchy requires the acceptance of two principles which grow out of the new physical and political conditions of international life: one is the right of free access, and the other is non-interference by force in processes of internal change.

The principle of free access reflects the fact that political control over territory is not necessary for economic access; it is not in fact a condition of successful and productive economic relations. This has been amply demonstrated by the decay of imperialism of the kind described by Lenin, and is being demonstrated today by the experience of the Soviet Union in Eastern Europe. The principle of free access permits nations to compete, not for the control of territory but for the establishment of mutually beneficial and non-exploitative relations, and thereby for political influence.

The notion of free access need not be in conflict with the vital security interests of the Soviet Union and the United States in territories where the establishment of hostile forces would be regarded as threatening, but it requires the acceptance of a distinction between security and hegemony. For the United States to define its vital interest in the Western Hemisphere, in Western Europe and in Japan means that it would feel a direct threat to its national security if these territories should come under the control of military forces hostile to the United States. It would hope for more—that relations with these countries would be amicable and productive, but it would seek that result by its diplomacy against competing influences, not by the exclusion of Soviet economic and political access to these areas.

Similarly, the Soviet Union would regard its vital interests as jeopardized by the establishment of hostile forces in Eastern Europe, but this legitimate security concern does not justify, and does not require, hegemonial control over the area. The establishment of productive relations between East and West Europe, far from being in conflict with Soviet interests, can make for a more stable and secure relationship, if Russia construes its interests in broader and less rigid terms than it now does.

Of course, it is understood that at the present time the Soviet leadership is far from prepared to accept such a distinction; any increase in external influences in Eastern Europe would now be regarded as an historical and ideological retrogression. The present Soviet outlook is in the other direction: toward obtaining from the West recognition of a Soviet sphere of influence in Eastern Europe. Perhaps time will be required to make it clear that spheres of influence, even if granted, cannot under modern conditions provide the basis for stable and productive relations.

Within these two vital zones, certain tacit rules of engagement have developed. The United States has made it clear, through a series of crisis situations, that it would not intervene by force in territory regarded by the Soviet Union as vital to its security interests. For its part, the Soviet Union has, since the days of the Berlin blockade, recognized certain less well-defined rules of engagement in Western Europe and the Western Hemisphere, with the partial and ambiguous exception of Cuba. Contrary to some popular misunderstanding, this mutual acceptance of tacit rules of conduct in security matters does not constitute a spheres-of-influence agreement, since it does not exclude the effort to extend political influence in each other's security sphere.

Outside these two vital zones, however, there is a need to work toward rules of engagement that shall apply in contested areas, if the competition for political influence is to be kept within reasonable and safe bounds. It is not a matter for conferences and treaties. Rather, these rules will evolve through the tacit codification of experience, a practical recognition of the restraints that each side comes to expect of the other; and their sanction will derive from the self-interest both nations have in avoiding direct involvement with the other in local conflict situations.

The Soviet Union is not, and the United States should not be, committed to the defense of the status quo. It would in any case be a vain quest. Our interests are best served if the processes of change can take place in an orderly way, with a minimum of violence, responsive to the wishes of the people involved, free of external compulsion. Perhaps the most that one can realistically hope for now is some increase in sober restraint where, as in the Middle East and in Vietnam, the forces of the two giant powers are partially engaged. Over a period of time, as a result of living through a number of such conflict situations, a codification of the common law of experience will define recognized limits of engagement for the conduct of our competition for political influence. As a concomitant development, the United States and the Soviet Union may resolve their dispute over the use of U.N. peace-keeping mechanisms, and develop a range of ad hoc techniques for containing and pacifying local conflict situations.

In a period of shifting relations and the emergence of some form of balance among the five major powers—China, Japan and West Germany (or Europe), in addition to the Soviet Union and the United States —what is required is an acceptance of a process of accommodation to relative degrees of political influence, in a post-imperial order committed to the fundamental independence of its constituent parts.

IV

Progress in these directions is not likely, however, if we neglect the present relationship between force and politics. Much current discussion on this point appears to be polarized between preserving the faith in military superiority as the guarantor of our security, and a strong tide of indiscriminate antimilitarism. What is needed—although admittedly difficult in the present acerbic climate—is a more measured judgment of our military needs, both nuclear and conventional, in the light of a broader conception of our true security interests.

For more than a year and a half, the Soviet Union and the United States have been engaged in Strategic Arms Limitation Talks—but meanwhile, the nuclear arms competition has continued to spiral upward, into new and more unstable weapons systems. The fault lies in the absence of an effective political leadership in either Russia or America capable of presiding with common sense over the pressures of military services and new war technologies. In the absence of a political judgment to cry enough, military procurement in both countries tends to be determined by interservice competition, compounded by misplaced prudence and bargaining zeal on the part of civilian planners. A continuation of the nuclear competition means less security for both nations, since many of the weapons now coming into sight are less stable, more costly and more tension-producing.

One barrier to a leveling off and reduction in the strategic competition is the argument—perhaps rationalization would be more accurate—that further strengthening of our military position improves our bargaining position, increasing the incentive for the adversary to negotiate an agreement. The effect, on the contrary, has been to provide dynamism for the military competition.

It has been psychologically difficult for the United States to accept the loss of its accustomed nuclear superiority, and its West European allies wonder aloud whether the American guarantee will be effective under conditions of parity. The mythology of nuclear weapons has not yet absorbed the realization that superiority has no practical meaning in any real context. The argument that parity would increase the Soviet propensity to take additional risks, or diminish the American resolution in responding, ignores the fundamental inhibitions of mutual deterrence, which are not substantially changed by disparities in the respective arsenals. The technical advantages of one system against another can be argued, but to allow these technical arguments to dominate policy-making in this field is to lose a sense of proportion about the limited usefulness of nuclear arsenals, however sophisticated.

In any rational perspective, security in the realm of strategic weapons would be best served by a stable equilibrium at as moderate a level as can be managed through explicit or tacit agreement with our adversaries. On this point, the interests of the two countries are not opposed, but on neither side is this fact yet fully appreciated.

Because conventional weapons are more closely related to political effects, the competition in this field is even more difficult to regulate. The hard question posed by the growth and global deployment of Soviet conventional forces, particularly at a time when the British military presence in Asia and in the Indian Ocean is being contracted, is whether an imbalance may develop in the next few years which will tempt the Soviet Union to use its forces in unstable and conflicted parts of the world to influence the outcome of political processes, whether by indirect pressure, military assistance or direct involvement.

If there is to be any possibility of moving toward moderating rules of engagement in the intermediate zones, rather than toward international anarchy and unbridled competition, as suggested earlier, it is evident that sanctions must be present in the form of military equilibrium in the regions involved. Only if the forces in the area are reasonably in balance, preferably at the lowest levels possible, are they likely to perform the function of negating each other—an extension to the conventional field of the balance of mutual deterrence.

What this implies is a more differentiated approach to the problem of conventional military capabilities than is now represented in the domestic debates. Military means cannot be our main reliance in seeking to maintain the non-hostile world environment necessary to our own security; other forms of power—diplomatic, cultural, political, economic, the successful resolution of our domestic problems—are more effective means of creating a favorable world environment. But in the present international system, military equilibrium, both general and local, is a necessary condition for the free and non-violent unfolding of processes of change. If we wish to move toward a world in which force does not dominate politics, a world of free access and nonintervention, we cannot escape the painful conclusion that a balance of conventional forces is needed.

The question that the United States faces is not whether to be a presence in the world but what kind of a presence. The values we wish to realize in our society will not maintain their vitality if we allow ourselves to become isolated in a hostile world. This can result as much from the neglect as from the abuse of power. What is required is restraint and wisdom in the use of power, toward ends consistent with the international order toward which we would like to see the world evolve.

TOBY TRISTER

TRADITIONALISTS, REVISIONISTS, AND THE COLD WAR:
A Bibliographical Sketch

I

American historiography on the Cold War is both voluminous and complex. Anyone seeking instant enlightenment regarding the origins and evolution of the Cold War is bound to be disappointed. New analyses appear every year, with each addition to the literature raising new questions of fact and interpretation. Within the existing material, a long and intense debate between "traditionalist" and "revisionist" authors continues on these crucial issues and factors: the causes of the Cold War; the influence of ideology on foreign policy; the impact of economic policies and domestic restraints on the formation of the Cold War mentality; and the inevitability of the great power confrontation.

How is the reader to untangle the mass of conflicting facts and interpretations and form a coherent picture of the Cold War debate?

One simple but telling way to identify the various schools of thought is to pinpoint the author's characterization of the principal actors in the Cold War—the United States and the Soviet Union—and ask which of the two the writer holds responsible for the conflict. Applying this criterion, traditionalist writers are those who cast in the role of villain the Soviet Union and revisionist historians are those who bestow a similarly sinister designation on the United States. Although such a dichotomy does not do justice to the many writers who have sought to apportion responsibility for Cold War antagonisms to both sides, it does at least help to establish parameters of the controversy among Cold War writers. Consider, for example, the following:

> The foreign policy of the Soviet Union is world wide in scope. Its goal is to have governments everywhere which accept the basic doctrine of the Soviet Communist Party and which suppress political and religious thinking which runs counter to these doctrines. Thereby the Soviet Union would achieve world-wide harmony— a *Pax Sovietica*.

So wrote John Foster Dulles, the future Secretary of State, in *Life* magazine (June 10, 1946, p. 119), expressing a widely held contemporary view that the Russians not only were untrustworthy negotiating partners, but that their ideology and domestic political system were sinister as well.

Two decades later, a revisionist author reached substantially the same conclusion about postwar *American* foreign policy:

> . . . the United States considered all political and economic blocs or spheres of influence that it did not control as directly undermining its larger political, and especially economic, objectives for an integrated world capitalism and a political structure which was the prerequisite to its goals. (Kolko, 1968, pp. 619–20)

While a "pure" traditionalist, like Dulles, blamed the Soviet Union or communism in general for causing the Cold War, a "pure" revisionist, like Kolko, blamed the United States, capitalism, or imperialism. Indeed, another revisionist author countered Dulles' notion of a *Pax Sovietica* by titling his analysis of the Cold War era—*Pax Americana* (Steel, 1967).

II

Even the writers who have scrupulously avoided these extremes were inclined to lean toward one or the other position. A majority of the authors whose foreign policy orientations were already formed when the policy of containment and the domino theory came under scrutiny (during the Vietnam War) continued to perceive the Cold War in traditionalist terms: through the prism of the Soviet march across Central Europe, the breakdown of four-power cooperation in Germany, and the anguished sense of betrayal experienced by many Americans after the irrevocable collapse of the Grand Alliance.

These events guided the conclusions of the early George F. Kennan (1951, 1954), Walter Lippmann (1947), and Hans J. Morgenthau (1951), as well as Zbigniew K. Brzezinski (1960, 1965), Herbert Feis (1960, 1970), Louis J. Halle (1967), Henry Kissinger (1957, 1961), John Lukacs (1966), Paul Seabury (1967), Marshall D. Shulman (1966), John Spanier (1960), and Adam B. Ulam (1968, 1971). Viewing the conflict as a great power struggle or as the inevitable clash of incompatible ideologies, several authors believed that the Soviets were nonetheless responsible for the conflict—such as Andre Fontaine (1968), Walter LaFeber (1967) and Arthur M. Schlesinger, Jr. (1967).

These books and articles—the core of American scholarship on post-war Soviet-American relations and the origins of the Cold War— were not uncritical of U.S. foreign policy. Their authors were clearly concerned with what they regarded as the unduly extensive obligations assumed by the American government under the Truman Doctrine to "support free people who are resisting attempted subjugation by armed minorities or by outside pressures." Indeed, both Morgenthau and Lippmann very early and strongly urged restraint, advocating what has since been called a "limitationist" approach to foreign policy (Gati, 1968). No nation, "however virtuous and powerful, can have the mission to make the world over in its own image," for "no nation's power is without limits, and hence . . . its policies must respect the power and interests of others," wrote Morgenthau in 1951 (pp. 241–42).

Walter Lippmann, opposing the seemingly unlimited mandate of the Truman Doctrine "to control events which we do not have the power, the influence, the means, and the knowledge to control" (p. 44), argued in The Cold War that, instead of a global containment policy on the peripheries of the Eurasian continent, the United States should provide assistance to its allies for postwar recovery and, additionally, seek to evacuate the Red Army from the heart of Europe by peaceful, diplomatic means. To ensure that primary goal, however, Lippmann's prescription extended beyond diplomacy: he was prepared to offer an American commitment to mobilize "the power of the United States to strike the vital centers of Russia by air and by amphibious assault" (p. 30) if necessary to block the return of the Red Army to Europe.

Morgenthau and Lippmann were concerned with the extent to which the U.S. should commit its national power and prestige in international politics. They did not necessarily take issue with the desirability of the goals of containment. Even Lippmann, whom the revisionists have incorrectly claimed as one of their own, believed that the crucial question was not whether we should pursue such goals, but whether we could operate a policy of global containment. His negative answer rested on the difficulty of implementation; global containment, he thought, would encourage a misuse of American power abroad and create instability at home.

For many other traditionalist authors, American foreign policy errors could be summed up as either too little or too late, or both. Some criticized the Roosevelt administration for having been indifferent to, or noncommittal about, the fate of East-Central Europe during World War II (Lukacs, 1966), others charged that the United States was gullible in accepting Soviet promises of self-determination for the countries of the region (Feis, 1970, Ulam, 1968), or that America failed to use economic leverage to win concrete political advantages from Moscow (Ulam, 1971). Still others (Herz, 1966; Spanier, 1960) suggested that our hope for an effective United Nations and the realization of a workable collective security system were inflated, and even anachronistic.

However, these works generally supported the thesis that

the policy of containment, the Greek-Turkish Aid Program, the Marshall Plan, and the subsequent Berlin airlift and the organization of the Western alliance on the whole represented appropriate and reasonably successful reactions to the situation in Europe. . . . Given the Soviet ideologically distorted interpretation of the Truman Doctrine and the Marshall Plan as American efforts to challenge the Soviet position in Eastern Europe and to establish an American hegemony in Western Europe, the Soviet conception of security could allow for no stopping place short of total domination over Eastern Europe. (Shulman, 1966, pp. 5–7)

III

By traditionalist thinking, the United States has been a reactive agent in the international system; that is, faced with the twin pressures of Soviet diplomatic intransigence and territorial expansionism, America acted defensively to assure the narrow goal of guaranteeing the West's security. By contrast, revisionists viewed American policy as dynamic and even aggressive. They claimed that the United States exploited its supremacy at the end of the war to press for the creation of sympathetic governments in Eastern Europe, despite previous understandings that governments friendly to the Soviet Union would be established in the region (Horowitz, 1967; Schuman, 1962); withheld Lend Lease from Russia as a lever to gain political concessions (Williams, 1959); and tried to extract further concessions from the Soviet Union through atomic blackmail (Alperovitz, 1965). United States actions in this view were scarcely the defensive reactions of a nation fearful of communist aggrandizement, then, but "an open-ended commitment to suppress revolutions" through calculated maneuvers to insure American postwar hegemony. (Horowitz, 1967, p. 10.)

Most revisionists argued that America's industrial might was mobi-lized in order to manipulate the international system in the direction of American interests. As a rationale for this policy, American decision makers cynically capitalized upon the fear of communism to stimulate public indignation. Moreover, they deliberately distorted Stalin's under-standable quest for national security through the creation of a limited East European sphere of influence by suggesting that it was the first step toward the formation of communist regimes in Western Europe. Under such circumstances, the Soviet response to America's provoca-tive policies was an understandable, if not unavoidable, stiffening of its own position.

Revisionist writers also agreed that American power in the postwar world has been disruptive. They explained it in terms of a globalist ideology—rooted in U.S. opposition to any political change beyond its control—and in terms of the American tendency to identify all such change with communist-inspired groups (Alperovitz, 1965; D. F. Flem-ing, 1961; Horowitz, 1965, 1967; Schuman, 1962; and Steel, 1964). Others assigned importance to America's desire to dominate all of Eu-rope economically and to make the world safe for "liberal capitalism" (Kolko, 1968; LaFeber, 1967; Williams, 1959). Wondering what ele-ments within the system prompted decision makers to conclude that any political change necessarily ran contrary to American security in-terests, several revisionists concluded that the answer must lie in the internal dynamics of a capitalist society. For example, Kolko, in The Politics of War (1968) pointed to the inevitability of America's ag-gressive reaction to political and social changes around the world:

> That there was something accidental or unintended about the American response to the world is a comforting reassurance to those who wish to confuse the American rhetoric and descrip-tions of intentions with the realities and purposes of operational power, but given the society and its needs American foreign policy could hardly have been different. (p. 625)

In their search for the origins of the Cold War, Fleming and Schu-man traced American hostility to Russia back to the Bolshevik Revolu-tion of 1917 and the subsequent Western intervention in the Russian Civil War. They argued that the West allowed its initial dislike for communist ideology to become an unrelenting campaign to isolate Soviet Russia and, when this effort failed, blocked the Soviet Union in its legitimate search for protection against invasion from the West. The Soviet Union had no plan to conquer Europe, argued Fleming, and the Red Army would never have advanced to the center of Europe, except for the purpose of defeating Nazi aggression. Once in possession of this territory, no Soviet leader could realistically abandon an opportunity to guarantee, at last, his country's security.

> A determined if not sympathetic comprehension of Russia's security complex is the beginning of all wisdom in the period after World War II. . . . No people in the world who had first suffered as the Soviet peoples have and then won a tremendous military victory would go into Eastern Europe merely for the ride. They would be bound to make sure that the invasion gate was closed, and by the methods which seemed sound to them, not those recommended by others living at a great distance. (Fleming, 1961, pp. 253–54)

Finally, the historian who inspired a generation of revisionist authors, was William A. Williams, whose writings have long sought to explain American foreign policy as an incessant quest for foreign markets. Since the purpose of our policy was to establish an international system open to unlimited American economic penetration, the U.S. felt threatened by Soviet control of Eastern Europe; hence Washington's belated and often coercive moves to compel Soviet acceptance of the American "Open Door" policy. As Williams interpreted past events, efforts to elicit East European participation in the Marshall Plan constituted an important step in the attainment of this objective. However, when it became clear that the United States would not succeed, anti-communism via containment was the necessary response of an angry and frustrated elite. The final irony of American Cold War diplomacy, noted Williams in a 1956 essay, was that it made the avoidable inevitable:

> Appearing as a classic and literal verification of Marx's most apocalyptic prophecy, the policy of containment strengthened the hand of every die-hard Marxist and every extreme Russian nationalist among the Soviet leadership. Those who defend containment as a necessity for America must also admit the validity of Stalin's argument that it was necessary for him to meet strength with strength, for justification by necessity knows no bounds of geography, ideology or morality. (p. 379)

This may well be the most important and perhaps most incisive indictment of American postwar diplomacy. Acting out of frustration to events they did not anticipate and could not forestall, American policy makers responded so as to precipitate the results they wished least and feared most.

IV

The attribution of blame for the origins and subsequent course of the Cold War has been the major theme of the traditionalist-revisionist debate. This always-emotional and often-hostile confrontation was rekindled with the publication of *The New Left and the Origins of the Cold War* (Robert J. Maddox, 1973). While the author expressed greater interest in examining the revisionists' evidence, the reliability of their sources and the accuracy of their scholarship—rather than engaging in explicit polemics—the revisionists greeted his work with unusual vehemence. For Maddox had not merely disputed their conclusions, but had cited what he thought were quotations taken out of context, deliberate omissions, and selected presentation of only those facts which substantiated their critical view of the United States. The major revisionist authors cited by Maddox had never been subjected to such devastating criticism, and they responded in kind.

However, other historians and political scientists have begun to move beyond the question of attributing blame. They are making a new effort to explain both Soviet and American foreign policy within the context of their domestic political environments and to analyze the strategies each developed to cope with the actions of the other. What kind of cause-and-effect relationship existed between the U.S. and the Soviet Union in the first years of the Cold War? How was their reciprocal relationship complicated by the interaction between domestic and international politics?

In addition to some of the studies published for the first time in this volume (especially those by Zimmerman, Zagoria, and Brzezinski), a new comprehensive analysis of *The United States and the Origins of the Cold War, 1941–1947* (John L. Gaddis, 1972), may constitute an example of the new direction in Cold War historiography. Although his book deals primarily with the input of domestic pressures on the making of American foreign policy, his measured conclusion also suggests that similar pressures were evident in both the U.S. and the Soviet Union.

> The Cold War grew out of a complicated interaction of external and internal developments inside both the United States and the Soviet Union. The external situation—circumstances beyond the control of either power—left Americans and Russians facing one another across prostrated Europe at the end of World War II. Internal influences in the Soviet Union—the search for security, the role of ideology, massive postwar construction needs, the personality of Stalin—together with those in the United States

—the ideal of self-determination, fear of communism, the illusion of omnipotence fostered by American economic strength and the atomic bomb—made the resulting confrontation a hostile one. Leaders of both superpowers sought peace, but in doing so yielded to considerations which, while they did not precipitate war, made a resolution of differences impossible. (p. 361)

In his *Aid to Russia,* a new study of Lend Lease and plans for postwar reconstruction, George C. Herring (1973) demonstrated the extent to which U.S. foreign economic policies were made within the context of domestic politics. Yet, he also concluded that even if the United States had continued aid after the war, the Soviet Union would not have pursued a substantially different political course.

Economic aid could have acted as a healing force only if accompanied by American willingness to accept, at least tacitly, predominant Soviet influence in Eastern Europe. The wisdom of such a course has much to commend it in retrospect, but history and experience had not prepared American leaders to act in this fashion. . . . In the absence of a broader Soviet-American agreement on postwar problems, economic assistance could not have accomplished much, and the wide divergence of attitudes and objectives rendered such an agreement impossible. (pp. 293 and 275)

Thus, Lend Lease and the promise of aid served as a symbol of the alliance which both sides may have wanted to continue after the war, but one which was easily sacrificed when allied cooperation collapsed over other issues.

These tentative and certainly less strident conclusions stand in contrast to at least some of the Cold War historiography of the 1960s. Undoubtedly, the opening of new archival material, such as those contained in the Roosevelt-Churchill correspondence of 1939–45, has facilitated the reinterpretation of old events in the light of new evidence. Perhaps the improved international atmosphere has also made an impact on our subjective perception of past American actions.

Whatever the cause, recent historiography seems to be moving beyond the traditionalist-revisionist framework toward a new phase. In this new phase, the active search for heroes or villains, for the existence of a *Pax Sovietica* or a *Pax Americana,* will not likely remain the central focus of scholarly investigation. Definitive assessments of Soviet intentions would require the opening of Soviet archives to Western scholars —an event no one expects to occur—and many documents dealing with American foreign policy during this period will remain classified. Therefore, there is no reason to conclude that more than tentative answers will ever be found to a historical problem as complex as the origins and unfolding of the Cold War. Despite years of intense debate and analysis, the soundness of Schlesinger's 1967 observation is likely to prevail:

If historians cannot solve their problems in retrospect, who are they to blame Roosevelt, Stalin and Churchill for not having solved them at the time? (p. 26)

SELECTED BIBLIOGRAPHY

* Acheson, Dean. *Present at the Creation.* New York: W. W. Norton, 1969.
* Alperovitz, Gar. *Atomic Diplomacy: Hiroshima and Potsdam.* New York: Simon & Schuster, 1965.
———. * *Cold War Essays.* New York: Anchor Books, 1970.
Aspaturian, Vernon V. *Power and Process in Soviet Foreign Policy.* Boston: Little, Brown & Company, 1971.
Bailey, Thomas A. *America Faces Russia.* Ithaca: Cornell University Press, 1950.
Barnet, Richard J., and Raskin, Marcus G. *After 20 Years: Alternatives to the Cold War in Europe.* New York: Random House, 1965.
Barrett, David D. *Dixie Mission: The United States Army Observer Group in Yenan, 1944.* Berkeley: Center for Chinese Studies, 1970.
* Bernstein, Barton J., ed. *Politics and Policies of the Truman Administration.* Chicago: Quadrangle Books, 1970.
Bohlen, Charles E. *The Transformation of American Foreign Policy.* New York: Norton, 1969.
* Brown, Seyom. *The Faces of Power: Constancy and Change in United States Foreign Policy from Truman to Johnson.* New York: Columbia University Press, 1968.
* Brzezinski, Zbigniew K. *Alternative to Partition: For a Broader Conception of America's Role in Europe.* New York: McGraw-Hill, 1965.
———. * *Between Two Ages.* New York: Viking Press, 1970.
———. * *The Soviet Bloc, Unity and Conflict.* Cambridge: Harvard University Press, 1960, revised edition, 1967.
Carr, Albert H. *Truman, Stalin and Peace.* New York: Doubleday, 1950.
* Clemens, Diane Shaver. *Yalta.* New York: Oxford University Press, 1970.
Davies, John Paton, Jr. *Dragon by the Tail: American, British, Japanese, and Russian Encounters with China.* New York: Norton, 1972.
* Deutscher, Isaac. "Myths of the Cold War." In *Containment and Revolution,* edited by David Horowitz. Boston: Beacon Press, 1967.
Donnelly, Desmond. *Struggle for the World: The Cold War, 1917–1965.* London: St. Martin's Press, 1965.
Dulles, John Foster. "Thoughts on Soviet Foreign Policy and What to Do About It." *Life* xx, June 3 and 10, 1946, pp. 113–26, 118–30.
———. *War or Peace.* New York: Macmillan, 1950.
* Fairbank, John K. *The United States and China.* 3rd edition. Cambridge: Harvard University Press, 1971.

* Feis, Herbert. *The Atomic Bomb and the End of World War II.* Princeton: Princeton University Press, 1966.

——. * *Between War and Peace: The Postdam Conference.* Princeton: Princeton University Press, 1960.

——. * *Churchill, Roosevelt, Stalin: The War They Waged and the Peace They Sought.* Princeton: Princeton University Press, 1957.

——. * *From Trust to Terror: The Onset of the Cold War, 1945–50.* New York: W. W. Norton, 1970.

Fischer, Louis. *Russia, America, and the World.* New York: Harper, 1961.

Fleming, D. F. *The Cold War and Its Origins, 1917–1960.* Two volumes. New York: Doubleday, 1961.

* Fontaine, Andre. *History of the Cold War.* Two volumes. New York: Pantheon, 1968.

* Friedman, Edward, and Selden, Mark, eds. *America's Asia: Dissenting Essays on Asian-American Relations.* New York: Pantheon Books, 1971.

* Gaddis, John Lewis. *The United States and the Origins of the Cold War, 1941–1947.* New York: Columbia University Press, 1972.

Gamson, William, and Modigliani, Andre. *Untangling the Cold War.* Boston: Little, Brown & Company, 1971.

* Gardner, Lloyd C. *Architects of Illusion: Men and Ideas in American Foreign Policy, 1941–1949.* Chicago: Quadrangle, 1970.

* Gardner, Lloyd C., Arthur M. Schlesinger, Jr., Hans J. Morgenthau. *Origins of the Cold War.* Waltham: Ginn & Company, 1970.

Gati, Charles. "Another Grand Debate? The Limitationist Critique of American Foreign Policy." *World Politics* XXI, no. 1 (October 1968): 133–51.

* Graebner, Norman. *Cold War Diplomacy: American Foreign Policy, 1945–60.* Princeton: Van Nostrand, 1962.

——.* *The Cold War: Ideological Conflict or Power Struggle?* Boston: Heath, 1963.

——. "Cold War Origins and the Continuing Debate: A review of recent literature," *Journal of Conflict Resolution* XIII, no. 1 (March, 1969): 123–32.

——. "Global Containment: The Truman Years." *Current History* LVII (August 1969): 77–84.

* Halle, Louis J. *The Cold War as History.* New York: Harper & Row, 1967.

* Hammond, Paul Y. *The Cold War Years: American Foreign Policy Since 1945.* New York: Harcourt, Brace & World, Inc., 1969.

Herring, George C., Jr. *Aid to Russia, 1941–1946: Strategy, Diplomacy, The Origins of the Cold War.* New York: Columbia University Press, 1973.

* Herz, Martin F. *Beginnings of the Cold War.* Bloomington, Ind.: Indiana University Press, 1966.

* Hoffmann, Erik P., and Fleron, Frederic J., Jr., eds. *The Conduct of Soviet Foreign Policy.* Chicago: Aldine-Atherton, 1971.

* Horowitz, David, ed. *Containment and Revolution.* Boston: Beacon Press, 1967.

——. * *The Free World Colossus: A Critique of American Foreign Policy in the Cold War.* New York: Hill and Wang, 1965.

* Jones, Joseph M. *The Fifteen Weeks.* New York: Viking Press, 1955.

* Kennan, George F. *American Diplomacy, 1900–1950.* Chicago: University of Chicago Press, 1951.

——. * *Memoirs: 1925–1950, 1950–1963.* Two volumes. Boston: Little, Brown & Company, 1967, 1972.

——. * *Realities of American Foreign Policy.* Princeton: Princeton University Press, 1954.

——. "The Sources of Soviet Conduct," (by X) *Foreign Affairs* XXV (July 1947): 566–82, reprinted as Chapter 2 in this volume.

Kissinger, Henry. *The Necessity for Choice: Prospects of American Foreign Policy.* New York: Harper & Brothers, 1961.

——. * *Nuclear Weapons and Foreign Policy.* New York: Harper & Brothers, 1957.

* Kolko, Gabriel. *The Politics of War: The World and US Foreign Policy, 1943– 45.* New York: Random House, 1968.

——. * *The Roots of American Foreign Policy: An Analysis of Power and Purpose.* Boston: Beacon Press, 1969.

* Kolko, Gabriel and Kolko, Joyce. *The Limits of Power: The World and United States Foreign Policy, 1945–1954.* New York: Harper & Row, 1972.

* LaFeber, Walter. *America, Russia and the Cold War: 1945–1966.* New York: John Wiley & Sons, 1967, revised 1972.

Lasch, Christopher. "The Cold War, Revisited and Re-Visioned," *New York Times Magazine,* January 14, 1968; and letters to the editor (especially John Lukacs), February 4, 1968.

* Lerche, Charles O., Jr. *The Cold War and After.* Englewood Cliffs, N.J.: Prentice-Hall, Inc., 1965.

* Lippmann, Walter. *The Cold War: A Study in United States Foreign Policy.* New York: Harper & Row, 1947.

——. *U.S. Foreign Policy: Shield of the Republic.* Boston: Little Brown & Company, 1943.

Luard, Evan, ed. *The Cold War: A Reappraisal.* New York: Praeger, 1964.

* Lukacs, John. *A History of the Cold War.* New York: Doubleday, 1962, revised 1966.

Maddox, Robert James. *The New Left and the Origins of the Cold War.* Princeton: Princeton University Press, 1973.

Marzani, Carl. *We Can Be Friends: Origins of the Cold War.* New York: Topical Books, 1952.

* McLellan, David S. *The Cold War in Transition.* New York: Macmillan, 1966.

McNeill, William H. *America, Britain and Russia: Their Cooperation and Conflict, 1941–1946.* New York: Oxford University Press, 1953.

Morgenthau, Hans J. "Arguing About the Cold War: A Balance Sheet," *Encounter* XXVIII (May 1967): 37–41.

——. *In Defense of the National Interest.* New York: Alfred A. Knopf, 1951.

——. *Politics Among Nations.* New York: Alfred A. Knopf, 1948.

* Oglesky, Carl, and Shaull, Richard. *Containment and Change.* New York: Macmillan, 1967.

* Paterson, Thomas G., ed. *Cold War Critics: Alternatives to American Foreign Policy in the Truman Years.* Chicago: Quadrangle Books, 1971.

——.* Ed. *Containment and the Cold War: American Foreign Policy Since 1945.* Reading: Addison-Wesley, 1973.

——. * Ed. *The Origins of the Cold War.* Lexington: Heath, 1970.

* Perkins, Dexter. *The Diplomacy of a New Age.* Bloomington, Ind.: Indiana University Press, 1967.

* Rapoport, Anatol. *The Big Two: Soviet-American Perceptions of Foreign Policy.* New York: Pegasus, 1971.

* Rees, David. *The Age of Containment: The Cold War, 1945–1965*. London: St. Martin's Press, 1967.

Schlesinger, Arthur M., Jr. "Origins of the Cold War." *Foreign Affairs* XLVI (October 1967): 22–52.

* Schuman, Frederick L. *The Cold War: Restrospect and Prospect*. Baton Rouge: Louisiana University Press, 1962.

——. *Soviet Politics at Home and Abroad*. New York: Knopf, 1947.

Seabury, Paul. "Cold War Origins." *Journal of Contemporary History* III (January 1968): 169–82.

——. *The Rise and Decline of the Cold War*. New York: Basic Books, 1967.

Service, John S. *The Amerasia Papers: Some Problems in the History of U.S.-China Relations*. Berkeley: Center for Chinese Studies, 1971.

* Shulman, Marshall D. *Beyond the Cold War*. New Haven: Yale University Press, 1966.

——. * *Stalin's Foreign Policy Reappraised*. Cambridge: Harvard University Press, 1963.

* Smith, Gaddis. *American Diplomacy During the Second World War, 1941–1945*. New York: John Wiley & Sons, 1965.

* Spanier, John. *American Foreign Policy Since World War II*. New York: Praeger, 1960, revised 1973.

Starobin, Joseph R. "Origins of the Cold War: The Communist Dimension." *Foreign Affairs* XLVII (July 1969): 681–96.

* Steel, Ronald. *Imperialists and Other Heroes*. New York: Random House, 1964.

——. * *Pax Americana*. New York: Viking Press, 1967.

Triska, Jan F., and Finley, David D. *Soviet Foreign Policy*. New York: Macmillan, 1968.

* Truman, Harry S. *Year of Decisions, 1945*. New York: Doubleday, 1955.

——. * *Years of Trial and Hope, 1946–1953*. New York: Doubleday, 1956.

* Tsou, Tang. *America's Failure in China, 1941–1950*. Chicago: University of Chicago Press, 1963.

* Tucker, Robert C. *The Soviet Political Mind: Studies in Stalinism and Post-Stalin Change*. New York: W. W. Norton, 1963.

* Ulam, Adam B. *Expansion and Coexistence: The History of Soviet Foreign Policy, 1917–1967*. New York: Praeger, 1968.

——. "On Modern History: Rereading the Cold War." *Interplay* II (March 1969): 51–57.

——. * *The Rivals: America and Russia Since World War II*. New York: Viking Press, 1971.

Williams, William A. "The Cold War Revisionists." *The Nation* CCV (November 13, 1967): 492–95.

——. "Irony of Containment." *The Nation* CLXXXII (May 5, 1956): 376–79.

——. * *The Tragedy of American Diplomacy*. New York: World Publishing Company, 1959, revised 1962.

* Zagoria, Donald S. *The Sino-Soviet Conflict, 1956–1961*. Princeton: Princeton University Press, 1962.

* Zimmerman, William. *Soviet Perspectives on International Relations, 1956–1967*. Princeton: Princeton University Press, 1969.

* indicates that paperback editions are available.

INDEX